PLANNING FOR COEXISTENCE?

T0330492

Planning for Coexistence?
Recognizing Indigenous Rights through Land-use Planning in Canada and Australia

LIBBY PORTER
RMIT University, Australia

and

JANICE BARRY
University of Manitoba, Canada

Routledge
Taylor & Francis Group
LONDON AND NEW YORK

First published 2016
by Routledge
2 Park Square, Milton Park, Abingdon, Oxon OX14 4RN

and by Routledge
711 Third Avenue, New York, NY 10017

First issued in paperback 2017

Routledge is an imprint of the Taylor & Francis Group, an informa business

British Library Cataloguing in Publication Data
A catalogue record for this book is available from the British Library

Library of Congress Cataloging in Publication Data
A catalog record for this book has been requested

ISBN 13: 978-1-138-49040-6 (pbk)
ISBN 13: 978-1-4094-7077-9 (hbk)

Typeset in Times New Roman
by Apex CoVantage, LLC

Contents

List of Figures and Tables

Acknowledgements

We respectfully acknowledge the Wurundjeri, Wadi Wadi, Tsleil-Waututh and Gitanyow peoples on whose lands the research for this book was negotiated and conducted and this book possible. As researchers and authors, it is a privilege to work alongside people for whom the messy challenge of working in planning contact zones is an everyday reality. We are grateful to all of the participants from these Indigenous nations and communities for sharing their time, expertise, and wisdom with us.

The research for this book was funded principally by the UK's Economic and Social Research Council (Grant number RES-061-25-1464) and without that funding support the research could not have been undertaken. Theresa Fresco helped to compile documents that contributed to our selection of case studies, while Joanna Stewart helped with the coding of policy documents as well as the transcription of interviews. To Fiona McConnachie and Krista Rogness, our thanks for assistance in the final stages of the book preparing maps and to Krista for all the tedious work on the reference list. A special thanks to Jody Smith for jumping in to help with the index. Beth McAuley and her team at the Editing Company in Toronto provided superb copy editing services. Our colleagues at various institutions including the Universities of Glasgow, Sheffield, Manitoba, Monash and RMIT who have supported us on this rather long research and writing journey: our thanks to all of you.

There are many others with whom we have conversed, debated, presented ideas to and exchanged correspondence with – too many people to count – who have helped us sharpen the insights and analysis we try to present in this book. Our thanks to you, also. Libby would like to thank her partner and daughters for their eternal patience: the time I had to spend either away on long overseas fieldtrips or poring over a computer to finish this work was not easy on any of us. You are always so patient with me, and I appreciate your support. Janice would like to thank her friends and family members who have listened intently, provided constructive advice and offered other forms of support during this research project.

Chapter 1

Introduction: The Challenge of Indigenous Coexistence for Planning

Dispossession, Planning and the Politics of Recognition

Indigenous peoples have been dispossessed – dispossessed of their lands, but also of the political, cultural and socio-economic responsibility to govern those lands according to customary ancestral law. These conditions of dispossession are particularly prevalent in settler-colonial contexts, where generations of colonial agents and migrants not only came to stay, but also worked to destroy and then replace Indigenous ways of being with a new political-economic order (Wolfe 2006; Cavanagh and Veracini 2013). As scholars working in the growing field of settler-colonialism studies note, these conditions are not confined to a discrete historic event (Wolfe 2006), but rather form a 'relatively secure or sedimented set of hierarchical social relations that continue to facilitate the *dispossession* of Indigenous peoples of their lands and self-determining authority' (Coulthard 2014, 7, emphasis in original). In other words, the fact of Indigenous dispossession in settler-colonial states is a contemporary phenomenon, and the conditions that enable it are persistently reproduced.

An extraordinary struggle has been underway for decades in the face of these conditions of dispossession, waged by Indigenous peoples in countless places across the globe to reconstitute themselves as self-determining peoples with a secure land base. This struggle has involved an encounter with settler-colonial states, an encounter that demands recognition from those states as a fundamental component of any effort to redress dispossession. The last 40 years has witnessed the emergence of an array of regimes of Indigenous recognition around the world, encompassing land settlements, treaties, reconciliation plans, compensation packages, partnerships and agreements. Although not legally binding, the *United Nations Draft Declaration on the Rights of Indigenous Peoples* provides some indication of the nature of these claims and of the models developed in response. It underscores the right of all peoples to self-determination in the pursuit of economic, social and cultural development, as well as Indigenous peoples' rights to maintain and strengthen their relationships to their traditional territories.

These efforts to respond to Indigenous claims are particularly pronounced in former British settler states (Australia, Canada, New Zealand and, to a lesser degree, the United States), countries that share a similar colonial history and similar systems of law. Many of these settler states have developed new legal and political mechanisms for responding to these claims: treaty negotiations in Canada,

Australia's native title regime, and the Treaty of Waitangi in Aotearoa–New Zealand are good examples. The language of rights and of rights-based recognition dominates much of the international, national and sub-national discourse on how settler states are responding to the claims Indigenous peoples are making. Planning has been one of the important public policy arenas where these new mechanisms have come to ground, and where other responses to Indigenous demands have been developed.

These responses, both in planning and in the wider body politic of settler states have attempted to settle the profoundly unsettling impact of Indigenous claims on settler-colonial authority. Yet they have also reignited an essential tension that lies at the heart of Indigenous-colonial relations between the sovereignty of Indigenous law and its associated responsibilities toward unceded Indigenous territories now enmeshed within settler-colonial jurisdictions, and the desire of settler-colonial states to reconcile these unique place-based relationships within existing colonial institutional and legal arrangements. As many Indigenous scholars, activists and leaders have shown (Taiaike Alfred, Glen Coulthard, Irene Watson, Aileen Moreton-Robinson, Michael Dodson, Patrick Dodson, Leanne Simpson), Indigenous demands inherently *challenge* the underlying authority of those very institutional and legal arrangements. Defining redress for dispossession through the very instruments that constitute that dispossession in the first place throws into sharp relief how the operations of colonial power are never transcended, but simply change register and shape. Dene scholar, Glen Coulthard argues that 'instead of ushering in an era of peaceful coexistence grounded on the ideal of *reciprocity* or *mutual* recognition, the politics of recognition in its contemporary liberal form promises to reproduce the very configurations of colonialist, racist, patriarchal state power that Indigenous peoples' demands for recognition have historically sought to transcend' (2014, 3, emphasis in original).

Given political and spatial characteristics, Indigenous demands place a specific onus upon planning systems. Planning, as an arena where issues about the use, management and future of place are contested, negotiated and settled makes an obviously important site where the finer institutional, legal and land-use arrangements of recognition are hammered out. It is not surprising then that planning has come to be a key forum where the politics of recognition comes to ground. Yet despite some fairly significant shifts, particularly in the field of natural resource management planning, how the politics of recognition plays out in different planning contexts and the factors that shape planning's responses to Indigenous demands are not widely discussed in planning research and practice (Hibbard, Lane and Rasmussen 2008). Perhaps more importantly, planning as a field of inquiry and practice has not yet sufficiently come to grips with its own complicity in the ongoing fact of dispossession in settler-colonial states.

This book is about what happens when Indigenous demands for recognition of coexisting political authority over territory intersect with environmental and urban land-use planning systems in settler states. Taking the complicity of planning in ongoing processes of Indigenous dispossession as a point of departure, this book looks closely at where and how Indigenous demands have become part of land-use planning systems and how those demands have been settled and managed. In doing so, the book is also about how planning processes themselves become sites for Indigenous resistance and resurgence, and the complex politics of recognition that unfolds.

Contribution, Purpose and Framing of the Book

Recognition of cultural difference has been a debate within planning for a long time; showing how this recognition unsettles the universalizing tendencies of planning (Sandercock 2003, 1998a) creates space for a critical reflection on the invisibility of certain cultural identities (Sandercock 1998b) and enables analysis of the socio-economic and political impacts of exclusionary practices (Hooper 1992; Sandercock and Forsyth 1992; Yiftachel 1998, 2009; Beebeejaun 2004; Harwood 2005). Cultural recognition often demands a more radical line of questioning about how planners should understand and then act in contexts of 'deep difference' (V. Watson 2006; see also Yiftachel 1998; Fenster 2003; Burayidi 2003; Beebeejaun 2004; Thomas 2000; Harwood 2005; Jackson 1997; Umemoto 2001; Porter 2006b). The onus Indigenous demands place upon planning significantly overlaps with, but is also distinctly different from, the recognition of other forms of cultural difference. For in contexts of Indigenous-settler encounters, planning is confronted with substantively different ontological and epistemological philosophies of human-environment relations, which give rise to unique systems of governance and a deep sense of responsibility and connection to places and the non-human entities that live in those places (see Alfred 1999; Langton 2002; I. Watson 2002). Tom Trevorrow, a Ngarindjerri Elder, states it in beautifully simple terms: 'Our traditional management plan was: don't be greedy, don't take more than you need and respect everything around you. That's the management plan – it's such a simple management plan but so hard for people to carry out' (*Murrundi Ruwe Pangari Ringbalin* 2010).

Indigenous scholars of planning have sought to express these differences and their implication for how planning is theorized and practised (see Jojola 2008; Matunga 2013). These expressions position planning as an essential element of the colonial project, directly implicated in the processes of Indigenous dispossession and colonial conquest. A small body of work attends to this important point (Porter 2010; Ugarte 2014; Dorries 2012; Stanger-Ross 2008), and has aimed to expose how planning continues, in its contemporary practice and theory today, to *reproduce* spatial relations in the interests of settler-colonial power (Lane and Cowell 2001; Howitt and Lunkapis 2010; Yiftachel 2009; Porter 2010). This often occurs in ways that erode Indigenous efforts to claim and *re*claim their political, cultural and economic sovereignties (Dorries 2012).

Acknowledging this erosion to be a real possibility in every planning situation, a growing number of authors are exploring the 'split personality' (Hibbard, Lane and Rasmussen 2008) of planning in Indigenous contexts, highlighting the ways planning might also be used to create space for the exercise of Indigenous self-determination (Lane and Hibbard 2005; Zaferatos 2004) and the reclamation of Indigenous modes of socio-spatial organization (Jojola 1998, 2003; Matunga 2013). Taking seriously that all outcomes and politics are contingent (they might always have been different) points to the importance of conceiving planning as a potentially transformative space. There are numerous compelling examples of planning processes that have been able to catalyze deep, cross-cultural learning about the legacies of colonialism and take significant steps toward the improvement of community relations (see, for example, Dale 1999; Sandercock and Attili 2010), if not the development of planning tools and practices that are more responsive to Indigenous customary law. A substantial body of literature and practice guides now exists, tracking how recognition of Indigenous rights and title has led to increased engagement with Indigenous stakeholders (Berke et al. 2002), and providing guidance on new modes of planning governance including the now well-established models of joint or co-management (Stevens 1997; Borrini-Feyeraband, Kothari and Oviedo 2004; Howitt, Connell and Hirsch 1996; Jaireth and Smyth 2003; Jentoft, Minde and Nilsen 2003; Lane and Williams 2008; Maclean, Robinson and Natcher 2014), or protection of cultural heritage (Jones 2007). More recent work is showing how a more advanced and scaled-up set of planning processes is now being conducted on a government-to-government basis, where settler states and Indigenous peoples mutually recognize their separate coexisting authority and create agreements to manage land-use planning responsibilities (Barry 2011).

The vast majority of these examples relate to environmental planning and natural resource management situations. The field has been much less responsive to the questions posed by Indigenous claims and Indigenous customary law for planning in *urban* contexts (for recent exceptions to this silence, see Porter 2013; Porter and Barry 2015; Dorries 2012). This is curious, as there are a variety of fields contributing to a rich set of debates that all speak very directly to planning on these questions. For example, there is significant work on the specific needs and socio-economic position of Indigenous people living in cities (Cardinal 2006; Peters 2005, 2006; Walker 2003). There is also important work on questions of urban governance, particularly about Indigenous self-government (Peters 1992; Walker and Barcham 2010; Walker 2006) and what that means for municipalities (Mountjoy 1999) and on urban citizenship debates (Wood 2003). Finally there is a robust and long-standing debate about the cultural politics and political economy of expressions of Indigenous identity and agency in the city as well as analyses that position urbanization as a key colonial process (Jacobs 1996; Edmonds 2010; Pieris 2012; Porter and Barry 2015; King 1990; Shaw 2007; Yiftachel and Fenster 1997), exposing how Indigenous people are often only engaged in urban governance processes when their protest movements present significant risks to the viability of major development projects (MacCallum Fraser and Viswanathan 2013).

This book seeks to address these gaps, especially the paucity of planning research on Indigenous recognition in urban contexts. To that end, the book speaks directly to the practice and theorization of planning, drawing on debates, concepts and theoretical lenses from a wide range of other fields. Our aim in this book is to examine *what actually happens* when planning systems meet the claims and struggles of Indigenous peoples, as well as when they interact with now well-established settler-state mechanisms that purportedly seek to redress those claims.

We do this from three points of departure: First, that planning as it is conceived and performed today in settler states is an innate part of the process that makes and remakes colonial spatial and political authority normal and coherent. Planning was intrinsically involved in historical processes of subjectification and dispossession, and remains one of the key policy arenas in which states seek to resettle the surety of their spatial jurisdictions. Second, that the variant of Indigenous recognition that liberal states have widely adopted in response to Indigenous claims reconfigures colonial domination and reproduces the conditions of dispossession. Third, that neither of the first two points should be conceived as monolithic or inevitable. The intersection of planning with Indigenous demands for recognition of sovereign political and spatial jurisdictions has enormous transformative potential. Understanding where that potential exists, how and when it can become foreclosed, and how the demands of Indigenous people might more effectively be used in planning for these ends requires a critical yet hopeful conceptual framing, and a close empirical attention to actually existing interactions between planning systems and Indigenous peoples.

This book adopts the struggle for *coexistence* as that critical yet hopeful conceptual framing. As the title of the book suggests, when the actions and agency of Indigenous demands can articulate planning as a practice and ethic of coexistence, we contend that a more transformative politics of recognition becomes possible. We use coexistence in this book as a normative, political and conceptual position. It is especially insightful for its commitment to holding onto a deep contradiction that underlies the contemporary situation of every settler-colonial state: Indigenous people and non-Indigenous settlers *co-occupy place*, and yet they do so in ways that are *rarely common* with each other, and often fundamentally different (Howitt 2006). Coexistence, then, immediately signals the profound challenge of, as Howitt calls it, 'being-together-in-place' (2006, 49) with an explicit acknowledgement that the geographies of settler contexts are constructed through 'social and geographical imaginaries in which the presence of others produces a sense of place that is simultaneously of belonging and alienation' (ibid.).

Coexistence, then, is a way of articulating a demand for sharing space in ways that are more just, equitable and sustainable (Howitt and Lunkapis 2010). Such an approach demands rejecting the politics of recognition that we have already flagged as highly problematic; the sort inspired by the work of Indigenous scholars in settler-colonial studies. Not only does coexistence require some kind of broadly conceived mutual recognition (Tully 1995; Fraser 1995) but also an acceptance of multiple and overlapping jurisdictions, where ontologically plural relations to and governance systems of place all have relevance and standing. Discomfort, unease and unsettlement are the inevitable psychologies and practices that emerge from a commitment to finding ways to accept and cherish these 'strange multiplicities' (Tully 1995). Conflict, incommensurability, ontological plurality and the discomfort of unsettling tension are all essential, if not constitutive, elements of a more progressive politics of recognition for planning.

How, then, to make this overarching political, ethical and normative frame analytically and empirically operational? To enable the close examination of actually existing interactions and politics of the unsettling and uncomfortable demands Indigenous people make to planning, we use the language of the 'contact zone'. This is language we have adopted from American critical linguist Mary Louise Pratt, who defines contact zones as 'the social spaces where cultures meet, clash and grapple with each other, often in contexts of highly asymmetrical relations of power, such as colonialism, slavery or their aftermaths as they are lived out in many parts of the world today' (1991, 34). As discussed in previous work (Barry and Porter 2012), thinking about planning and Indigenous peoples as a 'contact zone' adds two important dimensions to how cultural difference has hitherto been conceived in planning theory.

First, 'contact zones' orient attention toward the historically constituted colonial power relations that bring such zones into existence. Far from being simply 'there', contact zones are produced and mediated through the structural conditions and agency of social actors, institutions and discourses. Given our focus on land-use planning, we are particularly interested in the texts that define and perform these (post)colonial contact zones. Planning, as a key instrument through which the settler state organizes and standardizes socio-spatial orders, mobilizes a suite of distinct discourses that are produced and reproduced through formal laws, policies and procedures and that also circulate through the planning profession as informal norms and codes of practice. Attempts by state-based planning agencies to recognize the rights of Indigenous peoples are mediated by those socio-spatial orders. Contact zones call our analytical attention, then, to questions about how they come to be, why they appear in the shape that they do, and who is active in producing and reproducing them. Moreover, Pratt's underscoring of the ongoing effects of historically constituted relations of power challenges us to think about the conceptual and methodological tools that support rigorous analysis of the inter-relationship between the textual and everyday practice of the contact zone.

Second, Pratt conceives of contact zones as 'fundamentally asymmetrical' and open to all of the ambivalences of difference, expressions of power and modes of manipulation that are observable in other domains. We see contact zones not as solid sites inevitably heralding progress, but as fragile marginal spaces where the ideals of radically democratic social relations are far from guaranteed. While contact zones hold much potential for the negotiation of coexistence, they also signify possibilities that (post)colonial voices, identities and differences will be manipulated, dominated or categorically ignored. Contact zones keep us alert to the potential for colonial power relations of marginalization and repression to continue, and for existing planning laws, policies and procedures to erode Indigenous claims.

The research presented in this book addresses three sets of interrelated questions that establish the foundation for critical investigation of planning contact zones:

1. How do we see / conceive the spaces in which the struggle for coexistence unfolds? How might we better understand and critically interrogate the emergence and enactment of these zones of contact, as well as the everyday practice of struggles and intercultural negotiations that occur within them?
2. What are the discourses, structures and materialities that shape planning contact zones? How are the borders and spaces of the contact zone negotiated and produced, and with what effect? Do these look different between urban and environmental planning contexts?
3. What politics and practices might challenge and reconstitute the fundamental asymmetry of the contact zone? How should we co-create practices of coexistence and what are the implications for the recognition of Indigenous rights and title in planning?

This book is grounded in two specific settler-state jurisdictions: Victoria, Australia, and British Columbia (BC), Canada. The rationale for comparing these two former British settler states lies partly in their strong historical similarities and partly in the evolution of different ways of approaching recognition. Both places were shaped by violent, colonial acts of dispossession and assimilation, which stripped Indigenous peoples of land and political authority and sought to destroy their cultural practices. Yet Indigenous peoples in both places continue to assert their rights to land, as well as their political right to self-determination. And, in both places, these struggles over land and authority are increasingly playing out within the context of land-use planning, with individual planners (if not entire planning systems) often struggling to address coexistence with Indigenous customary law. These negotiations are ongoing and dynamic, and our interest in Victoria and British Columbia is precisely because these are places where the recognition of Indigenous rights and title is in flux, where Indigenous demands are clear and present upon planning systems, and where the planning profession is still trying to make sense of how to appropriately respond.

The comparative analysis of the two settler-state jurisdictions presented in the book operates at two spatial and political scales. Planning contact zones are produced at least partially at the state- or province-wide scale, where the legislative and policy regimes of the state impose certain demands and expectations. A significant component of this book, then, addresses this scale of jurisdiction. Yet Indigenous struggles and demands are place-based, attending as they do to highly specific spatial and political expressions of sovereignty. To understand how and where moments of Indigenous engagement with planning arise and work, and what they mean, we use local case studies; and so the book tells four different stories of the engagement of Indigenous people with state-based planning. Two cases are located in Victoria: one urban case, that of the Wurundjeri people's involvement in urban planning processes in metropolitan Melbourne; and one environmental case, that of the Wadi Wadi people's experience of forestry and protected area planning in northwest Victoria. Two cases are located in BC: one urban case, that of the Tsleil-Waututh Nation's relationship to strategic land-use planning conducted by one of the municipalities operating on their territory; and one environmental planning case, that of the Gitanyow Huwilp's role in the development of a strategic natural resource plan for the Nass River watershed in northwest BC. The locations where these stories are unfolding are represented.

The terms used to describe Indigenous people, are highly across contexts and sometimes contested even within and between the two jurisdictions we discuss in this book. We have chosen to mostly use the term Indigenous rather than Aboriginal where we are referring to a general identity position such as 'Indigenous people and planning'. We use Aboriginal where that has been requested by our participants or when we are referring to laws, politics and reports that use that terminology explicitly. When we are discussing the cases presented in this book, we use the specific name of the people: Wurundjeri, Wadi Wadi, Tsleil-Waututh and Gitanyow.

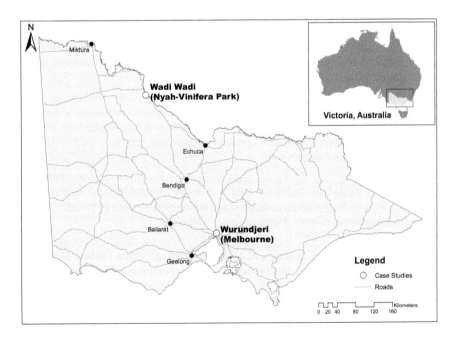

Figure 1.1   Location of case studies in Victoria

Source: Map created by Fiona McConnachie for the authors

The following paragraphs provide a brief orientation to each of these Indigenous groups, their story, and the very different state-based planning processes in which each became involved.

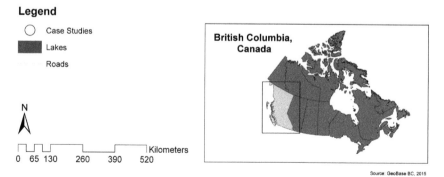

Figure 1.2   Location of case studies in BC

Source: Map created by Krista Rogness for the authors

Wurundjeri and Urban Planning in Melbourne

The Wurundjeri are descended from Wurundjeri-willam people of the Woiwurrung language group. Wurundjeri country[1] is now principally covered by the city of Melbourne, Australia's second largest city, and is therefore under heavy and mounting pressure from rapid urban and housing development in the city's expanding growth corridors. The Wurundjeri people have long asserted their continuing presence on country,[2] through their representative body, the Wurundjeri Tribe Land and Cultural Heritage Compensation Council Incorporated (hereafter Wurundjeri Council). A principal activity of the Council is the protection of cultural heritage, as well as land management, cross-cultural education and training programs, cultural consultations, music, dance, language and naming. The Wurundjeri story is about how, through the Council, they came to have significant statutory powers over certain urban development applications on their country, and what this highly regulatory form of recognition means.

Wadi Wadi and Co-Management of Nyah-Vinifera Park

The Wadi Wadi people are today made up of some 11 principal family groups with links through key apical ancestors and deep ancestral connections to the river red gum flood plains on both sides of the Murray River, which forms part of the boundary between Victoria and New South Wales. A key place of focus for the Wadi Wadi people is the Nyah-Vinifera Park, a 1,370-hectare reserve located on the Victorian side of the river that includes unique examples of river red gum trees, flood-plain biodiversity, and significant Wadi Wadi cultural sites. Having fought a long battle against timber harvesting in the area, the Wadi Wadi were instrumental in achieving a higher conservation status for Nyah-Vinifera in 2009. These efforts led to a formal process of negotiating with the Victorian State Government to agree to a co-management arrangement for governance of the park. This process, involving a lengthy series of meetings and negotiations with the Victorian Government's planning and land management agency, has as yet failed to produce an agreement. Although the negotiations are currently at a standstill, the Wadi Wadi continue their struggle for recognition and for greater control over the park.

---

1   The expression 'country' is used widely by Aboriginal and Torres Strait Islander people in Australia to refer to the lands and waters to which they belong: a 'place of origin in spiritual, cultural and literal terms' (Fredericks 2013).

2   To be 'on country' expresses a spatial and continuing relationship with those lands and waters.

Tsleil-Waututh Nation and Joint Planning Initiatives with the District of North Vancouver

The Tsleil-Waututh Nation, 'the People of the Inlet', is a Coast Salish Nation with territories in metropolitan Vancouver, over which 17 different municipalities and a regional authority all have overlapping jurisdiction. Tsleil-Waututh's primary reserve is immediately adjacent to the District of North Vancouver, one of several municipalities within Metro Vancouver, BC's largest city and the third most populous metropolitan area in Canada. All of Tsleil-Waututh's territory is under increasing development pressure and Tsleil-Waututh Nation has been engaged in a variety of initiatives to help them pursue their land-use interests, increase their visibility and become a more integral player in what is going on around them. These efforts have included the development of a bioregional atlas for their traditional territory and the creation of internal policies that articulate how they envision their relationship with businesses and government agencies operating in their traditional territory. Tsleil-Waututh Nation has also been involved in several joint planning initiatives with the District of North Vancouver, including a municipal park planning process and the development of the municipality's Official Community Plan (OCP).

Gitanyow Huwilp and the Nass and Skeena River Watersheds

Located in the Nass and Skeena River Watersheds in northern British Columbia, the Gitanyow is comprised of eight houses, or *Wilp*. Collectively known as the Gitanyow Huwilp, these houses own and have authority over a defined territory, or *Lax'yip*, and have been engaged in their own systems of land-use planning since time immemorial. This work has continued right up to the present day, including their most recent Wilp Sustainability Plan. The preparation of this plan began with the establishment of a formal planning relationship with the BC Provincial Government, and tied into two different provincial planning instruments and processes. These processes culminated in the signing of a *Recognition and Reconciliation Agreement* between the Gitanyow Huwilp and the BC Government, which includes written management objectives and designated resource management zones. Two key dimensions of the agreement are the recognition of the Gitanyow's traditional governance system and the maintenance of ecological and socio-cultural well-being for each individual Wilp as a major planning objective.

A Reflective Account of Our Research Methods and Procedures

In order to enable examination of planning contact zones at multiple scales, and in different settings, our research design was structured around two interrelated measures of analysis. We began with a detailed analysis of the settler-state documents that catalyze, and then powerfully shape, Indigenous recognition in the structures and processes of state-based planning. Both Canada and Australia adopt a federated system of governance in which the planning and regulation of lands is *primarily* an area of provincial/state responsibility. As a result, we focused significant attention on statutes, regulations and policy at the state/ provincial scale, being ever mindful that Victoria and BC have (to varying degrees) created entirely different policy directions for land-use planning for built and natural environments, with different government agencies overseeing their implementation. The planning systems in both locations also allow for some level of discretion (albeit with significant differences), which meant that the dataset also needed to include non-statutory texts (for example, guidance notes, fact sheets and best practice manuals). A total of 120 planning texts, across both jurisdictions, were analyzed.

This analysis provided a clearer sense of how the contact zone was conceived through the texts and helped to identify precisely where, to what degree and in what ways Indigenous rights, title and interests were recognized. We paid particular attention to when and at what stage Indigenous peoples were inserted into the planning process, over what substantive planning issues, and with what powers over intended process and outcomes of planning. We also looked for moments when planning documents were cross-referencing the case law, statues and policies that define the settler state's understanding of Indigenous rights and title. This textual analysis was structured through a series of linked questions. The first was an essential temporal dimension: was the intersection of Indigenous interests in planning seen as a product of a distant colonial past, or as an ongoing and contemporary concern? The second was the political dimension: are Indigenous people cast as 'objects' of planning, or as having their own agency in relation to strategic planning processes and goals? In a final stage of analysis, we looked at the spatial dimension of Indigenous recognition in planning systems. In what kinds of places was a legitimate 'Indigeneity' enabled under the gaze of planning? Was it tied to distinct sites or over entire territories? How was the relationship of Indigeneity linked to property, and especially of Indigenous title to private property rights?

This textual analysis was linked to and helped inform the second stage of the research design: the selection, negotiation and analysis of the four case studies. These cases were chosen because each represented not 'planning as usual' but a situation where unusual levels of Indigenous recognition were in play, and where it seemed that state-based planning agencies were being pushed by these four nations in innovative or potentially transformative ways. Having identified a number of possible case studies, we started to develop relationships with our Indigenous research participants. An important element of the discussions that unfolded was the identification of the formal mechanisms for engaging each of the relevant governing bodies. After extensive negotiations with Chiefs, Elders, Band Councils, professional officers and community members, we eventually signed individual research agreements with each. Those research agreements set out expectations and agreed-upon principles, covering intellectual property; verification of results and sign-off of findings; dispute resolution; confidentiality; reciprocity; and benefit sharing. Negotiations also dealt with funds to support and recognize the participation of each nation, paid to each out of the project budget from the funder, the UK's Economic and Social Research Council.

Once the research agreements were in place, we undertook in-depth interviews, collected relevant secondary documents and, in some cases, engaged in limited forms of direct observation. A total of 57 interviews across all of the cases were conducted with Indigenous and non-Indigenous informants directly involved in each planning contact zone. These interviews included Indigenous Elders and elected leaders, as well as any consultants and other advisors who supported their participation in a state-based planning process. Interviews were also conducted with state-based planners and other staff and elected officials involved in land-use management. The interviews were semi-structured in nature, lasting between one and two hours. All the interviews were transcribed, reviewed and approved by the interviewee prior to analysis. Documents ranged from strategic plans, internal reports and datasets where appropriate, Memoranda of Understanding or other kinds of agreement between planning authorities and participant groups.

The interview transcripts and case-specific documents were examined to construct a detailed narrative of the dynamics of each planning contact zone. Analytically, we focused on the specific practices and strategies used by our participants to catalyze the formation of a planning relationship between the Indigenous nation and the relevant state-based planning agency and to expand and/or deepen the scope of this planning contact zone once it was established. Because of the political and potentially sensitive nature of our investigation, all of the interviewees were given the opportunity to review their transcripts and to modify or strike information. The broad narratives of each case study (which became the basis of each of the four case study chapters in Part II) were presented and workshopped with each Indigenous participant group to obtain feedback on how we had understood and expressed their stories, and then to solicit approval. These were robust discussions that, in most instances, led to some revisions in our interpretation. Authorized representatives and/or the formal governing body for each of the participating Indigenous groups approved the findings before publication and dissemination of an online final project report. A final round of review, modification and approvals was activated prior to publication of this book.

On many levels, this account of the process of recruiting case studies and participants and collecting and analyzing data is insufficient. There were many nuances in each of the stories about how we came to settle on a research protocol with the people who agreed to work with us, and how the actual everyday work in understanding the story of each unfolded. What sounds standardized and relatively static in our account never actually felt or worked as such. We are not at liberty to discuss many of these nuances as they would reveal sensitivities and confidentialities that would contravene our principles as well as our agreements. It is clear that the very activity of research with, about and for Indigenous peoples is itself contested around the very questions our research was focused on: identity, positionality, power, relationships, agency and the politics of knowledge production. Our own study tripped over, reified and reconstituted unequal relations of power, resources and knowledge. It seems important, then, to offer a brief reflection on how our own project proceeded and provide some reasons as to why we proceeded in the way that we did. For we are mindful that, for good reason, this field demands research practices that attend patiently and carefully to these issues. Research agreements have become a relatively standard way to proceed on these matters, and are now standard practice for Indigenous research in Canada and Australia. More deeply, many Indigenous scholars and activists call for fundamental changes in research procedures, to achieve a more 'decolonizing' approach to the production of knowledge with, about and for Indigenous peoples (see, for example, Kovach 2009; Smith 1999; Wilson 2009).

Our own project is in many ways inadequate in relation to these imperatives. As researchers, it was we who controlled the parameters of the study, the way the funding and resources would be allocated, the questions being asked, the skills in analysis and dissemination, and the ultimate outcomes. This was primarily driven by practical reasons – a more grassroots, participatory methodology was not practicable. The project was funded by the UK Economic and Social Research Council, and both of us were based at the University of Glasgow. Conducting research of this nature from such a distance presented enormous challenges – practical and ethical alike. It was clear from the very outset that for reasons simply of distance and communication we would need to proceed in a relatively top-down way where we as researchers retained control over most aspects of the study. We were as consultative, open and transparent as possible and have maintained an ongoing relationship with each participant group over the years it has taken to produce this book. We acknowledge the limitations and problems that our approach signifies.

Structure of the Book

The book is organized into three parts. Part I sets the conceptual and methodological framing, fleshing out the debates and challenges briefly discussed in this Introduction. Chapter 2 addresses the core conceptual and material problematic of the book: how to understand the tricky, seductive politics of recognition in the contact zone. Beginning with a reading of Indigenous scholars and critics who are unpacking this politics and its impacts on contemporary Indigenous lives, the chapter then addresses the three linked problematics that arise when we take this framing to the debates about recognition in planning contact zones: the liberal framing of identity politics around rights, recognition and redistribution; the move toward procedural remedies that seek to extend participation and inclusion to Others claiming recognition; and the postpolitical fix of settling those claims through consensus-based models. In Chapter 3, we flesh out a methodological framework for studying planning contact zones. Arising from the ethical and political orientations charted in Chapter 2, we look at how to understand and frame contact zones as constructed by constellations of identity and power. The analytical process used in our research was discourse analysis, and so the chapter also provides a detailed discussion of this approach and how it was employed. Chapter 4 presents our analysis of the broad state/province-scale discourses that mediate planning contact zones in Victoria and BC. Sticking closely to the texts that call-into-being and then perform the two social fields of planning and recognition, we chart the underlying discursive threads that are recontextualized to mediate the politics of recognition that unfold across the rest of the book. As we will show in Chapter 4, while there are broad similarities between our two jurisdictions, some important differences begin to help explain the different experiences and outcomes in each.

Part II of the book focuses on the four case studies at the heart of this research and as such presents four substantive separate chapters, presenting the story of each of the Indigenous peoples with whom we worked. Chapter 5 is the story of the efforts of the Wurundjeri Council to better control aspects of their cultural heritage in the intensively developed environment of metropolitan Melbourne, by using the tools and limited recognition available to find new ways of asserting their interests. Chapter 6 is the story of the battle of the Wadi Wadi for Nyah-Vinifera Park, in northwest Victoria. Having successfully fought an anti-logging campaign and gaining higher conservation status for the park, the Wadi Wadi story is ultimately one of frustration and courage as they continue to negotiate for a co-management agreement over the park.

In Chapter 7 we move to BC and the story of the Tsleil-Waututh Nation in another intensively urbanized context, that of Metro Vancouver. The story focuses on the Nation's engagement in two very different planning processes with the District of North Vancouver. Chapter 8 is about the Gitanyow Huwilp and their struggle for recognition and control of their lands and resources in the Nass River watershed in northern BC. The story describes the twists and turns of their efforts to achieve recognition of their political authority and their traditional planning governance approach. All of these case studies follow a similar structure in that they all highlight the catalysts, strategic actions and contextual factors that gave rise to the enactment of these planning contact zones. Each chapter then progresses through the development and everyday practice of each of these zones of contact, drawing attention to key moments when boundaries were enforced, narrowed, challenged, reinterpreted or transformed.

Part III places the four cases together in a comparative analysis. Drawing together the essential details provided in each of the stories in Part II and also in Chapter 4, and the conceptual framing established in Part I, we interrogate the different dimensions of these four planning contact zones that arise. Chapter 9 begins by identifying and linking the different expressions of agency present within each of the case studies. Drawing together the different forms of strategic actions that catalyzed and expanded each of the four contact zones, the chapter begins to theorize how the pursuit of coexistence unfolded and where it was thwarted by pre-existing and highly resistant conceptions of the desired process and outcomes of planning. This line of analysis is intended to draw attention to the potential role of text and discourse, which is the subject of Chapter 10. Here, the inter-relationship and recontextualization of the discourses present with the state-based 'systems' of recognition of Indigenous rights and title and the state-based systems of planning are analyzed, showing how Indigenous peoples' relationships to planning in each of our case contexts are mediated. Importantly, this chapter shows the limits and costs to the politics of recognition in planning contact zones.

In Chapter 11, we address the difficult problem of understanding the actions of state-based planners in these planning contact zones and the intercultural relationships that have emerged. Turning the standard idea of 'capacity development' on its head, we show the urgency and importance of building decolonizing intercultural capacity among non-Indigenous planning actors. The concluding Chapter 12 draws the threads and debates of the book together and attempts to tease out what it would take to puncture and transform the problematic politics of recognition in planning contact zones as they are currently manifest in settler states like Victoria and BC. Returning to the problem of the costs and seductions of a liberal politics of recognition, we discuss what might be required to imagine a planning for coexistence: a relational, decolonizing formulation of planning where self-determining Indigenous peoples invite settler states to their planning table on their own terms.

PART I
Concepts and Contexts

Chapter 2
'We Are All Here to Stay':
A 'Meditation on Discomfort'

Introduction

The purpose of this chapter is to lay the foundations for a critical understanding of the struggle for coexistence: one that attends more deeply to the mutual responsibilities held by both settler and Indigenous societies, responsibilities that arise from living together in shared space that demand an unsettling of deep colonial power relations. The chapter title is, therefore, a very deliberate fusion of the words of Canadian Supreme Court Justice Antonio Lamer with those of Irene Watson, a Tanganekald and Meintangk legal scholar from South Australia. 'We are all here to stay' is the oft-cited statement made by Justice Lamer in the 1997 *Delgamuukw* ruling, a watershed decision in terms of the recognition of Indigenous rights and title. This simple observation underscores the need to engage in deep and meaningful negotiation regarding the coexistence of Indigenous and settler societies. In the words of Irene Watson, any such negotiation is a 'meditation on discomfort', in that it demands acknowledging uncomfortable questions about white sovereignty and the dominance of white culture through its political and legal orders (2007, 30).

To do this work, we listen carefully to the voices of Indigenous scholars and activists, who have been (over successive generations) collectively charting a course for Indigenous decolonization. Reading their work alongside that of other theorists enables a critical framing of the logics that produce, intimately regulate and sometimes co-opt Indigenous claims in relation to planning. This framing will help explain why planning contact zones emerge as they do, and will point to the possibilities for moving toward more decolonizing practices. Planning scholarship has been discussing related themes about recognition and cultural difference for a long time (Barry and Porter 2012; Porter 2014; Porter and Barry 2015; Fincher and Iveson 2008; Sandercock 2000; Watson 2006; Agyeman and Erickson 2012). Our approach is situated within this debate but seeks to extend it by developing a more critical conceptual framing than has yet been articulated.

To begin, the chapter sets out why it is necessary to pursue a more critical approach to understanding contact zones between settler states and Indigenous peoples. Our point of departure, as we stated in Chapter 1, is that we urgently need a framework that is alert to the politics produced by dominant modes of recognition. In planning, this requires paying attention to three 'problematics', which this chapter addresses in turn: first, a liberal framing of identity politics around rights, recognition and redistribution; second, the presumption of procedural remedies that seek to extend participation and inclusion to Others who are marked by difference and make claims for recognition; and third, the postpolitical fix of settling those claims through consensus-based models.

Indigenous Sovereignty, Coexistence and the Illusion of Decolonization

On the question of what exactly is at the heart of Indigenous claims and struggles for recognition and redress to colonial violence, the voices of Indigenous peoples are very clear:

> I want to hold the same privilege that is held by the loud and the heard voices so that we (Aborigines) can speak about our own things for ourselves. I want to occupy spaces of governance where I would have the capacity to protect my country against the state that eats it and pours its pollution back onto the lands of my ancestors while it starves our future into assimilated submission. I want to unsettle spaces held by the powerful so as to resettle the future of millions of peoples globally in their access to good food and clean drinking water and to continue the sustainable lifestyles of our ancient ones. (I. Watson 2007, 32)

Yet the contemporary mode of recognition in settler states frames the 'problem' as one presented *to* an undifferentiated and acultural Western democracy by the unsettling claims of cultured, different Others. Those claims are enfolded into, and accommodated within, existing systems of dominance and power in such a regressive way that such inclusion 'promises to reproduce the very configurations of colonial power that Indigenous peoples' demands for recognition have historically sought to transcend' (Coulthard 2007, 437). Watson concurs. She suggests that, although major Australian court decisions and other attempts to 'recognize' Indigenous title 'are represented as offerings to the possibility of de-colonizing colonial myths', these 'illusions of recognition and success' simply provide opportunity for 'the state to take a bow for efforts it has not made, for work not yet done' (2005, 16).

These quite fundamental concerns with the contemporary politics of Indigenous recognition are echoed in the work of other Indigenous scholars and activists. Corntassel frames Indigenous recognition as a 'politics of distraction' and rejects outright 'the performativity of a rights discourse geared toward state affirmation and recognition' (2012, 89). Alfred, writing over 10 years earlier, notes that while aspects of the 'rusty cage' of colonialism have been broken, 'a new chain has been strung around the [I]ndigenous neck; it offers more room to move, but it still ties our people to white men pulling on the strong end' (1999, xiii). His manifesto for realizing Indigenous self-determination goes on to capture the problem explicitly:

The state has shown great skill in shedding the most onerous responsibilities of its rule while holding fast to the lands and authorities that are the foundations of its power. Redefining without reforming, it is letting go of costly and cumbersome minor features of the colonial relationships and further entrenching in law and practice the real bases of its control. It is ensuring continued access to indigenous lands and resources by insidiously promoting a form of neo-colonial self-government in our communities and forcing our integration into the legal mainstream. (xiii)

What Watson, Coulthard, Corntassel and Alfred are exposing here is the enormous between Indigenous expressions of self-determination and sovereignty and the impoverished, deeply regressive way by which those expressions come to be managed and co-opted through contemporary forms of recognition politics. Consequently, underneath the appearance of a more benevolent, recognizing liberal state lies not just ignorance but a *denial* of Indigenous sovereignty.

This is a very significant charge. Moreover, when this kind of critical framing is applied to planning, it demands consideration of the potentially regressive nature of planning contact zones. Although Pratt (1991) has already drawn attention to the 'highly asymmetrical relations of power', the work of these Indigenous scholars and activists demands more critical consideration of the dangers of conceiving planning contact zones as some sort of universal and socio-culturally non-specific forum, capable of simply accommodating 'Others' into an ever-expanding democratic realm. The asymmetry of these power relations runs deep, producing and reproducing colonial ways of being, seeing and acting. Under these conditions, the struggle for coexistence is reduced to a struggle for inclusion: something that can be recognized through a procedural or institutional fix and can accommodate an Indigenous Other within an existing legal or political order. This way of understanding the struggle fails to 'unsettle spaces held by the powerful' and does little to create spaces for Indigenous peoples to 'speak about our own things for ourselves' (I. Watson 2007, 32). In other words, just because planning has noticed Indigenous peoples and has been required – or in some cases voluntarily willing – to bring Indigenous interests to the planning table, the politics of recognition do not automatically guarantee the unfolding of a more socially just and culturally aware planning approach. It most certainly does not herald a decolonization of planning. How, then, might we conceive of what those dominant modes of recognition in planning are actually doing, and develop a more critical perspective on their outcomes?

Developing a More Critical Framing of Recognition and Rights in Planning

One critical step toward that conception is to name those modes of recognition so that we can expose the work they do. Tully (2004) provides a useful vocabulary, calling such modes of recognition 'monological'. In doing so, he identifies two important components: first, that monological recognition fixes the object of struggle 'for' recognition and in doing so reifies existing power relations where the state is always the subject assessing the claim for recognition, and the Indigenous group is always in the role of subjecting itself to scrutiny to win its claim. The struggle is not over the terms of recognition itself (who will recognize who, and under what conditions), but simply 'for' being recognized. The second component is that the terms of the claim have to be expressed in essentializing ways chosen by the recognizing subject and consequently demand outcomes that fix and render static for all time the recognition and rights achieved. Thus – monological, because the discourse is unidirectional, shaped by one speaker only in the language of the master, fixed and static. Monological recognition does not express shared coexistence. Rather, the contemporary politics of recognition is an insistent dominance by settler states and non-Indigenous peoples over those whom it has dispossessed and oppressed with respect to ongoing access to land and resources and the rights to determine the processes and framings through which such claims for recognition will be heard.

Writing from the Australian perspective, Povinelli (2002) describes monological modes of recognition as 'cunning'. She shows how the specific performativities required of Aboriginal people by the Australian nation-state to prove their claims to native title are seductive incitements to recognition specifically designed to distract, distort and misrecognize. She argues that these moves are a constituent part of the contemporary configurations of how settler states engage with dispossessed and colonized peoples. They are not perversions or misinterpretations of a somehow 'more proper' or 'more just' liberal recognition. It is not that something went wrong in the translation of liberal ideals about rights into policy practice and that a more full and just recognition of rights could be achieved if only we could get the legislative framework and the policy guidance to work better. The injustice arises from the very hegemony of the liberal democratic order itself (Zizek 2009; Butler and Athanasiou 2013), an order that incites the fantasy of things being otherwise than they are.

As Spivak (1993) teaches us, any victory of liberation demands a stance of persistent critique toward the dogmas we inherit through those victories. Recognition, then, is not an 'end in itself' but must instead be seen as a field of political struggle. This is true whether that recognition is hostile, affirmative, or non-existent. Thus, the second vital step in developing a more critical apprehension of the politics of recognition is to divert attention away from 'winning' recognition from the state and instead cultivate analysis of *what recognition costs* (Spivak 2003) and who bears those costs. The first of three inter-related costs of the cunning configurations of monological recognition relates to distortions that arise from the liberal framing of identity politics through the language of rights and redistribution. It is to that first problematic that we now turn.

Problematic I: Recognition, Rights and Redistribution

'Claims for the recognition of difference now drive many of the world's social conflicts', Nancy Fraser said in her famous *New Left Review* essay (2000, 107). Since the 1960s, identity politics around cultural, sexual, gender and religious differences have been a site of considerable social struggle both on the streets and in the writings of scholars and social commentators. Those claims, and the resurgence, reclamation and empowerment of identity they seek, are framed in what Fraser calls the 'identity model', following Hegel, where realizations of the self can only be achieved through the recognition of another self-determining conscious agent. Human freedom, then, rests in an intersubjective, mutual recognition with *other subjects who are also free.* Misrecognition of a group's subject identity becomes classifiable as an essential component of social injustice (Young 1990, 2000), giving rise to the possibility of social struggles framed as a series of demands upon nation-states to properly recognize the right of social groups marked by difference to *be* different.

What is qualitatively distinct about these kinds of demands, vis-à-vis struggles around the minimum wage or working conditions, is that they appear to exist more in the realm of identity than in the realm of material economic resources. They appear to raise questions of cultural (mis)recognition rather than questions of class exploitation. This supposed, yet problematic, fracturing of the 'merely cultural' (Butler 1998) has been the subject of considerable debate in political theory (Butler 1998; Fraser 1997a, 1997b; Young 1997). We raise it here because it becomes important to an understanding of how claims for recognition have been (supposedly) settled in planning and other areas of public policy. We see questions of cultural misrecognition and economic marginalization as two components of the same dynamic of political-economic-ecological exploitation. It is impossible to decouple questions of identity and sovereignty from questions of material resources, especially *land,* for the political economy and the political ecology of Indigenous marginalization and oppression is produced through the intertwining of economic exploitation, land dispossession, environmental degradation and racism. Alfred conjoins it to the specific problematic of Indigenous alienation in this way: 'material poverty and social dysfunction are merely the visible surface of a deep pool of internal suffering. The underlying cause of that suffering is alienation – separation from our heritage and from ourselves' (1999, xv). Alfred goes on to assert that '[a]ttempting to right historical wrongs by equalizing our material conditions is not enough: to accept the simple equality offered lately would mean forgetting what indigenous nations were before those wrongs began' (1999, xv). The question, then, as Fraser observed, is not one of cultural recognition *or* economic redistribution, but of the inter-articulation of each with the other.

The problem that emerges is that the monological mode of recognition, and its tendency to fix and stabilize the claims Others make upon the nation-state, has proven itself largely unable to deal with the inter-connected nature of these demands for recognition and redistribution. In the realm of Indigenous-state relations, public policy responses to such claims are generally fixed through three types of policy intervention. The first is employment and economic development programs that seek to redress economic marginalization. Such programs are usually developed with little to no reference to questions of Indigenous identity and sovereignty. The second and third types of intervention do address, albeit partially, those issues. Tangible mechanisms to deal with Indigenous claims, usually to territory, are a second type of intervention. The modern-day treaty-making process in British Columbia and the native title regime in Australia are both examples of this, where a procedure is established to manage, hear and determine Indigenous claims. A third intervention is to develop collaborative or partnership approaches to decision making and resource allocation. This is now common practice in many Indigenous-settler relations and includes models such as joint management of protected areas or environmental planning utilizing traditional ecological knowledge alongside Western scientific knowledge. Given their connection to issues of cultural (mis)recognition, these last two kinds of intervention tend to be understood as questions of rights: both the *rights to use* and otherwise express an ongoing cultural connection to lands and resources, as well as the *right to participate* in decisions about those lands and resources. This connection to rights is not surprising, as rights are the mechanisms through which monological recognition is operationalized – rights make recognition 'real'.

It is not surprising then that rights have become the most important language in global Indigenous politics today. Rights are the cornerstone of international conventions, such as the UN *Declaration on the Rights of Indigenous Peoples*, they are at the heart of almost all Indigenous claims for recognition, and they appear (usually in watered-down fashion) in the variety of responses to those claims by non-Indigenous nation-states. In general terms, rights can be conceived as 'securing or protecting fundamental human interests' (Tully 2000, 3). In the domain of Indigenous-settler relations, those interests are usually focused on rights to land and self-determination. Consequently, claims about rights– their expression, recognition and protection – are also always struggles identity and recognition. Rights-based recognition is the mode through which Western settler states relate to their citizens. It is not surprising then that Indigenous peoples have mounted extraordinary efforts and struggles through courts, legislative change, and changes to governance or procedure, to seek redress.

What does it mean for the nation-states of a dominant culture to recognize and accommodate the rights of a different culture? What does such recognition cost and who bears that cost? Recognition and accommodation under the common conditions of Indigenous rights claims in settler states are achieved within the systems of legal and moral order *of those settler states*. The very terms of what rights are, how they can be recognized and who gets to do the recognizing are controlled by settler states, as Tully identifies in his framing of monological recognition. Indigenous people find themselves claiming rights in a way that demands they subject their cultures, histories and claims to the scrutiny of Western configurations of power and under terms that are not of their own making.

One of the outcomes usually sought both by settler states willing to recognize and by Indigenous peoples bringing their claims is an authoritative statement that determines and fixes Indigenous rights and non-rights. Native title in Australia is an excellent example of this. A consent determination of native title draws a boundary on a map demarcating where native title 'exists' and where it has been extinguished, and then lists the people and their descendants who can legitimately be recognized as holders of that native title. This fixes the spatial and identity authority of the recognized native title owners in order to provide certainty and stability to other interests. It also fixes the authority and rights of the state and other landowners, a point that is often overlooked. In recognizing its colonial Other, the settler state is also finding ways of reconstituting its own authority elsewhere. A companion component of this dimension of monological recognition is the imposition of false choices upon the peoples being recognized by a supposedly benevolent state. Often represents little more than a thoroughly compromised trade for: the recognition of some rights in some places at the cost of forever signing away rights in other places or other times (Woolford 2005). Chapter 4 takes up these points in more detail.

The 'meditation on discomfort' for planning involves an acknowledgement and critical understanding of how these politics of recognition and the tension between rights-based and redistribution-based policy interventions play out in planning systems. Where and how does planning tend to produce monological forms of recognition, where the urge is to resettle and make certain the rights of others in the face of the unsettling claims made by Indigenous people? How can planning become more reflexively aware of, and accountable for, the way its regulatory impulse confines Indigenous claims to certain predetermined categories, never allowing those claims to puncture the underlying premises of planning or challenge its ultimate authority? When and how does planning become complicit in taming fundamental claims about sovereignty to a reduced question about better employment opportunities, or an occasional partnership on a plan of management? This book sheds important light on these questions.

Up to this point, we have been discussing the particular manifestations of recognizing concrete, material rights, such as rights in title and use of land. The other important domain of rights recognition between settler states and Indigenous peoples is around the question of participation, or 'procedural rights'. This is equally important, for what use are rights and title if they do not also operationalize the right to speak for those places? It is to that second problematic that we now turn.

Problematic II: Participation, Voice and Inclusion

One of the other ways the 'cunning of recognition' (Povinelli 2002) works – one that is especially pronounced in planning – is through the easy, seductive presumption that involving 'more voices' and 'more stakeholders' in planning solves injustice (see Porter 2014). Questions of voice, participation and inclusion are abstract concepts important to political theory, but they are fundamental to planning practice. Participation is assumed to be a straightforwardly 'good thing' and that a more inclusive planning system is better than a less inclusive one. These assumptions about including all stakeholders, voice and participation have become normalized in planning, both in our thinking about it and in the evidence of recent changes to different planning systems around the world (see Brownhill and Carpenter 2007; Innes and Booher 2004). A rich seam of thinking in planning takes pains to point out the not-necessarily productive proliferation of this model in all sorts of settings, such as contexts of profound segregation (Murtagh, Graham and Shirlow 2008) or what Vanessa Watson terms 'deep difference' (2006).

Participation in one form or another has been one of the most common shifts in planning where systems are responding to the claims of Indigenous peoples. Particularly pronounced in natural resource management and environmental planning, the institutional design and decision-making forums of planning have expanded to incorporate Indigenous peoples on boards of management, advisory committees, working groups and taskforces. In some cases, Indigenous peoples have equal or dominant shares in decision-making powers, such as through co-management arrangements or leaseback arrangements for protected areas. In urban or redevelopment settings, the focus is very much on including Indigenous peoples in planning processes, at planning decision tables, and in institutional arrangements with varying degrees of success.

Modes of recognition that merely invite Othered peoples into a system to perform certain kinds of roles within it, without ever changing or challenging the operations or logic of that system, are problematic. Those Others simply become incorporated into a dominant order, without that order itself ever shifting. For example, changes that give Indigenous people full or equal control over decision making in a protected area sounds seductively like a shift in colonial power relations. Yet such an approach leaves intact the privilege of non-Indigenous perspectives about what is worth conserving and how it should be done. Enabling Indigenous people to sit at a decision-making table is a nice gesture, but it doesn't fundamentally change the decisions being made at the table, what is on or off the agenda for those decision-makers, how the table is constituted, or where power is located.

Moreover, the notion that political decisions can be reached on the basis of deliberation between free and equal deliberative citizens ignores the reality of power and hegemony. Any kind of social order, including a deliberative 'order' of democratic actors taking political decisions in the name of a public good is an expression of hegemonic power. This is because any order is an expression of a particular configuration of power relations pressed into the contingencies of social reality at a point in time. It might always have been different – the order itself (a political institution or process for example) is the product of certain power relations coming to ground and sticking firm to create the illusion of an order (Mouffe 2005).

Indigenous peoples are demanding not the right to be included in someone else's order, but the authority to *co-determine that very order*. Claims about sovereignty and self-determination expose this 'stakeholder model' not only as insufficient, but as a mechanism employed to resettle non-Indigenous governance as a final authority (see Alfred 1999; Dodson 1994; I. Watson 2002). Situated as they are within monological modes of recognition, they seductively incite Indigenous people to join in the participatory field in order to hold existing relations of power and control over land and resources constant.

This is achieved in part through language, especially in the privileging power of the dominant language, or as Laclau and Mouffe (2001) would say the 'language of the master'. This language and the practices it enables, presents itself as 'a universal vocabulary of understanding and reflection' (Tully 2000, 37). Indigenous domains, replete with their own approaches, languages, practices and strategies, are positioned, 'when noticed at all ... to be some kind of minority language within the dominant language of western political thought' (Tully 2000, 37). Moreover, the problematic of this dominant language is more than one of comprehension or conversation. Language expresses and enables worldviews, sensibilities and rationalities. Seeing how the language of the master dominates these participatory moments in planning contact zones at the same time identifies which rationalities about space, place and human-land relations are hegemonic.

Taken seriously and recognized properly, Indigenous claims are more than a polite request for the accommodation of interests. They should, and do, unsettle the very basis of Western sovereignty in settler states. The 'meditation on discomfort' for planning is to become critically aware of how the impulse toward participation in planning systems tends to produce these cunning forms of recognition. There is much already in the planning literature about how problematic a simplistic 'inclusion' is in the recognition of difference for planning (Harwood 2005; Quick and Feldman 2011; Rahder and Milgrom 2004; Sandercock 2003; Agyeman and Erickson 2012). That problematic is particularly stark in planning situations where there are deep and abiding 'conflicting rationalities' as Vanessa Watson (2003) has shown and to which the fundamental tension inherent in recognizing the co-existence of ontologically plural place-making speaks (Howitt 2006; Howitt and Suchet-Pearson 2003). How can planning become more reflexively aware of, and accountable for, the way its participatory structures assume that culture is a category that other people bring to the system (rather than also being built into those systems)? Under what circumstances can participation and inclusion be transformative, and when does it co-opt and tame Indigenous claims? This book seeks to answer these important questions.

Modes of recognition that simply identify an Othered Indigenous group to bring to the planning table are clearly monological, and thus very shallow, contact zones. Yet there is one more aspect to the 'stakeholder model' of participation and inclusion that has become a near-universal feature of planning generally and in the contact zone especially. This is the presumption toward consensus-based outcomes, a presumption that strips away the inherent conflict between values (what Chantal Mouffe [2005] calls 'the political') and in doing so evacuates dissent from public policy (and so Erik Swyngedouw [2009] diagnoses a 'postpolitical' condition). This third problematic is our focus in the next section.

Problematic III: Settling Claims through Consensus

The question that participation raises is how to achieve an effective outcome, because it does make decision making rather difficult. Planning in the contact zone, or anywhere else for that matter, is conflict-ridden, and so it should be. We are talking about nothing less than the imagination of our future cities and neighbourhoods, towns, streets, mobilities and socialities. Far from the happy, clean, shiny impression of planning forums that the profession sometimes likes to paint, planning, especially in contact zones, is a deeply contested slog, riven with misunderstandings, mistakes, deliberate obfuscations, political engineering, strategic alliances and uncomfortable encounters. And so, the other side of the coin of the participatory, stakeholder model of planning has been the rationality of consensus-based decision making – of 'getting to yes'. This model, of getting all the right people around the table, designing appropriate institutional or process arrangements, giving those people sufficient voice, and then working towards consensus on a decision has become something akin to articles of faith.

These are all important, yet in (post)colonial contexts they can easily signal the rearticulation of yet another exclusionary, dispossessory logic because their tendency is to represent a specific operation of monological recognition. The identity positions from which 'consensus' is sought are assumed to be natural categories that exist prior to the moment of consensus. In this way, the consensual approach merely addresses the appropriate correlation between interests at the decision-making table rather than the conditions under which the original dispute arises. The trajectories, discourses and terms of engagement (beyond the immediate ones within the consensual forum itself) are never considered a 'stake'. Seen as such, the consensual setting is already heavily mediated and manufactured, falsely articulating itself as an ontological reality. Where planning meets Indigenous claims, the outcomes that might be possible from consensus-based approaches are always already heavily mediated, in the interests of white privilege. For example it is possible to come to a consensus on the techniques and personnel involved in managing a natural resource, but the larger questions of 'what is a natural resource?' and 'why is the particular natural resource under discussion defined as such?' cannot be articulated. Consent about what place is and should be has already been manufactured. Consequently, the presumption of consensus has a clear and undeniable tendency to co-opt Indigenous frames of reference and undermine sovereign Indigenous polities and jurisdictions.

An empty signifer, consensus turns out to be '"nothing at all" ... which nonetheless causes a gigantic commotion all around' (Zizek 2001, quoted in Hillier 2003, 50). Consensus operates as a seduction, a fantastic desire brought to ground and materialized in a set of accepted practices and methods (Hillier

2003, following Lacan). These practices are precisely the politics of distraction Corntassel (2012) identifies – the 'gigantic commotion' produced by the will to achieve consensus causes attention to be drawn away from what is really going on. For these reasons, consensus has been diagnosed in other contexts as an essential component of the postpolitical condition in planning (Pløger 2004; Allmendinger and Haughton 2012).

Linked to this distracting, cunning seduction is the more precise outcome of consensus as 'an action of exclusion' (Mouffe 2005, 11). In order for the mirage of consensus to appear, the dissenting voices with their struggle and their claims and their marginalized values have to be displaced. Consensus is manufactured in an entirely fantastical manner, because its manufacture depends on the silencing of dissenting voices. The mechanisms through which this is achieved are varied – for example the framing of an agenda for participation or consultation that excludes certain items from discussion. Or the design of a participatory process that demands certain participants behave and speak in certain kinds of ways and thus excludes those who differ in that regard. These are all operations of power, as a solid body of critical work on the communicative paradigm in planning has attempted to expose (Huxley 2000; Huxley and Yiftachel 2000; McGuirk 2001). In planning contact zones, where the power relations are so asymmetrical, and so deeply cast in histories of violence and dispossession, to ignore them amounts to the same action as reifying and reproducing them. Moreover, dissent does not disappear from such situations, but has simply been displaced, waiting to resurface in future contestations. As Mouffe (2005) notes, the political will always return. Merely from a position of effectiveness, then, it is clear that when conceiving of planning, especially where planning meets its Others in highly asymmetrical relations of power marked by histories of violence, dispossession and oppression, the presumption toward 'consensus' is fundamentally flawed.

The 'meditation on discomfort' for planning demands acknowledging that the impulse toward consensus in planning systems is enormously costly for Indigenous people. How can planning become more reflexively aware of, and accountable for, its will to consensus? Under what circumstances can consensus, and the methods used to achieve it, be transformative, and when does it co-opt and tame Indigenous claims? This book will deal comprehensively with these questions.

Conclusion

This chapter has laid the foundations for how we might critically appraise the dominant framing of recognition in settler states today. In exposing this mode of recognition as monological, the chapter has explored three precise mechanisms through which that recognition operates within planning: it fixes rights and non-rights and misses the link between sovereignty and economic marginalization, as if Indigenous sovereignty claims could be addressed by a traineeship program; it offers seductive and cunning forms of inclusion that render the cultural presumptions of the settler state invisible; and by denying the inherent conflict that is essential in an ontologically plural world it manages claims through the postpolitical dynamic of consensus building.

The politics of recognition and the manifestation of contact zones between planning and Indigenous peoples cannot, then, be seen as automatically progressive, or stable. Colonialism is a *present* phenomenon, and this holds for planning as much as it holds for the more prominent questions about the legal and constitutional status of Indigenous peoples. In this understanding, contact zones will always be shaped by ongoing colonial processes of control: always potential sites for co-optation, domination and oppression; never neutral or innocent. In planning, where the ever-present pressure is to 'get something done', the fantasy of closure and certainty built on participatory, consensus-based decision making is strongly seductive. This chapter has contributed to a body of work that exposes this concept as not only a fantasy, an impossible mirage, but as potentially hegemonic – containing logics that co-opt the worldview of Others and simply accommodate them within the existing system.

Yet as the voices of Indigenous scholars and activists attest, Indigenous peoples are contesting, resisting and 'talking back' to these fixing effects of monological recognition. They are especially doing so in planning contact zones, where the real implications of recognition come to ground in concrete ways. Recognition through planning really matters because it affects Indigenous access to a land base; enjoyment and use of land; and the extent of threats from other undermining or impacting activities. Consequently, one of the spaces in which Indigenous people are increasingly operating to push for alternative, more mutual or relational modes of recognition is through planning systems. This is why it is of vital and urgent importance that planning becomes attentive and reflexive about the costs and seductions of the politics of recognition.

The orientation we have mapped out in this chapter informs our approach to study the contact zone. Seeing the contact zone as a thoroughly co-constituted and power-full space, the critical importance of designing analytical frameworks that emphasize the relational and entwined constitution of different subjectivities ('Indigenous', 'planner') should be obvious. Our starting point is to be able to see analytically how and where the boundaries of contact zones come to be drawn, and what forces shape their delineation. The next chapter sets out the analytical tools for examining the ways in which monological recognition is enacted and enforced, especially through text; and then for understanding and explaining struggle against those forces.

Chapter 3
Seeing the Contact Zone: A Methodology for Analyzing Links between Everyday and Textual Practice

Introduction

The research we present in this book began from two vitally important ontological departure points. First, planning contact zones are constituted at the intersection of two social fields: the recognition of Indigenous people by settler-states and the planning system itself. Both have discursive and material power in mediating the possible and the impossible, the thinkable and the unthinkable, the contours of the politics of recognition and coexistence. Both fields, therefore, have to be present in the analysis. Second, both these social fields are heavily textual in that they are prescribed and bounded by texts, with policies, legislation, court rulings and regulations saying what can happen, under whose authority, and where. Consequently, a significant part of the analysis has to be oriented toward the heavy textuality of contact zones, looking carefully at how texts constitute and shape their boundaries, as well as the role of texts in reconfiguring and recontextualizing different kinds of discourses. Both fields are also the sites of social agency and action – replete with heavily contested practices. Those practices take all kinds of forms from the mundane to the explosive, from the textual to the non-textual, from the material to the symbolic.

How should we approach the study and analysis of the messy everyday practice of planning where it is being contested, challenged, co-opted and reimagined by the recognition claims that Indigenous people are making? What methodological approaches are useful for grasping and explaining the extraordinary variety of interactions, discursive reformulations, misunderstandings, strategic alliances, overt confrontations and quiet dragging of feet that characterize these contact zones? The purpose of this chapter is to answer these questions in relation to our particular study. In doing so, the chapter addresses two objectives: first, to offer a broad methodological approach that springs from the ethical and political orientations mapped out in Chapter 2 and that seeks to identify how contact zones are 'called into being' (to paraphrase Butler 1999) through reiterations and reformulations of power, authority, identity and recognition. This methodology has been designed to help unpack where change (especially transformative or progressive change) comes from: how does the unsettling and resettling of planning unfold? Second, the chapter seeks to develop a detailed analytical framework for understanding the particular work that discourse does in shaping and mediating the struggle for coexistence.

We begin by theorizing the critically important nexus in planning contact zones between text and practice, using insights from Interpretive Policy Analysis (IPA) and Institutional Ethnography. Having established some of the core tenets of our overall methodological approach, the chapter then teases out a range of theoretical and methodological tools for unpacking and critically interrogating the textual and everyday practices of the contact zone. It approaches this task from two distinct vantage points: first, how the practices of insurgent agency can be better understood when situated in the broader institutional *habitus;* and, second, how the shaping, constraining, authorizing and regulating potential of texts can be better understood when situated within a broader discussion of the performance of power. In the second section, we think critically about the specific role of discourse in constructing, maintaining and unsettling the contact zone and provide an account of how we operationalized concepts from Critical Discourse Analysis (CDA) to enrich our analysis of both the textual and everyday practices at work in our four case studies.

Textual and Everyday Practices of the Contact Zone: Seeing the Links

Interpretive methodological approaches are now well established in planning and other public policy fields, particularly with reference to the more established field of Interpretive Policy Analysis (see Fischer 2003; Hajer 2003; Wagenaar 2012; Yanow 2007, 2000, 1996). Our research design has also been informed by that tradition, which influenced a large part of our approach. IPA seeks to develop conceptual and methodological understanding of the both phenomenological and heurmeneutic dimensions of policy and policy development (Yanow 2007). Yet the planning literature has tended to focus on the former, privileging the deliberative elements of the everyday practice of policy and plan making (see, for example, Forester 1999, 1989 Healey 1998; Innes and Booher 2010). Our work partially sits within, but also seeks to extend and challenge this literature. As discussed in Chapter 2, our conceptual and ethical orientations eschew the presumption of planning as a consensual or level playing field. A first methodological challenge, then, is to expose the relations and fissures of power, especially the particular articulations of power that frame (post)colonial contexts. These relations include the power to influence, frame and control how the entire project of planning is conceived and operationalized. Such power is partly constituted through the maintenance of deep-seated values and norms (Lukes 1973; and as applied to planning Healey 1997; Forester 1989). Or, put differently, through hegemonic discourses that performatively enable social fields like 'planning' or 'Indigenous recognition' and shape their meaning (Bourdieu 1977; Butler 1999).

A second methodological challenge concerns the relationship between the textual construction of the contact zone (both in planning and in the field of

Indigenous recognition) and the everyday practice of people interacting with each other in specific local instances. This is a challenge that relates both to the tension between structure (context) and agency (practice), and to its scalar dynamics, for example between provincial/state regulations and their actual operation 'on the ground' in real place-times. Again, there are established traditions of studying planning and other areas of public policy as textual constructions of one kind or another and as the sum of minutiae of daily practices. What began to emerge, then, was the importance of an open methodological approach that enabled us to hold both textual and other kinds of practices together. Seeing the lines of connection and complexities of interaction between what at first blush looks like a highly textual 'system', but is also very practical, became central to our analysis.

To this end, we found the methodological frame offered by Institutional Ethnography, and the work of Dorothy Smith in particular, extremely insightful. Emerging out of studies that focused on the experiences of subordinated groups in social services and other bureaucratized structures, the focus of Institutional Ethnography is on how everyday practices and experiences map to broader institutional structures and relations. It provides a methodological approach for identifying how local practices are drawn into entire complexes of social relations (Campbell and Gregor 2002; Smith 2005). Texts are intrinsically important to an Institutional Ethnography approach, but only insofar as those texts authorize, legitimate and create different kinds of possibilities for action. This is a quite specific framing of texts as discursive as well as active, which has shaped an ontological focus on the textually mediated character of social relations. Institutional Ethnographers call these 'ruling relations' or how 'people's doings in particular local settings are recognized and attended to as participating in relations in which they are active and through which their local doings are coordinated with those of others elsewhere' (Smith 2001, 162).

'Ruling' in this context does not mean that texts operate in a unidirectional way, or that there is no room for reinterpretation, subversion and failure. Instead, texts are interpreted through a phenomenon Institutional Ethnographers refer to as 'text-reader conversations'. The text side of that conversation is of course fixed and static – it is the materiality, the words, or the 'black and white' print of written documents (Smith 2001, 191). But the other side is open and fluid, positioned in the agency of all kinds of actors who are variously activating and reconstituting the meanings of those texts (Smith 2005). Texts themselves, then, are active agents – 'activating social fields, shaping their form and content, prescribing and directing what happens within them' (Porter and Barry 2015, 28).

We found these methodological insights sat comfortably alongside our broader conception of the relationship between structure and agency, context and action, and the interaction of actors and texts across different institutional scales. Our approach is heavily influenced, then, by the idea that social fields, identities and relations are 'hailed into being' (Butler 1999) rather than pre-existing or determined. We might best characterize this methodological approach as open and performative, enabling a conception of planning contact zones as constituted and maintained through ongoing 'performances' (of both text and practice) about identity, resources and authority. In short, struggles that unsettle and resettle the politics of land.

This performative and rather hybrid methodological approach is deliberate and vital for a number of reasons. There is a kind of positivism that often underpins analyses of processes and struggles that begin from very delimited understandings of state, civil society, and differentiated subordinate groups. The fields and social positions of 'planners' or 'Aborigines' or marginalized groups, or the state more generally are often seen as static and pre-existing. Methodologically, we are committed to countering this with a different way of conceiving the politics of land-use, ownership and authority in (post)colonial contexts. Understanding and adequately conceptualizing how contact zones unfold and emerge demands seeing them not merely as interactions between different cultures, but as 'performative ensembles'.

A further important reason why this stance is vital is that it brings methodological life to theories that inform our thinking. The term 'contact zone' suggests margins and edges, borders and centres. While Pratt never enters into a discussion of these matters, we see contact zones as neither pre-determined nor static spheres. Instead, the margins, borders and centres are in perpetual construction and contest. They are then an inherently hybrid or even 'third' space (following Bhabha 1994), neither one thing particularly nor the other, always open to reconstitution albeit under highly mediated conditions. Cultural conceptions, such as those about planning or land or space and place, are translated and negotiated in these spaces, and the emergence of new positions and ways of being (not necessarily transformative or progressive) is always possible. Haig-Brown and Archibald (1996) refer to these negotiations as 'border work': a practice that involves both border crossing, through the creation of hybrid spaces, and border maintenance, through more hegemonic practices of domination. As Somerville and Perkins note, making visible the processes of border construction is as important as recognizing the 'strategic possibilities' (2003, 257) that lie on both sides of borders.

Seeing the contact zone as fluid yet textually mediated also enables analysis to hold open the possibility that the new discourses and practices that might emerge from this continuous performance are neither necessarily transformational nor repressive. State-ordained practices and texts contain all sorts of repressions and possibilities, as do the practices and discourses that emerge from other domains. Moreover, while framing Indigenous claims within existing planning texts and discourses may trigger at least a partial recognition of Indigenous rights and title, such a strategy can always foreclose other opportunities and may only serve to perpetuate colonial ways of articulating and organizing human-environment relationships. In this way, the performance of the contact zone through everyday and textual practice might simultaneously be involved in maintaining and expanding its boundaries.

The methodological framework we have developed for this study is thus itself a rather open, fluid hybrid of a number of components. Each lends insights and tools for the study of the contact zone: the conception of contact zones as performative assumes no predetermination of the agents of change, the provenance of transformation or the contours of marginalization. IPA's attention to the phenomenological and hermeneutic dimensions of policy exposes how institutional and policy change can be seen as a discursive contest or interaction (Hajer 1993). Methodologically, we are inspired by Institutional Ethnography as an approach particularly well suited for exploring how the everyday practice of the contact zone (and the strategic actions taken to modify and transform it) are shaped and constrained by broader discursive structures and frames. We found that augmenting this with the analytical techniques of Critical Discourse Analysis (CDA) was helpful, and later in the chapter we provide detail as to how we operationalized CDA in our study. Before we get to that, however, a brief discussion on practice and text as two intertwined dimensions of our methodology is needed.

Everyday Practice in the Contact Zone

One thing is very clear from Indigenous scholars, critics and activists: stories of struggle in colonial contexts that render colonizers fully present, voiced, and always triumphant oppressors, and Indigenous people mute, silent, and only ever victims are partial stories at best. At worst they reconstitute colonial power relations and underpin many of the more paternalistic and disempowering uses of knowledge and scholarship in the name of Indigenous rights. Indigenous agency in its various expressions and manifestations must therefore be central to any analysis of either historical or contemporary expressions of struggles marked by relations of colonial power.

Mary Louise Pratt, to stay close for a moment to our operating concept of the contact zone, identifies the ways that Indigenous peoples have worked to 'write back' to the colonial centre as one such form of agency. Her terminology is the 'arts of the contact zone' (1991), a notion that draws attention to the diverse strategies colonized peoples have used – and continue to use – to negotiate, find voice within and potentially disrupt the asymmetrical power relations of colonial and (post)colonial encounters. In her work, Pratt conceived the 'arts of the contact zone' as the strategies different actors use to communicate across lines of difference. These 'arts' are united through the ways in which they all 'involve a selective collaboration with and appropriation of the idioms of the metropolis or the conqueror. These are merged or infiltrated to varying degrees with indigenous idioms to create self-representations intended to intervene in metropolitan modes of understanding' (1991, 35). Pratt's observations are an instructive starting point, and we look carefully in Parts 2 and 3 at the 'arts' and practices that the four Indigenous nations who participated in the study used in their own daily struggles. These constitute the bulk of our analysis of practice in the contact zone as we try to unpack and explain how and why the stories in our four case studies are unfolding. It is vitally important to examine the various conditions under which certain kinds of practices of resistance or everyday struggle are variously subversive, co-opted or transformative. Part of this task demands formulating ways of understanding why particular modes of resistance or avenues of struggle are chosen, how they work and who practices them with what effects.

Yet these questions give rise to some deep ontological and epistemological dilemmas. First is that particular kinds of action or moments of agency are not determining of any specific outcome. In our case studies, as we will describe later in the book, all manner of agency, struggle, practice and action are present, but their effects and outcomes vary widely. Some seem to lead to genuine success, other actions fall on deaf ears or wither away. Aspects of the social movement literature are insightful around questions of charismatic leadership (Lovell 2003; Weber 1979) political opportunity structures (Tarrow 1994), shifting access to power and forms of quiet, everyday resistance (Scott 1987, 1990). All are at work in our cases, as we will show. Yet any analytical framework that suggests there is a 'best practice' or a 'way to' struggle against and within regimes of power that firmly mediate the contact zone we find deeply unsatisfactory in analytical and political terms. If agency could be pinned down in this standardizing and universalizing way, then it would always be the case that any marginalized group could eventually achieve recognition of their rights and entitlements as long as there was good leadership, a window of opportunity and some resources to back the fight. This is so obviously not the case, and so starkly an inaccurate account of the incredibly fractured, heterogenous relations between Indigenous people and settler states around the world, it becomes indefensible as a framework.

Second is that the question of agency is not only one of the practice of a subordinate group against a hegemonic order or a dominating interest. There seems more to gain analytically by not limiting agency and practice to the various methods of resistance and struggle waged by Indigenous peoples. Indeed, to line up 'agency' as the everyday practice of the subordinated Indigenous groups and 'text' as the realm of the state and its oppressive tendencies would rather work against the more performative, relational and mediated approach we have taken. Consequently, we sought to expand the notion of agency to *everyday practice* and ask about the ensemble of actions and performances by all kinds of actors in the contact zone. Practices as we conceive them in this research have an everyday mundane quality as much as they have an extraordinary or explosive quality. Practice is as intrinsic to the maintenance of hegemonic orders as it is to fighting against them and there is nothing intrinsic to agency that defines it as a disposition to resist or a guarantee of political effectiveness. Theories of performativity (Butler 2010; Butler and Athanasiou 2013; Christophers 2014) and to a lesser extent the *habitus* (Bourdieu 1977) both recognize the contingent qualities of agency, and the interconnections with structures, histories and context.

Structures and actions do not exist as discrete categories, but instead are constitutive of one another – either through disposition-producing *habitus* (Bourdieu 1977) or through the kinds of subject performativity that Butler conceives. Agency, or practice, is deeply embedded within and mediated by existing contexts, structures and relations such that we cannot see the one (practice/agency) without the other (context/structure). Bourdieu's constitutive dispositions that emerge from actors' position within a *habitus* are close to the 'ruling relations' that Smith and Institutional Ethnographers see as coordinating the practices and behaviours of social actors. Just as text does not causally define action for Institutional Ethnography, nor does the *habitus* unilaterally determine dispositions or practices. But they certainly *mediate* that practice. The point is that the 'structure' or context (the *habitus* for Bourdieu, the social field for Butler) is generative at the same time as never fully formed.

On the question of effective and transformative agency, however, we begin to break with the explanatory power of the *habitus*. Bourdieu contends that the effectiveness of the various speech acts performed by social agents in their *habitus* depends on the positionality of those subjects and their listeners. To be effective, in other words, practices and actions have to be performed by subjects already invested with authority in regard to those practices (Bohman 1999). While this is to some extent defensible, what it doesn't explain is how subject positions once deemed completely illegitimate in a social field (such as Indigenous people at planning tables) can transform that illegitimacy into a form of authority. In other words, at some level, while the contact zone can be seen in itself as a *habitus*, Bourdieu's assumptions about the positionality of subjects and listeners can't explain how the contact zone comes to be.

The view that effective agency arises from certain subject positions also seems to hide the possibilities for transformation, particularly where subversive practice might use the discourses and tools of the very structures against which the subversion is directed (Butler 1999). This is precisely Pratt's point in her 'arts of the contact zone' and in line with our broadly (post)colonial critical stance, a commitment to the possibilities of hybrid reformulations and reimaginations of social relations is vital. As our case studies will show, Indigenous peoples have very successfully adopted, in some instances, 'planning techniques' such as maps, policy requirements or zoning to subvert and transform the land-use outcomes those techniques in other formulations sought to impose. Yet in other instances, comparatively similar attempts to subvert the 'language of the master' have barely rippled the surface of planning hegemonies around spatial authority and order. What we have tried to develop, then, is an analytical framing of transformative political agency that can expose these contingent, performative dimensions.

Textual Practice in the Contact Zone

Texts play a clear and very powerful role in shaping, constraining, authorizing and regulating the day-to-day experience of an institutionalised *habitus*. In Institutional Ethnography, texts are key references, though not necessarily final determinants, for regulating and authorizing institutional behaviours. Proscriptive texts in particular, like regulations or statutes, enable or constrain action, standardize sequences of steps, identify appropriate actions, create different kinds of roles and responsibilities, and appropriate local practices by inserting them into already established modes of behavior (Smith 2001). In other words, they authorize, legitimate and create different kinds of possibilities for action.

In our study, we defined text as the laws, regulations, policies, guidelines and procedures governing planning in our two case jurisdictions. Land-use planning, as an administrative instrument of the state that seeks to categorize, rationalize and standardize social-spatial relations in both urban and natural resource management contexts, is inherently textual. Planning texts are powerful enactors of discursive orders. The textual nature of planning comes in different forms, a point we will begin to address in Chapter 4, be it the highly codified and hierarchical regulatory system that shapes Victorian land-use planning or the unwritten 'texts' that run throughout British Columbian planning in the form of norms or orders of practice that circulate within the profession.

At the same time, texts also fundamentally shape how settler states conceive of the peoples they continue to colonize and their responsibilities towards Indigenous rights and title. This is the recognition field that together with planning systems constitutes the planning contact zone. These texts include court decisions and resultant statutory changes, as well as a plethora of best practice guidelines, statements of intent and codes of practice. Collectively, and sometimes in contradictory fashion, the texts that define how 'Indigenous' is recognized in settler states and what planning means powerfully define and regulate the contact zone.

Understanding these complexities and nuances in the operation of text as a practice, and practices as agency is quite demanding of a methodological framework. We have been especially focused on ensuring the study design was able to expose and analyse the (post)colonial relations of power that are surely at work. As Foucault teaches us (Foucault 1980, 1984, 1988a), understanding power in these terms demands a particular focus on discourse, and how discourse operates across a range of social practices (see also Fairclough and Fairclough 2012; Smith 2005)

Partly for reasons of practical study design, much of which was set out in Chapter 1, we have conceived of discourse as both textual and material, written and practiced. Practices are as much discursive as discourses have material, practical and affective dimensions. To that end, our analytical approach in the study has been to look for the operations of discourse across the dataset we co-generated. In doing so, we adopted some of the concepts and procedures of Critical Discourse Analysis. We turn to a discussion of our approach to discourse, and CDA in particular, in the next section.

Analyzing the Practice and Text of Discourse

Approaching both practice and text as discursive is a key methodological tool for studying the expressions of power and struggle in the contact zone. This is because a focus on discourse enables an examination of the narratives, dispositions and articulations that carry meaning, and through that meaning shape and change social reality. Discourses regulate particular decision-making episodes by determining what is included and excluded, and how. It is through discursive practice that meanings of what is 'planning' and what is 'Indigenous' become normalized – made self-evident and legitimate. As Bourdieu (1977) explains:

> Official language, particularly the system of concepts by means of which the members of a given group provide themselves with a representation of their social relations ... sanctions and imposes what it states, tacitly laying down the dividing line between the thinkable and the unthinkable, thereby contributing towards the maintenance of the symbolic order from which it draws its authority. (21)

In relation to agency, subject positions like 'planner' and 'Indigenous activist or leader' are also constituted through that ensemble of performances, such that the individuals who come to act in those roles 'become what they are' (Lovell 2003, 6).

Yet it is also at least partly through discourse that those same hegemonies are contested and unsettled. Text and discourse are not static and are often an area of struggle, contestation and transformation (Fairclough and Fairclough 2012; Smith 2005). As Foucault stated:

> Discourses are not once and for all subservient to power or raised up against it, any more than silences are. We must make allowance for the complex and unstable process whereby discourse can be both an instrument and an effect of power, but also a hindrance, a stumbling-block, a point of resistance and a starting point for an opposing strategy. Discourse transmits and produces power; it reinforces it, but also undermines and exposes it, renders it fragile and makes it possible to thwart. (Foucault 1988b, 101)

This understanding of the struggles over and within discourse demands consideration of whether and how discourse connects to a more generative understanding of power that underscores the *powers to* or the capacities to enact change. Our work grapples with the idea of discourse as both a *power over* the conception and enactment of the contact zone and a *power to* struggle for coexistence. Consequently, our research is designed so as to critically apprehend institutionalized forms of power (material, discursive and linguistic) as real and pervasive, while at the same time remaining alive to the utterances and discursive formulations performed by different actors that might variously pierce, support, reinforce or re-signify those structures. More specifically, we ask: how, to what degree and with what costs might the strategic and careful use and adaption of existing discourses connect to the struggles for coexistence and recognition?

This interest in discourse is not simply a response to such theoretical treatments of the role of discourse in the operation of power, but is also grounded in an understanding of how planning is conceived and performed in each of our research contexts. In this sense, discourse as a textual and everyday practice aligns with our ontological conception of the performative and relational nexus between structure and agency. Discourses are as much a practice as material practices are often discursive.

Aspects of both Interpretive Policy Analysis and Institutional Ethnography are focused on discourse, though in slightly different ways. Both can be seen as complementary methodologies for analyzing the role of text. Yet each, in separate spheres, has been criticized for under-theorizing the structures of discourse (Chouliaraki and Fairclough 1999), and for a lack of precision in setting out how ethnographic and textual data might be interpreted. It is for this reason that we sought to integrate more precise analytical procedures in our design, and so turned to Critical Discourse Analysis (CDA). We found CDA helpful in its ability to expose the structuring powers of texts at the same time as acknowledging the 'causal powers' of agents. Developed by Norman Fairclough and others (Fairclough 2003; Chouliaraki and Fairclough 1999), and extensively adopted and developed in a range of fields, CDA provides a way of thinking about both the structures of the discourses that are already present within and come to dominate a social field, as well as the ways in which these discourses evolve and change. Like IPA and Institutional Ethnography, CDA allows the compilation of a range of data for analysis including documents, interviews, observations and other ethnographic approaches. Indeed, as Norman Fairclough (2003) acknowledges, CDA is probably best undertaken using a range of data sources and techniques.

CDA identifies a relatively stable and durable combination of three particular elements that together operationalize 'orders of discourse' (Chouliaraki and Fairclough 1999; Fairclough 2003). These are ways of representing (which CDA rather confusingly names 'discourses'), ways of acting (genres) and ways of being (styles). Taken together, these orders of discourse are sometimes able to 'articulate and subsume' (Fairclough, Jessop, and Sayer 2004) other discursive fields to form what are called by critical discourse analysts 'nodal discourses' (Chouliaraki and Fairclough 1999; Fairclough 2005). The term 'nodal' identifies their power to form a 'condensation' (Harvey 1996) around a complex social reality by organizing and shaping other ways of representing, acting and being.

While Institutional Ethnographers may not see ruling relations as necessarily discursive, we see a resonance between 'nodal discourses' and 'ruling relations', albeit their constitution from slightly different intellectual lineages. Analytically, nodal discourses or ruling relations are possible to trace, in text and in the institutional and social practices of and about texts. For Institutional Ethnographers, they can be seen in two ways: '[t]hrough the categories of objects, subjects/agents and forms of actions of the text itself which presuppose and rely on other texts; and ... in a complex co-ordinating the work sequences that produce organizational outcomes' (Smith 2001, 187–188).

Somewhat similarly are the analytical orientations for CDA, where nodal discourses can be rendered available for analysis through: text and its linguistic features; discursive practice such as interdiscursivity and the various moments of the production and consumption of text; and through social practice particularly how discursive events are placed, performed and change institutional contexts (Fairclough 1992) In both IE and CDA, then, there is a particular role for analysis of interdiscursivity and the work discourse does to coordinate and articulate practices and social relations.

Yet as with ruling relations, the control that nodal discourses exercise is never complete, nor is it pre-determined. Discourses, both written and practiced, evolve and change as new discourses are introduced to and reinterpreted within the context of any given social field. This work of *interdiscursivity* occurs when discourses seep beyond the boundary of one social field and begin to permeate another. For CDA, this occurs specifically through the operations of text, where one text reworks or re-accentuates another and in so doing contributes to a wider process of social change. In that new social field, whether it be across a different structural, sectoral or scalar boundary, they are not simply reproduced but are appropriated. This is a co-producing, dialectical relationship where discourses apparently 'external' are appropriated and made meaningful within another social field.

The outcome of interdiscursivity is rarely a supplanting of existing ways of representing, acting and being, but rather the creation of hybrid discourses, an 'irreducible characteristic of complex modern discourse' (Chouliaraki and Fairclough 1999, 59). Hybridity is seen as a 'resource in interaction' (58) because it creates possibilities for expressing and practicing different genres, styles and representations. Using multiple orders of discourse within a single text, for example, also heightens the power of that discourse to speak to multiple and potentially competing or conflicting social fields.

Operationalizing any of these quite abstract theoretical constructs into an analytical framework is a matter of interpretation and judgement, as evidenced by the very diverse application of both discourse theory and CDA in a range of fields. Our approach has been a strategic selection of some key analytical constructs that were insightful for exposing and explaining the relations between social change, social practice and text as it is performed in planning contact zones. We see discourses as powerfully mediating, but not finally determining, the conditions and the boundaries of the contact zone between Indigenous people and state-based planning systems. They are both textual and non-textual: established planning texts authorize and regulate the contact zone by assigning positions and responsibilities and by legitimizing appropriate courses of action. They also appropriate practices undertaken in the contact zone by assigning pre-existing institutional categories and situating those practices within established bureaucratic structures.

Both interdiscursivity and hybridization are salient to how we analytically identify the performative construction and maintenance of the contact zone. This is because certain discursive formulations, through a highly mediated but nonetheless contested set of social practices, come to powerfully organize key 'nodal discourses'. It is in the articulation of texts and social practices from a number of discursive fields that shape planning contact zones where discourses appropriate and internalise Indigenous recognition within planning systems.

Contact zones are, therefore, inherently the products of recontextualized discourses. And more importantly, it is those nodal discourses as we will begin to show in the next chapter that powerfully mediate the possibility of particular subject positions and their authority to speak.

Those discursive formulations operate across each of the three elements of 'orders of discourse' that CDA identifies: ways of representing, ways of acting and ways of being. Our approach has been to attend to the operation of these different elements at various scalar levels in our analysis. The representation of Indigenous interests, authority, agency and legitimacy is the basis of the field of recognition, and becomes interdiscursively articulated with planning systems in certain highly circumscribed ways. Within the particular episodes of planning that we have studied, it is clear that there is contest about various ways of acting, and of framing acting. There are ways of acting that produce knowledge, contest knowledge, seek to negotiate, assert, or dispossess. All are important discursive dimensions of planning contact zones. Finally, subject positions within contact zones are called into being through discursive formulations of what it is to 'be' a planner, an Elder, a Chief, a negotiator, a consultant, a lawyer or an advocate.

The ontological and epistemological basis of CDA also aided greater precision in what we came to define as text and practice for the purposes of data collection and analysis, and how we operationalized that analysis. Texts are all the regulations, statutes, court decisions, policy, guidance, maps, strategies and official reports that together mediate how Indigenous recognition and how planning is conceived and enacted in both BC and Victoria. In analysing selected texts, we were particularly looking for how planning contact zones emerged through the interdiscursive articulation of planning and recognition systems. Practices, we came to define as how people talked in retrospect about what they did and how. For practical reasons we were limited in the amount of observation and ethnographic work we could undertake in our four case study areas. Our analysis of practice, then, is a discursive interpretation of how people talked about their practice, and how that talk then aligned with what appeared to be their material outcomes as expressed in changing institutional and organisational practices. The interviews and limited observation we undertook with research participants enabled us to look for how hegemonic and counter-hegemonic strategies were enacted and materialised 'on the ground' in practice. Greater detail about these research procedures was provided in Chapter 1.

Conclusion

If planning research and practice are to begin a process of decolonization, a critical component of that journey will be building appropriately critical and ethical methodological frameworks for appraising what is actually happening. This chapter has attempted to make a contribution to that end. Utilizing a hybrid methodology built from components of Institutional Ethnography, Critical

Discourse Analysis and Interpretive Policy Analysis, we have set out how planning research might begin to tangle with the intersection between agency and the messy everyday reality of practice in the contact zone, with the more structuring effects of textuality imposed by the policy and regulatory regimes through which planning system and recognition domains are operationalized in settler states. In particular, we have focused in this chapter on building a methodological approach that is especially focused on the text and practice of discourse. For discourse is the lens through which the politics of coexistence in contact zones is refracted in our case study areas. The next chapter looks closely at how those discourses operate in the planning system and recognition domains that mediate the contact zone in Victoria and British Columbia.

Chapter 4

Constructing Contact Zones: Planning and Recognition Discourses in Victoria and British Columbia

Introduction

Planning contact zones occur at the confluence of two social fields, or domains, of settler-state activity: the more-or-less formal systems of planning and Indigenous recognition. What happens at this confluence is a largely unstudied question and one this book seeks to address. It is a question that requires understanding of the structures and discourses through which both planning and Indigenous recognition are made manifest: how they are made operable by the state, what defines them and how they are practised. The first two sections of this chapter, therefore, provide details on the systems of planning and recognition that exist in Victoria and British Columbia, highlighting key similarities and differences. The final section looks at the confluence: what the formal intersection of planning and Indigenous recognition in these jurisdictions looks like.

While these first two sections provide important background information that will help readers make sense of subsequent chapters, the contribution is not solely substantive. This material also begins to reveal particular ways of seeing, being and acting in these two social fields. Consequently, the shapes of the contact zones in Victoria and BC reveal some key tensions in how settler states respond to alternate claims to space and place. The specific policy discourses, regulatory tools, procedural approaches and governance arrangements are different, but the systems of planning and recognition in Victoria and BC are all informed by a persistent desire to 'settle '(limit, contain, reconcile) Indigenous claims and create certainty for private property rights, controlled land-use and the management of the public interest. As will become apparent in the third and final section, the tensions have particular implications in terms of the discursive construction of the contact zone.

Our focus in this chapter is (primarily) on the broad structure of the contact zone at the state and provincial levels in Victoria and BC. The material presented is solely the texts (legislation, policy and court decisions) that together produce the structural frameworks of planning and Indigenous recognition. We begin with describing the relevant state/provincial planning systems in a general sense, and then the specific systems that pertain to the four types of planning context within which our case sites are situated: urban planning and public land or conservation planning in Victoria; and urban planning and Crown land planning in British Columbia. Each substantive section weaves the necessary backdrop for understanding the story of Indigenous contact with each of these planning contexts that are presented in Parts II and III. For that reason, the text places a particular focus on urban planning in Melbourne, where additional layers of government authorities, planning legislation and policy come to structure the contact zone than might occur in urban planning contexts elsewhere in Victoria. In the mirroring section outlining urban planning in BC, the focus remains at the provincial level, as it is within that generic system that we find the discursive formulation of urban planning processes in the province. All of this material is framed within a lens of planning as a manager of competing claims for space and place, often expressed through property rights.

In the second major section, we describe how Indigenous recognition is currently operationalized in these two settler states. Again, we proceed in turn, first describing how the recognition of Indigenous rights and title has come to be performed in Australia and Victoria, and then in Canada and BC. Using landmark court decisions, and related legislative regimes, we frame this discussion through the lens of Indigenous claims the certainty of settler-state jurisdictions and property regimes. The recognition regimes that result are settler-state responses that seek to manage and limit those unsettling claims. In the final section, we look more precisely at the point where these two domains of planning and recognition meet: what we call the contact zones of Victoria and BC. We describe where and how Indigenous rights, title or interests appear in planning systems in these two jurisdictions. The discussion is framed to enable a perspective on why these contact zones appear as they do, the answers lying in how the nodal discourses at work in each intersect and are recontextualized.

Planning and the (Un)Settling of Property Rights?

Planning is often conceived as a way to manage conflicting land-use and property rights, by regulating and qualifying the rights to use, develop, build on and extract resources from land according to a broadly conceived public interest. This story of the profession, one that emerged in response to an ongoing tension between private development and common goods should be very familiar to any student of planning. Many planning textbooks continue to identify this progressivist, interventionist and normative role (for Australian and Canadian examples, see Gleeson and Low 2000; Hodge and Gordon 2013). Different planning systems enact different strategies and mechanisms to perform this perceived role. In urban areas these strategies often include by-laws and land-use zones that limit the type and density of development; urban design standards and guidelines; and requirements for developers to build daycares, parks or social housing. In non-urban areas, the strategies tend to focus on creating designated protected areas (for example, national parks), as well as various buffers and setbacks that limit development around sensitive environmental values and features. In these ways, it is possible to see planning as a system of governance that *unsettles* the primacy of private property by purposefully intervening in struggles over who can do what, where they can do it and who gets to say.

Yet the relationship between planning and private property rights is less innocent and straightforward than this would suggest. The enjoyment of private property and its benefits rests on the security and certainty of the rights of individual owners vis-à-vis the certainty and stability of a broader public interest. Owners and investors have to be certain of their exclusive rights of access, use and enjoyment; citizens have to be certain of their rights where there might be an abrogation of the public interest. Planning systems, then, attempt to make certain the rules under which particular kinds of actors and citizens can make claims.

Victoria's Planning System

As in all settler states, the presumption of Victoria's planning system is that underlying land ownership, and the authority to control and regulate the use and development of land, rests with the state. Lands in Victoria belong to the Crown unless they have been alienated by deed or grant, such as in the allocation of freehold title. Regulation of the use, development and conservation of all lands in Victoria is the jurisdiction of the Victorian State Government, with the exception of 'matters of environmental significance', which are the preserve of the Commonwealth Government under Australia's federal system.

The legislative basis of the land-use planning system in Victoria is the *Planning and Environment Act (Vic) 1987*. This Act incorporates every land-use designation in use across the state, and establishes the objectives of planning in Section 4 as to provide for the 'fair, orderly, economic and sustainable use, and development of land'. There are strong objectives to protect the public interest and overall to 'balance the present and future interests of all Victorians'. These objectives are seen to be in the public interest, an interest that is protected and enhanced by the activities of the state and its agencies as the arbiter on these questions of balance, fairness and growth. A suite of State Government agencies and authorities implement this responsibility. Local government authorities in Victoria, created under the *Local Government Act (1989)*, are also intrinsically involved in planning at the local level. In general terms, the system of planning is relatively heavily prescribed by statewide policy direction and a significant standardization of the content, process and form of planning.

Urban land-use planning in Melbourne
The system of land-use planning as it pertains to Melbourne is a complex negotiation of delegated power and authority between the state and local levels of government. Through delegation by the state, local governments are responsible for most land-use and development decisions in their jurisdiction, and are also

required to prepare municipal-level strategic plans. The system is substantively hierarchical. Overarching policy direction is the remit of the State Government, which produces a state planning policy to which all municipal-level plans must comply (for more discussion on the structure of Australian governments in relation to planning, see Thompson and Maginn 2012). Decisions on particular land uses and developments – that is, the statutory control system – are operated mostly at the local government level but again are heavily standardized and prescribed through a system of standardized zones and a hierarchy of planning policy.

Strategic urban planning at the regional and metropolitan scales – and especially that which pertains to the case of metropolitan Melbourne, as we will outline in Chapter 5 – is mostly the remit of the State Government and its agencies. While there is no statutory requirement for metropolitan-scale strategic planning, there has been a long, if somewhat patchy, history of metropolitan planning. Melbourne, which is Victoria's capital and its largest city, has a history of non-statutory metropolitan planning dating back to 1929, and in its current iteration is called *Plan Melbourne*, a document produced in 2015.

This most recent revival of metropolitan-scale planning in Melbourne needs to be understood within the context of substantial urban and population growth. Melbourne has become one of the world's most expensive cities for real estate and a highly desirable location for property capital internationally. Inflated land values, extremely high housing costs and ongoing growth on the sprawling fringe are some of the consequences. Metropolitan planning strategies are a response to these trends. One particularly controversial trend in Melbourne is urban sprawl, and in 2006 the Victorian State Government created a Growth Areas Authority (GAA) to manage and plan for growth in designated peri-urban growth areas. That authority has since been disestablished and folded into a new Metropolitan Planning Authority (MPA), which also has responsibility for inner-city urban renewal. For purposes of accuracy, we refer in this book to the GAA, as that was the agency in operation at the time the data was collected in 2011. The GAA was responsible (as the MPA now is) for the preparation of strategic planning in the growth areas at three different spatial scales: the corridor scale, where broad land-use and development direction is set; the precinct scale, where more detailed planning across neighbourhoods is established; and the local scale, where plans for specific sites are drawn up. The objectives of the planning undertaken at this level accord with the more general planning policy direction in Victoria: to coordinate and facilitate growth and public infrastructure provision, to 'promote sustainable development' and to generally balance the needs of certainty for private investors and developers with the provision of public goods.

Public land management and conservation planning
Planning for public lands and protected areas is solely the jurisdiction of the State Government, through a variety of public land management authorities, under its powers to reserve land for public purposes as set out in the *Crown Land (Reserves) Act (1979)*. At the time of this research, the Victorian Government's

Department of Sustainability and Environment (DSE) had primary responsibility for the management of public lands (the department has subsequently changed names several times, in this book we will refer to the agency as the DSE). The *Conservation, Forests and Lands Act (1987)* sets out the structure and process by which such public lands are managed, directing ministers and their respective departments to prepare plans, establish codes of practice and undertake land management activities.

Since 1998, the strategic planning and day-to-day management of lands reserved for conservation purposes has been undertaken by an arms-length government agency called Parks Victoria. The DSE provides the overarching strategy and policy for conservation lands, and Parks Victoria implements these through its planning and management activities. Planning functions, then, are undertaken by both these agencies, although the DSE is the more powerful, as it sets the broad policy direction to which Parks Victoria is accountable. Strategic land-use planning for conservation areas occurs at the level of specific parks and protected areas. Plans of management are a statutory requirement for any park proclaimed under the *National Parks Act (1975)* and are also usually in place for other conservation areas. In keeping with Victoria's generally more hierarchical planning structure, these plans all have standard content and are based on data in standardized datasets, and the process by which they are developed is prescribed by State legislation and policy.

A strongly hierarchical designation of land uses is inscribed within the public land and conservation management legislative regime in Victoria. National Parks, deemed less modified and with higher conservation values, are deemed worthy of full protection and placed at the top of a hierarchy. State Forests, deemed already modified and valuable for natural resource extraction, are at the bottom of the conservation hierarchy (see also Porter 2010 for a more detailed analysis).

British Columbia's Planning System

According to the Canadian constitution, lands and resources are *primarily* an area of provincial authority. The BC Provincial Government is therefore formally responsible for almost all lands within the province (National Parks, Indian Reserves and military lands being three notable exceptions, as these are all areas of federal responsibility). However, the provincial level of government is not directly involved in land and property issues that fall under incorporated municipalities – which include cities, towns, villages and district municipalities (such as the District of North Vancouver, which we will discuss in Chapter 7). The relationship between the province and municipalities is articulated in the *Community Charter* [SBC 2003], which affords municipal governments the 'fundamental power' to address wide range of issues that are broadly planning related. On Crown lands (a highly contested term that many Indigenous peoples reject), the province has full authority, and it discharges that authority in a non-statutory planning regime that grew out of a long history of environmental conflict lacking ideas of alternative dispute resolution or multi-stakeholder decision making. This system soon encountered a growing trend toward (neo)liberalization, with private forest management companies playing an increasingly important role (Barry and Porter 2012). Therefore, both municipal and Crown land planning are shaped by the delegation, by the province's constitution authority, of land and resource management to other levels of government and even to private entities.

Municipalities and urban planning
The *Local Government Act* [RSBC 1996] is BC's primary piece of planning legislation, which allows municipalities to largely self-determine the desired outcomes and processes of planning. Municipalities are required to express their five-year vision through the completion of Official Community Plans (OCPs): strategic planning documents that must address the entire suite of public and private land use and establish policies for housing and the reduction of greenhouse gas emissions. The *Local Government Act* goes on to specify some of the details regarding the preparation, approval and amendment of an OCP, but it is not overly directive. Municipalities simply need to 'consider whether consultation is required' with other stakeholders. Furthermore, the Act also does not contain any precise requirement regarding the specific forms and intensity of the consultation process, though each OCP is required to undergo a formal public hearing before being enacted as a by-law.

BC's urban planning system also includes a rather non-hierarchical approach to regional and intermunicipal issues, which further underscores this lack of provincial engagement in determining the character of major acts of strategic planning. Whereas the *Local Government Act* only *encourages* municipalities send their OCPs to one another for comment, municipalities in designated regional growth areas are *required* to work together to create Regional Growth Strategies (RGSs). An RGS must address the social, economic and environmental health of the entire region, with a particular focus on the reduction of urban sprawl. As in the case of OCPs, the Act contains only minimal requirements with respect to the nature of the planning process and the level of consultation. Each municipality is, however, legally required to ensure that its own OCP is written within the context of the RGS. This rather unusual cooperative approach to regional planning relies on individual municipalities coming to some sort of agreement (through the RGS) about what larger values they want to protect and will agree to uphold in their OCPs. The individual OCPs still create certainty for property development (as these are the documents that drill down questions of specific land-use zoning), but the RGS creates certainty for adjacent municipalities in the sense that they always have at least a general idea of their neighbours' major development plans.

Provincial Government and the planning of Crown lands
Like land-use planning in incorporated areas, the planning and management of BC's Crown lands occurs at multiple scales, but it is more hierarchical. Crown land planning is guided by a commitment to develop broad regional direction before

engaging in more localized and often sector-specific acts of planning (for example, protected area plans, forest management plans). Unlike in the case of planning in incorporated areas, there is no statutory requirement to produce strategic plans; BC's *Land Act* simply allows the establishment of land-use designations. A number of planning policies and procedures have been created to guide these planning processes, but these guidelines have changed quite dramatically over the program's approximately 20-year history. Not only have the policies changed, but there has also been very little consistency in terms of the oversight provided by government and quasi-government agencies. The now defunct Commission on Resources and Environment, Land Use Coordination Office, Ministry of Sustainable Resource Management, Integrated Land Management Bureau (ILMB) and current Ministry of Forests, Lands and Natural Resource Operations have all been tasked with the responsibility of mediating public and private (resource-development) interests. At the time of this research, very little attention was being given to creating and revising strategic plans.

The policy and procedures that were developed to support natural resource planning were quite purposefully written to allow for variation – a decision that was justified by the tremendous variation in the size and the ecological, economic and demographic conditions of each of BC's approximately 30 different natural resource planning areas. The Integrated Resource Planning Committee and, later, the Land Use Coordination Office worked to produce a series of policy documents that articulated the core principles of strategic natural resource planning. These core principles included the comprehensive assessment of resource values (that is, the ecological attributes, as well as other socio-economic and cultural interests), the use of scenario-planning and extensive public participation, including the adoption of a consensus-based approach.

The current policy direction is contained in the 2006 document *A New Direction for Strategic Land Use Planning in BC*. This document suggests that, while the basic principles of strategic natural resource planning have remained the same, they have also been heavily modified to provide certainty and remove policy impediments to the economic health of BC's forest industry. Under the *New Direction* document, all acts of strategic planning must be predicated on the establishment of a strong 'business case'. Plan initiation and amendment will be conducted only when there is a statutory imperative: 'major emerging land use conflicts or competition among different user groups; a need to identify new economic opportunities; and/ or a need to address FNs' [First Nations'] opportunities, constraints and values and interests in areas where strategic plans have not been completed' (BC ILMB 2006). In other words, planning is no longer seen as an inherent public good and will occur only when the financial risks outweigh the time and resources needed to complete a plan.

The *New Direction* document also stresses that each initiative should be tailored to explicitly address the unique set of conditions that led to the establishment of a 'business case'. The only constraints are that all strategic plans need to provide certainty for the different resource users; retain the province's role as final decision maker; operate within current fiscal constraints; ensure that land is being used to its 'highest and best use'; involve 'key stakeholders' and incorporate First Nations' 'interests and values' (BC ILMB 2006). Therefore, although the overall logic and rationality of natural resource planning has changed, there is now even greater latitude in terms of designing the planning processes and outcomes that might be used to achieve these goals.

Indigenous Recognition and the (Un)Settling of Property Rights?

Indigenous claims unsettle the exclusive and privileged access to privately and collectively held (that is, Crown) lands. What was once held to be undeniably certain suddenly looks less secure. The weight of evidence of dispossession is exposed through those claims, demand recognition that such exclusive and privileged ownership *is built on* the theft of lands from other people. Thus, Indigenous claims not only unsettle the certainties of Western jurisdiction and notions of property, they challenge the very constitution of Western liberal sovereignty. Settler states respond to these threats by extinguishing Indigenous rights and title in certain places in a number of inter-related ways: by rendering Indigenous peoples 'too modern' to make a claim for their traditional territory; by rendering their territory too modernized to enable legitimate recognition of a living Indigenous cultural association and/or by reducing their ancestral responsibility and authority to care for their traditional territories to procedural power. It is through these acts of containment that Indigenous claims are resettled.

While Indigenous recognition and its potential implications for planning have already been discussed in broad conceptual terms Chapter 2, here we take a more focused look at how the recognition of Indigenous rights, title and governance systems manifests in our two research locales. This discussion will include key shifts at both the national and state/provincial levels. For although land and resource management are firmly areas of state/provincial responsibility in both Australia and Canada, as we have just outlined, it is the federal authorities in these two settler states that are charged with negotiating the state's overarching relationships with Indigenous peoples.

Indigenous Recognition in Australia and Victoria

Australia does not have a system for recognizing Indigenous rights and title to land and sea country according to Indigenous law and custom. Neither British nor Australian governments have ever entered into a treaty with Aboriginal or Torres Strait Islander nations, despite a long history of Indigenous activism and pressure for a treaty. Instead, what Australia has might be best described as a patchwork that is differentiated by State and Territory jurisdiction as a result of the different legislative frameworks that have been put in place. South Australia was the first Australian government to enact land rights legislation in 1966, after which all jurisdictions followed with the exception of Western Australia, but adopting widely varying systems. The picture is extremely complex, and the patchwork remains, despite the existence of an overarching and nation-wide regime of recognition called 'native title'. This regime of recognition arose from the High Court of Australia's decision in the historic *Mabo* case (*Mabo v. State of Queensland No. 2 [1992]* 175 CLR 1) of that year, and is our principal focus for understanding the recognition regime in Australia in this book. This decision brought about the most significant marker of recognition by overturning the presumption of *terra nullius* (empty land) that had held for more than 200 years of Australian colonial history and recognizing that Aboriginal and Torres Strait Islander title once existed and may still exist in some places where it has survived colonization. In response, the Australian Federal Government passed the *Native Title Act (Cwth) (1993)*, which established a legislative framework through which such Indigenous people can claim native title, and where successful have their native title recognized under Australian law. This Act, and following that specific legislative responses then passed in most states and territories, together establish a series of procedural rights for Indigenous people to be at the land-use decision-making table where decisions might potentially impact on native title. While the legislative frameworks are quite distinct in each State and Territory, for our purposes in this book, taken together they produce a particular discursive framework through which recognition politics in Australia, and especially Victoria, are framed.

Native title, then, constitutes a landmark shift in Australian land law. Yet despite the apparent significance of this decision as a moment of recognition, the reality is rather different. A generation of research and commentary now exists from the post-Mabo era, documenting and clarifying how the native title regime effectively operates at worst as a system of extinguishment and at best as a highly limited recognition space (see Smith and Morphy 2007; I. Watson 2005; Dodson 1996; Langton 2001). Native title can be recognized only on lands that have not been alienated from the Crown by deed of title, grant or (some) leases. After a backlash of fear and hostility following the *Mabo* decision, Australian governments moved swiftly to extinguish native title on freehold properties. This leaves only Crown lands (including leasehold lands) available to claim. That extinguishment is of course most spatially intense in cities, where most land is owned privately under freehold title. But it is also spatially intense in the places where dispossession through processes of colonization was early, swift and resulted in the absolute removal, often by force, of all Aboriginal people from their territory. One such example is the case of Victoria, where within only 15 years of the establishment in 1835 of the first small (illegal) squatter camp at what is now Melbourne, 20 million hectares of land had been stolen from Aboriginal peoples, and the massive combined toll that smallpox, genocide and loss of lands and economy took on Aboriginal people had reduced the population by some tens of thousands (see Boyce 2011; Clark 1995; Clark 1998; Barwick 1988).

Aboriginal and Torres Strait Islander claimants are required to pass two essential proof tests for their claim to be recognizable under the native title regime:

(1) ancestral connection to the claimed country (usually via written accounts of early white settlers) and (2) a 'continuing connection' to that country that is demonstrably based in 'traditional laws and customs' that predate colonization (for legal analysis, see Brennan 2011). These proof tests, combined with the conditions for extinguishment, create an enormous gap between how Indigenous people understand their relationship with their land and how that relationship might be recognized in Australian law. The ongoing dispossessory intent and outcome of this regime is widely recognized (Dodson 1996; Smith 2001; Atkinson 2002; Moreton-Robinson 2004; Watson 2015) and it produces a very particular spatial expression across the Australian continent as shows.

It is this extremely flawed native title regime that forms the principle base of contact between Indigenous rights and planning. In legislative terms, this is expressed as the Future Acts regime, as set out in the *Native Title Act (Cwth) (1993)*.

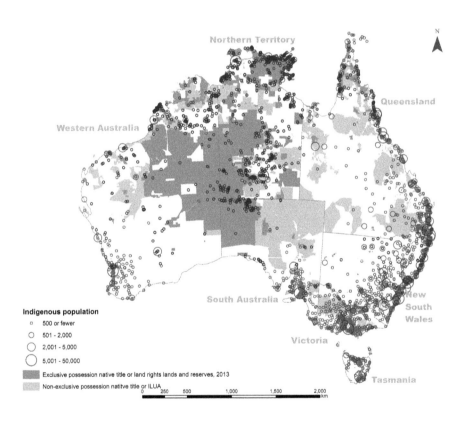

Figure 4.1   The Indigenous estate in Australia, as at 2013

Source: Map courtesy of Jon Altman and Francis Markham 2015, used with permission

Here, native title claimants or holders have procedural rights to be consulted, or negotiated with, on activities taking place within their claim area. This includes planning and land management activities.

Victoria has its own legislative framework responding to native title, in the form of the *Traditional Owner Settlement Act (Vic) (2010)* (TOSA). Aboriginal people in Victoria played a very significant role in agitating and pressuring for this legislation. Having seen the need for a different legislative framework than native title for the Victorian context (see Bauman et al 2014), Aboriginal people across the state came together to form a Traditional Owner Land Justice Group. A first action of the group was to publish, in 2005, a communiqué demanding recognition of rights and title, restitution and compensation, and practical actions to restore control over land planning and management. That communiqué began the negotiation and development of a traditional owner settlement framework, based on the principle of 'right people for country', which became the TOSA.

The TOSA departs from the national native title regime in that it envisages an agreement-based approach to settling native title and other land justice claims. Four different agreement types are made possible under the act:

1. A recognition settlement agreement
2. A land management agreement (joint management)
3. A natural resource agreement (which enables sharing of profits)
4. A land-use activity agreement.

Adopting the language of 'traditional owner' has in part been a push by Aboriginal people in Victoria who have sought alternatives to 'Aboriginal', and 'native title'. Use of the word 'owner' signals the intention to place Aboriginal ownership on a more equal footing with other ways of owning, and to signify the unique qualities of that ownership through the word 'traditional'. Nomenclature of this nature remains highly contested in Victorian Aboriginal politics and is constantly shifting.

To be a 'traditional' owner, however, also creates an implicit connection to the discursive construction of native title. Although there is no requirement within the TOSA to provide the same conditions of proof as the national native title regime demands, the complicated politics involved solicit demands from both traditional owner groups and from government for some kind of proof of their ancestral and ongoing connection to that particular country. This sometimes involves the assemblage of detailed anthropological evidence of the ancestry of each individual claimant, as will become clear in Chapter 6.

Indigenous Recognition in Canada and BC

Unlike in most parts of Canada, the initial waves of European settlement in BC were *generally* not preceded by the negotiation of treaties. Indigenous peoples were forced onto 'Indian Reserves' (as they continue to be referred to in federal legislation). These reserves represent an incredibly small and marginal portion of the broader traditional territory and tended to provide little opportunity for the land-based practices that are the lifeblood of many Indigenous cultures. Notably, these reserves are not owned by First Nations but are federal lands that have been 'set apart' for their 'use and benefit' (*Indian Act R.S.C. [1985]*, c. I-5, section 18[1]) and that were historically managed by a federal 'Indian agent' (Coates 2008). As we will see, greater authority is now being transferred from the Federal Government to First Nation Band Councils (which are themselves creations of and highly regulated by the federal *Indian Act*).

These violent acts of settler-colonialism were facilitated, at least in part, by the assumption that Indigenous peoples' political and territorial rights were completely extinguished upon the establishment of Western systems of law and property (Tennant 1990). These colonial assumptions have been successfully unsettled through a series of precedent-setting rulings from the Supreme Court of Canada, beginning with the 1973 *Calder* decision. This decision had profound impacts on Canadian Aboriginal policy (Godlewska and Webber 2007), not the least of which were constitutional amendments to recognize and affirm all existing Aboriginal and treaty rights. The *Calder* decision also led to the establishment of a Federal Lands Claims Office, which would not only seek resolution Indigenous claims in areas not covered by historic treaties (comprehensive lands claims) but also use a negotiated approach to resolving any disputes over entitlements and other lawful obligations arising out of the treaties (specific land claims) (Indian and Northern Affairs Canada 2003).

It was the Supreme Court of Canada's 1990 *Sparrow* decision that prompted the BC Provincial Government to consider its responsibility to engage in comprehensive land claims. Although that case did not concern Indigenous title, but rather the broader notion of Indigenous rights (Tennant 1990), it did find that '[h]istorical policy on the part of the Crown can neither extinguish the existing aboriginal right without clear intention nor, in itself, delineate that right' (*R. vs. Sparrow [1990]*, 1 S.C.R. 1075, para. 2). In other words, all Indigenous rights (including title) could no longer be seen to have been extinguished by the application of federal or provincial law – the very issue that the *Calder* case was unable to conclusively address. It was this finding that 'put an end to 130 years of denial of aboriginal rights by the BC government' and provided the necessary stimulus for the establishment of BC's own approach to comprehensive land claim negotiations (BC Treaty Commission 2010, 1).

Officially established in September 1992, the BC Treaty Process is a tripartite one, involving the federal and provincial governments and each individual First Nation that elects to participate. Negotiations progress in six stages, from the preparation of a simple Statement of Intent through to long-term implementation plans. Notably, the BC Treaty Process adopts a very low threshold for 'proving' traditional use and occupancy. The Statements of Intent simply must provide enough information for the BC Treaty Commission to determine that their traditional territory 'is *generally* recognized as being their own' (BC Treaty

Commission 2009, point 7, emphasis added) and it is up to the First Nation to resolve any issues of overlapping claims. Aboriginal governance, lands, resources and financial compensation were identified as some of the issues that the parties would likely want to address. Like the broader comprehensive land claim process, BC treaty negotiations generally include identification of specific settlement lands, development of appropriate mechanisms of compensation, provisions for self-government and opportunities for engagement in environmental decision making within the traditional territory.

The BC-specific and broader federal approaches to land claim negotiations and modern treaty making adopt a similar approach to the thorny question of extinguishment. Originally, the final outcome of a comprehensive land claim was conceived as a 'blanket extinguishment' of Indigenous claims to all but the small portion of their traditional territories that had been agreed upon as suitable treaty settlement and/or reserve areas. The *Comprehensive Land Claims Policy (1987)* later acknowledged the need to allow for the persistence of certain 'defined rights' (9). This policy went on to acknowledge the possibility of engaging First Nations in the environmental management of their land claim area, even after the signing of treaty, but continued to stress that these kinds of benefits were 'in exchange for relinquishing rights relating to the title claimed over all or part of the land in question' (9).

Canada and BC's approach to treaties, therefore, needs to be understood not as an attempt a mutual recognition and coexistence but rather as an exercise in achieving certainty (Woolford 2005; Alfred 2001). Applied to Canada's approach to recognizing Indigenous rights and title, certainty is not about current and future use but rather certainty of ownership and, ultimately, jurisdictional authority. These discourses and approaches have not gone unchallenged, with many First Nations electing to opt out of the process entirely and look to the courts as a potential avenue for negotiating their coexistence with the settler state. Although this form of Indigenous recognition is steeped in settler-colonial law – a reality that suggests that it needs to be understood as monological as opposed to mutual recognition (Chapter 2) – it nonetheless works to unsettle the primacy of Western notions of property and political jurisdiction by demanding increased attention to the territorial connections and responsibilities that Indigenous peoples never surrendered.

To understand these unsettlements, we must look to another series of closely related high court rulings, beginning with the 1997 *Delgamuukw* decision. It included not only recognition of rights to use the land, but also 'the right to the land itself' (*Delgamuukw v. British Columbia [1997]* 3 SCR 1010, para. 138). This latter recognition of Indigenous title rights is also seen to include 'the right to choose to what uses land can be put' (*Delgamuukw [1997]*, para. 166), a finding that led the Supreme Court Justices to conclude that Indigenous people need to be engaged in land-use decision making in a manner that will often 'be significantly deeper than mere consultation' (*Delgamuukw (1997)*, para. 168). The courts have also allowed for a certain degree of flexibility as to who holds the right to be consulted. These Indigenous rights holders are not confined to a specific body and may include Indigenous individuals, bands (political bodies formally established by the federal *Indian Act*) and traditional governance structures (Newman 2009). This approach stands in stark contrast to Victoria's *Traditional Owner Settlement Act*. In fact, the *Delgamuukw* decision quite firmly states that Indigenous peoples' 'right to occupy and possess' is framed in broad terms and, significantly, is not qualified by reference to 'traditional and customary uses of those lands' (para. 119).

Subsequent court decisions have gone on to extend, but also contain, this more advanced form of consultation. The *Haida Nation v. British Columbia (Minister of Forests)* [2004] 3 SCR 511, (2004 SCC 73) and *Taku River Tlingit First Nation v. British Columbia (Project Assessment Director)* [2004] 3 SCR 550 (2004 SCC 74) decisions stated that the level of consultation must be in proportion to the strength of the Aboriginal claim and the extent of the possible impacts, and is also seen to demand a certain 'level of responsiveness', which has been defined as 'accommodation' (2004, para. 32). Indigenous peoples would not, however, have veto power over Crown decisions. The threshold for triggering the duty is really quite low. The courts have been quite clear that First Nations claims to space and place are *prima facie*, meaning that government duties arise when they 'could meaningfully form an idea of there being Aboriginal title, an Aboriginal right, or a treaty right' (Newman 2009). Not entirely unlike the BC Treaty Process, the form of certainty that is being expressed in these duties is not directly about the certainty of ownership but rather the establishment of clear principles and procedures – and, most significantly, limits – for addressing how to make land-use decisions when the nature of ownership is not very clear.

Constructing Contact Zones: An Intersection and Re-contextualization of Discourse

As the previous sections show, state-based systems of planning and Indigenous recognition reveal similar tensions in the response of settler states to unsettling claims. Each of these systems (re)settles these challenges through the discursive boundaries that are produced and reproduced in various statutes, regulations, policies and procedures. We return to this issue of boundaries in Chapter 10. In this last section, we focus on a related issue: how the resettling discourses that are present within systems of recognition are *recontextualized* (see Chapter 3) according to the resettling discourses already present within systems of planning. We draw attention to how this recontextualization is occurring within the context of urban and environmental planning in Victoria and British Columbia.

In doing so, this section offers *preliminary* commentary on the basic tenets and characteristics of the four contact zones being examined in this book. We deepen and extend this commentary in Parts II and III of this book, using our four case studies to show how actual contact zones unfold, manifest and are made active. None of these cases exist in isolation; all are informed by and deliberately contest the ways in which the contact zone is conceived and constructed at the provincial/ state scale. It therefore remains important to interrogate that wider scale in order to understand its implications for the everyday practices of the contact zone.

The Contact Zone in Victoria

Although the Australian approach to Indigenous recognition and the requirements of the Future Acts regime, in particular, create a broad legislative intersection between native title and planning, there is no high level within planning legislation of what impacts this intersection heralds. The urban context shows a particularly shallow and limited form of recognition of Indigenous peoples in planning. In the urban planning system there is relatively little recognition that Indigenous peoples exist, much less any sense of rights and title, or even 'interests' in the activities of planning. There is no overt intersection of native title in urban planning in Victoria apart from, in some plans, a disclaimer that a plan may need revision to ensure minimal compliance with native title. In the planning system for public lands and protected areas, the contact zone is wider and more explicit and exhibits a more direct engagement with native title and traditional ownership. We detail both in the two sections that follow.

Urban planning and Aboriginal cultural heritage

In 2006, a new regime for managing Aboriginal cultural heritage was enacted in Victoria and brought about the first explicit and direct link between Aboriginal interests and the system of development control in Victoria. The *Aboriginal Heritage Act (Vic) (2006)* amended the *Planning and Environment Act (1987)* and the Victoria Planning Provisions to give statutory powers to authorized Aboriginal organizations called Registered Aboriginal Parties (RAPs) on urban development proposals that trigger the requirements of the Act. The system works where proponents of developments over a certain size and in certain areas must prepare, as part of their planning application, a Cultural Heritage Management Plan (CHMP). These are submitted to the relevant RAP, who assess the impact of the development on cultural heritage and the measures that developers propose to address that impact. RAPs, then, become in the language of planning statutory consultees on planning development applications, and have significant statutory powers and responsibilities. This includes the power to veto a cultural heritage management plan (and by extension, the development application) if cultural heritage management has not been addressed to their satisfaction.

This is the first time that Aboriginal interests have ever featured in the planning system of Victoria. What is recognized here, however, is a procedural right to be involved in a planning decision-making process, as well as a limited form of political right to decide on development proposals in relation to their potential impacts on cultural heritage. It is a recognition of neither title nor innate political rights, as it is only those organizations identified as RAPs (by the Victorian Aboriginal Heritage Council) that can have these decision-making rights.

Moreover, there are threshold tests similar to those for determining native title. To become a RAP requires proving a legitimate traditional connection to country. Indigenous cultural heritage interests are simply inserted into the planning system as another layer of consideration.

Other than this highly specific formulation of a contact zone in Victoria, a limited symbolic acknowledgement exists of Aboriginal peoples' prior occupation on Victorian lands. In 2004, the Victorian Constitution was amended to incorporate a high-level statement that recognizes the prior occupation and ongoing attachment of Aboriginal peoples to land and waters in Victoria. Adopting a similar language, some planning documents also have a statement of symbolic acknowledgement on their inside front cover. These statements never explicitly recognize rights or title, nor do they explicitly tie planning functions or assumptions with recognition of the Indigenous domain. The use of bland, depoliticized language such as 'acknowledgement', 'past occupation' and a 'contemporary association' undermines the claims that Aboriginal people make in Victoria to land ownership and political sovereignty.

Indigenous joint management and conservation planning in Victoria
Native title has had a larger impact in planning for public lands, particularly in relation to conservation areas. The *Traditional Owner Settlement Act (Vic) (2010)* made a series of consequential amendments to the public land and conservation management legislative framework in Victoria. Under this framework the State Government expressed a commitment to, and a process for, entering into agreements with Indigenous people regarding land management and planning over lands reserved for conservation and resource management purposes. Section 82(b) of the *Conservation, Forests and Lands Act (Vic) (1987)* was amended by the TOSA to enable Traditional Owner Boards of Management to govern specific parks and reserves. These boards, of between 9 and 11 members with a majority of traditional owners, would be appointed by government and supported by an executive officer. This form of joint management would give recognized traditional owners a majority stake in decisions about the development and conservation of a park, within the existing legal and policy framework of land conservation and management.

The TOSA represents a different approach to settling Aboriginal title claims, pursuing negotiated agreements as settlement, rather than the litigation approach the native title regime tends to inculcate. Indeed, development of the TOSA arose directly from an explicitly observable gap emerging in the jurisdiction of Victoria where native title claims were having little success (see Bauman et al 2014). The TOSA in that sense directs both the State and Traditional Owner groups to engage in negotiated agreement-making around the key question of who should be recognized as the 'right people for country', and thus considerably loosens the proof tests for recognition that are embedded in the Federal native title regime. Having said this, links remain to those proof tests, both tacit and more explicit. A tacit link is the requirement, as will become important in the story of the Wadi Wadi people, for the ratification of land management agreements to the satisfaction of the Attorney-General and Department of Justice, rather than the land management agency making the agreement. This tends to raise the requirement of further 'proof of connection' evidence to be shown, at least in some cases. The TOSA does make explicit links with the registration test requirement of the Native Title Act where particular dimensions of settlement packages are being negotiated. Significant efforts have thus been made to move away from more adversarial and proof-based approaches (see Bauman et al 2014), including the development of 'threshold guidelines' by the Department of Justice (2013). Nonetheless the TOSA has not been able to entirely unsettle some of the limitations faced by Aboriginal people in densely settled places like Victoria.

A further limitation in the regime is that this is a principally procedural contact zone. While the *Traditional Owner Settlement Act (2010)* allows for the recognition of Aboriginal use and enjoyment of rights in lands and waters, the planning framework in response does not acknowledge these. Instead, it focuses only on procedural rights with some decision-making powers and incorporates these more limited rights into the existing planning framework. Traditional Owner Boards of Management have powers and remits quite similar to other protected area governance approaches, and become implementers of the established conservation and land management framework – its policies and regulations – for Victorian lands and waters.

Ever since the *Mabo* decision put Aboriginal land rights more visibly within land policy, public land management agencies began to realize that many of their activities should include Indigenous people as stakeholders. Organizations such as Parks Victoria, the DSE and some of the catchment management authorities have established partnership frameworks and 'Indigenous strategies' of one sort or another to express a higher level of commitment to Aboriginal communities, even where formal Traditional Owner Boards of Management do not exist. Parks Victoria has been at the forefront of this agenda and has led the public sector in Victoria in terms of progressive approaches to building relationships with Aboriginal people, regardless of native title possibilities or outcomes. Indeed, Parks Victoria staff express a fundamental principle that 'as the designated manager for the State's parks it has clear responsibilities for managing Country of Victorian Traditional Owners' and that this should be achieved by 'working through [traditional owner] organizations and respecting free, prior, and informed consent'. Partnership frameworks and guidelines for working with Indigenous communities imply a symbolic recognition of Aboriginal 'prior occupation' of lands and waters, and a varyingly explicit recognition of the requirement of governments to redress ongoing socio-economic disadvantage. They do not recognize rights and title, nor do they explicitly recognize formal political authority, even within the symbolic language. Most partnership frameworks are consensus focused and seek to 'work with' Indigenous communities on issues such as cross-cultural education, service provision, reconciliation and the boosting of Aboriginal employment opportunities.

The Contact Zone in British Columbia

As previously highlighted, Indigenous peoples are acknowledged as having a role to play in the planning of both municipal and Crown lands. The *Local Government Act* acknowledges the potential for (and, in some instances, mandates) Indigenous consultation during the preparation of municipal and regional plans. The *New Direction* document also acknowledges the potential necessity of using planning to address Indigenous interests – a statement that needs to be read within the context of the legal duty to consult and accommodate Indigenous peoples. Yet, as the following sections will illustrate, significant differences emerge in terms of the overall nature and depth of the contact zones. The urban contact zone is informed by a much more limited form of Indigenous recognition, oriented around the geographic and political boundaries of the 'Indian reserve'. The contact zone that informs the planning of Crown lands is much broader and *begins* to envision ways to address the political rights and responsibilities that arise out of a recognition of Indigenous rights and title.

Municipal coordination and the interface with treaty and reserve lands in BC
In urban contexts, the recognition of Indigenous rights and title that has been underway at both the federal and provincial level contributes only indirectly to the construction of a planning contact zone. Many municipalities (including the District of North Vancouver) opt to include stock phrases about how their plans have 'been written without prejudice to First Nations' assertions of aboriginal rights and title to their traditional territories' (District of North Vancouver 2011, 2) the specific term 'Aboriginal rights and title' is absent from almost all of the policy documents that guide the creation of these plans. The term appears only in the policy and procedural documents related to the small number of municipal functions for which there is a statutory requirement for provincial approval (for example, municipal boundary extensions). Similar statements are completely absent from both the *Community Charter Act* and the *Local Government Act*.

These rather glaring omissions are at least partially due to the ongoing legal uncertainty as to whether the duty to consult applies to municipalities. Recent decisions by the BC Supreme Court and Court of Appeal have found that these duties rest solely with the Crown (that is, federal and provincial governments). The procedural responsibilities for fulfilling those duties may be delegated to other parties, including municipalities. At the time of writing, this legal precedent had not been challenged in the Supreme Court of Canada, though there had been some critical commentary that exposed significant flaws in the current precedents (see, for example, Imai and Stacey 2014).

Aboriginal rights and title do still play a significant role in shaping the relationship between local governments and First Nations, but only with respect to the BC Treaty Process. According to the Union of BC Municipalities (UBCM), there are already 75 First Nation reserves within or immediately adjacent to existing municipality boundaries (Union of British Columbia Municipalities 1994). For

First Nations participating in the treaty process, these and other treaty settlement lands will provide new urban development and income-generating opportunities in areas that could historically be developed only to meet the basic housing and infrastructure needs of First Nation communities. Such changes have prompted municipalities to seek greater information exchange and coordination with neighbouring First Nations in terms of service provision and growth management.

Organizations such as the UBCM (which represents all BC municipalities and acts as a powerful lobbyist) have also been promoting active dialogue, dispute resolution and coordinated planning efforts between municipalities and adjacent First Nations, including a consistent land-use zoning system on adjacent municipal and treaty settlement lands. While these kinds of planning relations offer a clear recognition of Indigenous political authority when treaty settlement land abuts a municipal boundary, municipalities have actively resisted (through various UBCM policy resolutions) any suggestion that Indigenous rights and authority might continue to be exercised outside of treaty settlement lands. It is, however, acknowledged that Indigenous people may continue to have interests in cultural sites within municipalities – though there is also a very strong assertion that selection and designation of such sites needs to occur within 'very specific parameters' (Union of British Columbia Municipalities 1997). While there is no formal law, policy or procedure to guide BC's urban contact zones, there is a strong expectation that the approach accord with existing municipal norms and practices.

Government-to-government planning on BC Crown lands
Unlike the contact zones that exist in urban areas, the relationships that are beginning to emerge between Indigenous peoples and the provincial government within the context of planning for public lands are heavily framed and influenced by the duty to consult. This is not to say that the BC Treaty Process is irrelevant, as many of the participating First Nations are using this process to assert interests in both the conservation and economic development of forested lands. But when the idea of strategic natural resource planning was first introduced (notably in the very same year that the BC Treaty Process was initiated), there was a strong desire to keep these two issues as separate as possible (Barry 2011). This separation has been difficult to maintain, especially in the face of the 2004 *Haida* decision, which drew specific attention to consulting and accommodating Indigenous interests during strategic planning.

The provincial response to the *Haida* decision was to work with key First Nation political organizations to develop the 2005 *New Relationship Policy Statement*. This document identifies a need for a 'new government-to-government relationship based on the respect, recognition and accommodation of aboriginal rights and title'. These rights are not limited to customary use but rather include 'the inherent right for a community to make decisions as to the use of land and therefore have the right to a political structure for making those decisions' (British Columbia 2005, 1). Although the government-to-government relationship applies to all areas of provincial governance, it has particular relevance to strategic natural resource planning. As previous research has shown (Barry 2011), the *New Relationship* provided an additional imperative to engage in bilateral negotiation to identify and work to address any issues related to Indigenous rights and title. Notably, the policy and procedure that guides strategic natural resource planning rarely makes reference to distinct rights and title, but rather to the provincial government's legal obligations and 'commitment to a New Relationship with First Nations' (BC ILMB 2006). None of these documents contain any specific guidance on how this relationship ought to be enacted within the context of natural resource planning, suggesting that these planning contacts zones are quite malleable and can be tailored to meet specific circumstances and interests.

Conclusion

Indigenous recognition meets planning systems in a variety of ways – as sites of consultation and accommodation envisioned by court decisions, as statutory requirements for planners to consider Indigenous interests and as zones of contestation where the practice of Indigenous claims unsettle Western planning's long taken-for-granted authority over land use. This chapter has provided an overview of both the systems of planning and Indigenous recognition as they currently operate in Victoria and BC, highlighting how each is mediated and shaped by its own internal set of discursive pronouncements. It also explored how planning contacts zones emerge out of a recontextualization of state-based discourses (and associated laws, policies and procedures) of Indigenous recognition and planning. Although the intersection of systems of recognition and planning is a confluence, an intermingling of one with the other, planning contact zones are still fundamentally about planning. As such, they reconfigure existing approaches to managing the tension between public and private property claims. But Indigenous claims are not 'public interest' claims. They are of a different order entirely. In failing to imagine a more effective way to grapple with the coexistence of rights and title that those claims express, planning instead works to *resettle* the certainty of property in the interests of white, 'owning' actors.

It is through these processes of recontextualization that we can begin to see how planning is the system of governance employed by the settler state to contain the unsettling claims that Indigenous peoples pose to the certainty of property and to (re)settle non-Indigenous power over land, reconstituting ongoing processes of dispossession. In both BC and Victoria, there is a presumption that settler-governance systems are the final arbiters of land-use contests and the keeper of the public good. Woven together, discourses that construct planning and recognition as domains of settler-state jurisdiction neatly interlock to create a widely varied zone of contact between Indigenous people and planning. This interface is especially shallow and thin in urban planning contexts, where Indigenous interests are limited to highly specific spatial areas and managed through procedural technologies. On public lands, contact zones seem more expansive, sometimes indicating a willingness to accommodate Indigenous rights and title, but only as a reconstitution of Western sovereignty. The recontextualization of discourses from the domain of recognition into planning explains why so much ground appears to have been won by Indigenous people in the domain of natural resource and environmental planning in contrast to urban areas. Indigenous people are more obviously and easily accommodated into an existing tension between public interest and private development in non-urban places. Private interests are by definition already highly constrained on lands allocated for a wider common interest such as biodiversity conservation or natural resource use. Indigenous claims can be easily brought to bear on a conception of planning that already privileges different values and multiple publics on the question of how to manage common natural resources.

Unsettling and resettling in these ways is never complete and always contested. It is a process of endless negotiation and struggle that represents the constellations of power and contingency in any one space-time. To understand these processes, their varied manifestations and outcomes, it is vital to look at the everyday practices that work to produce contact zones in different kinds of spatial, political and cultural contexts. It is to that purpose, and our four local case sites, that we now turn.

PART II
Stories of Planning in (Post)colonial Victoria and British Columbia

Chapter 5

The Non-Recognition of Indigenous Rights in Metropolitan Melbourne

Introduction

Like all Australian cities, Melbourne is built on the unceded and unrecognized country of Aboriginal nations, with Melbourne's built-up area largely over the country of Wurundjeri people. While there is often quite prominent symbolic recognition of this, there is no formal recognition of rights and title, and indeed little prospect of such recognition given the constraints presented by the native title regime (see Chapter 4). Moreover, Indigenous people in Melbourne experience quite profound marginalization – they are usually poorer, experiencing high levels of unemployment and homelessness, much like the urban experience of many Indigenous peoples in other settler states.

In this chapter, the focus is on the work of the Wurundjeri people, through their organization the Wurundjeri Tribe Land and Cultural Heritage Compensation Council Incorporated (hereafter, Wurundjeri Council). Dispossession remains a central fact in contemporary Wurundjeri society. With little recourse to restitution of their title to that country, and coming from such a marginalized position, Wurundjeri people have nonetheless found ways to assert their rights and interests, particularly their right to access a land base in this heavily urbanized context. While such recognition is partial, limited, fragmented and vulnerable, it gives rise to two kinds of planning contact zones. One is the incorporation of Wurundjeri interests into a variety of partnerships and plans for the management of public lands and waterways in Melbourne. The other is the role of Wurundjeri Council as a Registered Aboriginal Party (RAP) with statutory powers to protect Wurundjeri cultural heritage, where a development application triggers the *Aboriginal Heritage Act*. Wurundjeri Council has harnessed this role and power to great effect.

Working in these partial, limited contact zones, the Wurundjeri Council has emerged as an important player in the planning of Melbourne's rapidly growing peripheral corridors. In the remainder of this chapter we look at each of these particular zones of contact, how they have come about, what they look like and the ways that the planning system tries to close down the wider recognition spaces that Wurundjeri Council are creating.

Wurundjeri Country and Governance: The Context

All living Wurundjeri people are descended from Wurundjeri-willam people of the Woi-wurrung language group. Wurundjeri Country is identified as extending across what are principally the Yarra River and Merri Creek Catchments (see Presland 2010), from 'the Great Dividing Range to the north across to Mount Baw Baw in the east, to Cranbourne and Mordialloc in the south, and the portions of Port Phillip Bay between the Mordialloc Creek to the mouth of the Werribee River' (Wurundjeri Tribe Land and Cultural Heritage Compensation Council Incorporated 2012, 2).

It was with the Wurundjeri people that John Batman and his company 'negotiated' his infamous treaty in 1835. This began an extremely rapid and violent process of dispossession, as the 'treaty' and the actions of Batman and his company opened up the excellent country around what is now known as Port Phillip Bay as pasturelands. The so-called treaty was 'the ultimate legal and ethical fantasy for both land grabbers and philanthropists' (Boyce 2011, 58) It was of course Wurundjeri land management practices that had created such excellent and prosperous country. Rapid dispossession, murder, violence, impoverishment and incarceration of Wurundjeri and other Aboriginal peoples constitute the history of colonization in this region. Just 15 years after Batman and his crew arrived and founded Melbourne, famously declaring 'this is the place for a village' (Boyce 2011, 74), Wurundjeri people had been dispossessed of their lands, economic base, ceremonial grounds and were utterly marginalized.

This story remains palpably present for Wurundjeri people today. It is a powerful source of identity, but also lives on as a sense of deep, unresolved injustice. As one Elder described it, the question of land theft is 'that burning question that still needs to be resolved and that's never been addressed' (pers. comm. 30 May 2011). Land is of course central to Wurundjeri society: land is identity, lore,[1] culture and economy as it is across Aboriginal societies. Consequently, the fact of this total dispossession of Wurundjeri people from their land base – and it is indeed an ongoing and total dispossession – is central to their claims: 'we're a land based culture and we've got no land so it's very hard to keep it alive ... [you must] capacity-build us, lend [us] some land, allow us to access country and do our cultural practice ... (pers. comm. 12 July 2011).

Connections to country are partly drawn from that history of dispossession and partly from contemporary practices that are revitalizing Woi-wurrung language as a living expression of Wurundjeri lore, culture and economy. Places of particular significance feature prominently in Wurundjeri expressions of these ongoing connections and practices: the Bolin Bolin Billabong, the Sunbury Rings complex, Mt William (one of the few greenstone quarries in Victoria), Dights Falls (listed as an Aboriginal Place on the Aboriginal Cultural Heritage Register – pers. comm. 12 July 2011), and the river systems especially around the area now reserved as Yarra Bend Park. Of great importance is Coranderrk, on Melbourne's northeastern fringe,

---

1   The term for law preferred by Wurundjeri people.

established in 1863 as a mission that housed more than 300 Aboriginal people from around Victoria and New South Wales including Wurundjeri survivors. Coranderrk was the site of a rich history of struggle and entrepreneurialism by its residents. Now in ownership by the Wurundjeri people, it is an important land and cultural base.

It is a long history, then, that the Wurundjeri people draw on to frame their struggles for identity and restitution of their lands. The most recent expression of that struggle is the establishment in 1985 of the Wurundjeri Council, the representative body of Wurundjeri people. In establishing the Council, Elders were responding to significant threats to cultural sites and artefacts from urban development pressures. One of the first of its kind, the Council's goal was to protect that cultural heritage and retain control and ownership of cultural landscapes within their own hands, to: 'revive our culture, who we are, our identity and that led into dealing with government departments, the protection of sites through developments (pers. comm. 12 July 2011). This was a visionary move, because at that time the cultural heritage legislation, in the form of the *Aboriginal and Torres Strait Islander Heritage Protection Act (1983) (Cwth)*, was more limited. Little ownership or control was vested, under that former system, in Aboriginal people themselves, and there was little scope for consultation or partnership with the people to whom these artefacts belonged. Despite these limitations, Elders had identified there was sufficient scope under that previous legislative framework to set up a process where Wurundjeri people worked alongside archaeologists on development sites take possession of artefacts identified as a result of archaeological survey and excavation. This offered a modicum of recognition that something here was legitimately Wurundjeri-owned. Importantly, it built capacity by providing an income stream and some limited employment.

Today, Wurundjeri Council is the representative body for Wurundjeri interests. Governed by an Elders Committee of Mangement, the Council is made up of descendants of the three principal family groups (Nevin, Terrick and Wandin), and a CEO appointed by the Elders Committee of Management. These three family groups all trace their lines of descent to the Wurundjeri man named Bebejan, through his daughter Annie Boorat and her son [Robert][2] Wandoon. Currently, there are over 100 members of the Council and around 50–55 members of staff, approximately 45 of whom are Wurundjeri people. A significant area of Council's activity comprises cultural heritage management. However, Elders and staff are also active in many other programs, including land management through the Country or 'Narrap' team; cross-cultural education and training programs, especially with schools and local Councils; providing cultural practices for public events, particularly 'Welcome to Country' and smoking ceremonies; music and dance; language and naming; and cultural consultations (pers. comm. 18 August 2015). A small number of Wurundjeri

---

2   Wurundjeri Elders consider it likely that the name 'Robert' was a further Anglicisation as Wandoon would have been his birthname. Note also that his name is also commonly given (incorrectly in the view of Wurundjeri Elders) as Robert Wandin.

Elders are quite well known, as the Council is highly visible at important events like NAIDOC (National Aboriginal and Islander Day Observance Committee Week), National Sorry Day, Wurundjeri Week, National Reconciliation Week, Indigenous Literacy Day and Melbourne's annual Moomba festival. As will be discussed later in the chapter, a significant piece of work undertaken in recent years was the preparation of a strategic plan, called the Narrap Country Plan.

This prominence has given rise to quite widespread symbolic statements and gestures of recognition of Wurundjeri prior ownership of much of Melbourne. Most of the non-Indigenous municipal councils who operate on Wurundjeri country publicly acknowledge prior ownership of lands by the Wurundjeri people and recognize that a vaguely defined 'connection' continues. These statements are to be found at the opening of any public event, or the inside front cover of a variety of municipal and other government department documents. Increasingly, those sentiments translate into genuine respect by non-Indigenous Melburnians for Wurundjeri people. One Wurundjeri Elder spoke about this change permeating social and policy practices: 'people now are coming forward and they know the protocol and procedure. They know they've got to speak to the Indigenous people of the land and they're doing the right thing ... ' (pers. comm. 18 July 2011).

One mechanism that has catalyzed a statutory requirement for planners and land developers to 'speak to' Wurundjeri people is the *Aboriginal Heritage Act*. This Act creates the only contact zone with urban planning in Melbourne (see Chapter 4), by requiring the proponent who is seeking to undertake an activity, and therefore sometimes also local planning authorities, to consult and engage with recognized Aboriginal organizations through approval of a Cultural Heritage Management Plan when the activity triggers the need for such a plan under the Act. How this statutory mechanism has been harnessed by Wurundjeri Council, is the subject of the next section.

Wurundjeri Council Statutory Powers in Urban Development

When the Victorian Government introduced a new legislative framework for the protection and management of Aboriginal cultural heritage across the State, this represented a new opportunity for Wurundjeri Council. The *Aboriginal Heritage Act (2006)* (AHA), as described in Chapter 4, established a process for the state to recognize approved Aboriginal organisations as 'Registered Aboriginal Parties' (RAPs). To use the language of development planning, these organizations effectively become statutory consultees on some development planning decisions by virtue of changes the AHA made to the planning system. Indeed, the Act provides RAPs with significant statutory powers in some urban development proposals. Wurundjeri Council applied to become a RAP with approval first granted in 2008 and later across a further extension of area in 2009. An application for another extension remains under review by the Victorian Aboriginal Heritage Council.

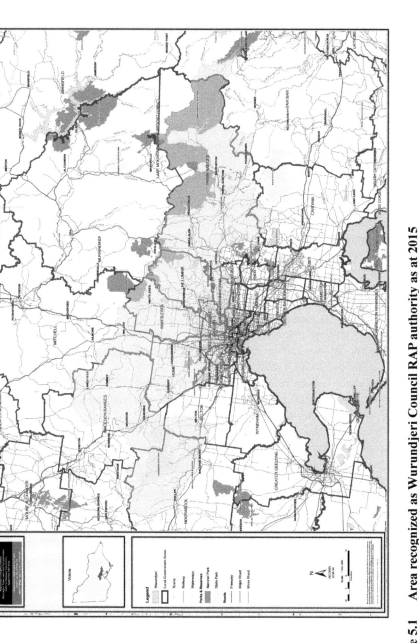

Figure 5.1   Area recognized as Wurundjeri Council RAP authority as at 2015

Source: Map courtesy Office of Aboriginal Affairs Victoria, used with permission

Gaining RAP status is a form of recognition of ancestry and the right to control tangible and intangible aspects of Wurundjeri culture related to that ancestry. Wurundjeri were required to make a case to the Victorian Aboriginal Heritage Council showing that their organization constituted traditional owner members, that disputes over territory and lineage had been resolved, and that the organization had appropriate (that is, non-Indigenous) governance structures in place.

Status as a RAP provides Wurundjeri Council with substantive procedural rights and a set of statutory powers regarding the approval of land-use and development planning applications. The AHA legislatively requires local Council planning offices and development proponents to engage with Wurundjeri Council on proposals that trigger the regulations. In that regard, Wurundjeri Council holds statutory powers on some planning development applications and has the right to request that the proposal for development be significantly amended or even rejected.

This role has been very significant for Wurundjeri Council in a number of ways, particularly concerning capacity and financial sustainability. When the AHA regulations are triggered, the proponent of the development must fund an archaeologist to prepare a Cultural Heritage Management Plan (CHMP), and then must fund the relevant RAP to evaluate that plan. Proponents are also responsible for funding any cultural heritage site works that are required by the RAP. This creates a real and ongoing income stream for Wurundjeri Council. Where once there was reliance on goodwill relationships with agencies and developers, and a rather fraught attempt to monitor developments where cultural heritage might be disturbed (or as one staff member described 'heritage was managed with a handshake, a nod and a wink' (pers. comm. 11 July 2011) the legislative requirement expanded the sheer volume of cultural heritage work being done by the Council. Today, Wurundjeri Council has a dedicated Cultural Heritage Unit, comprising Elders supported by non-Indigenous staff (archaeologists and an anthropologist). More sustainable income streams and increased employment opportunities for Wurundjeri people have been positive outcomes.

There is no doubt that such shifts have been extremely positive, indeed some Wurundjeri staff expressed the view that 'we don't feel like it's just something set up just to appease us, we think it's real and meaningful' (pers. comm. 30 May 2011). The AHA demands compliance because of its legislative teeth, and thus brings about a contact zone between planners, developers and Wurundjeri people. As we will see in the next section, those powers have very effectively been harnessed by Wurundjeri Council to enable a range of other very positive outcomes.

It is worth outlining, however, as we set out in Chapter 4, that while the AHA provides significant statutory powers and authority to Wurundjeri Council, it cannot of course provide access to a land base for the practice of Wurundjeri lore and culture. The AHA, while welcomed across Victoria, is driven from within government, and particularly the State Government agency, the Office of Aboriginal Affairs Victoria (OAAV). While there was high-level Aboriginal representation leading up to the writing and implementation of the AHA, Wurundjeri themselves felt largely left out of the process. It can also be read as operationalizing settler-state power that seeks to resettle and contain Aboriginal influence over urban development (see Chapter 10). This is visible in the various ways that the AHA contains and bounds Wurundjeri authority and interests.

Spatially, that bounding operates through the threshold trigger requirements of the AHA. A development proponent must prepare a CHMP when three threshold tests are passed:

1. The development is in an area of known Aboriginal cultural heritage sensitivity;
2. The development involves 'significant ground disturbance';
3. The development is in an area that has not seen 'previous significant ground disturbance'. (*Aboriginal Heritage Regulations 2007* S6)

Each of these three triggers is precisely defined in the Regulations. Areas that are 'known' as having cultural heritage sensitivity are those that have usually been made subject to state inspection and legitimation. Any places or areas that are listed on the Victorian Aboriginal Heritage Register – that is, mapped and recorded by an archaeologist according to established standards of categorization – are sensitive areas, as are waterways, coasts, prior waterways, ancient lakes, declared Ramsar wetlands, high plains, greenstone outcrops, stony rises, volcanic cones, caves, dunes and sand sheets (*Aboriginal Heritage Regulations* Part 2, Division 4). Places 'unknown' or unrecorded under this gaze of the state and its authorized archaeological experts are not usually considered to be culturally sensitive. Having said this, there is provision in the legislative framework for cultural places to be identified without archaeological recording and only according to Aboriginal lore and culture. However, it is usually the case that specific sites are recorded through archaeological investigation. It is, then, possible to identify cultural places in accordance with Aboriginal tradition, but it is much harder to do so. To that extent, then, expert knowledge about culture is overly institutionalized within the state, and other knowledges or experts are seen by the state as more difficult to include (L. Smith 2004; Porter 2006a).

Moreover, any of these 'known' places are excluded from the authority of Wurundjeri Council as a RAP if those places have previously undergone "significant ground disturbance". This means that any land that, since colonization, has been mined, quarried or excavated is exempt from the AHA. It is important to note that the Act provides significant powers to Wurundjeri Council where it is triggered. What is interesting, though, is the spatiality of where the Act is *not* triggered. The exemption appears to uphold a view that Aboriginal people have long-contested: that Aboriginal culture is somehow in stasis, fundamentally unchanging and vulnerable to modernity. In this sense, when the Act exempts certain spaces from its remit because the ground has previously undergone 'significant ground disturbance' can be viewed as a rather powerful declaration of the places where Wurundjeri lore and culture can be identified in the landscape of Melbourne. The

AHA and its regulations thus tend to operationalize the incorrect non-Indigenous assumption that places in Victoria are no longer legitimately Aboriginal places. By this route, planning systems then become involved in regularizing the recognition of real, authentic Aboriginal places and excluding those where the settler state has deemed that evidence to have been wiped away. Conveniently, it also works to provide certainty to the development industry and ensure that many places in Melbourne are precluded from the legal requirement to work with Wurundjeri. This spatially limit Wurundjeri Council's statutory powers only to those places where the Act is triggered.

Politically, the AHA also works in ways that try to contain and bound Wurundjeri authority. RAPs can only react and respond to development proposals brought forward by proponents. This means that while Wurundjeri Council has significant powers, those are much more difficult to wield if many of the decisions and the wider development agenda is retained by proponents and government authorities. The site protection and management process is also heavily prescribed by the Regulations. Wurundjeri Council receives a CHMP and then initiates a set of negotiations within proscribed limits about the proposal, it's siting, impact, and any works needed to salvage artefacts prior to construction. Again, while there is significant power, the agenda tends to be set beyond the remit of Council.

Yet while these legislative frameworks might constrain in some ways, they also offer potentially significant ways to deepen that contact zone and shift established ways and processes of working. Wurundjeri Council has very successfully harnessed their statutory powers to enable a significant deepening of the contact zone partly because of their RAP status and a more general shift to see Aboriginal groups as stakeholders in land management and planning. This dimension of the Council's work is the focus of the next section.

Harnessing Procedural Power to Widen the Contact Zone

While the legislation is highly prescriptive and procedural, from it springs the possibility of relationships. Wurundjeri Council is keenly pursuing relationships as the best way forward for achieving the kinds of recognition, access to land, and community capacity development they seek. One way that the Council has sought to develop such relationships is through the model of different government agencies funding a liaison post that remains within the organizational structure of the Council. As noted above, Parks Victoria and Melbourne Water were two of the first agencies to adopt this approach in around 2009, when they jointly funded a post to take forward the Merri Creek Cultural Values Assessment. VicRoads, the State's road and vehicle licensing agency, has also funded a post in the same way.

The increase in volume of workload for Wurundjeri Council also precipitated some thinking about governance and process in working with these stakeholders. Early experience of working with archaeologists and development proponents prompted a rethink of just who was involved in those conversations and how those conversations should be structured. While not required by the legislation, Wurundjeri developed a model that is now standard practice in their consultation with CHMP proponents and which they have now rolled out to govern other interactions. The model involves the engagement of CHMP proponents, once they have notified their intention to Wurundjeri Council to prepare a CHMP, in a series of mandatory consultation meetings with Wurundjeri so that the Council can discharge its responsibilities under the AHA. Sponsors and proponents meet with Wurundjeri Elders representing each of the three family groups, and Council's archaeologists and anthropologists at the initial stage to discuss the project, and then to discuss the results from the field assessment and options for cultural heritage management, after a field assessment has been undertaken by the RAP staff and Cultural Heritage Advisor (an external consultant). Wurundjeri staff, Advisors and Elders carefully review the draft CHMP once lodged for evaluation, and provide notification of refusal or approval of the CHMP. The model also includes scope for additional meetings for more complex or important projects, and there are a series of steps post-CHMP approval for Wurundjeri staff to monitor compliance. The process is designed to build relationships with proponents, who are often volume house builders or large development corporations, and to engage early to indicate where there might be issues or challenges. In so doing, Wurundjeri cleverly invoke the discourse of certainty so central to the presumptions of planning and private urban development in Melbourne. The approach is to ensure early consultation so that no 'surprises' spring up for proponents later, resulting in a swifter more certain outcome of the CHMP evaluation process.

Additionally, Wurundjeri Council now allocates three Elders, representing the three family groups, to be involved in each of those meetings, and some of the onsite visits and negotiations where they consider it appropriate. Such an important development exemplifies the desire of Wurundjeri people to confirm the authority of Elders across all of the business of the Council. Moreover, it is a move that unsettles some assumed ontological categories within the system, including the widely held but normalized presumption that Elders have only ceremonial roles and that cultural heritage management is really the preserve of 'experts'.

What RAP status also catalyzed for Wurundjeri was a much deeper engagement with the fundamental problem of where Indigenous interests come to be inserted in the multi-scalar system of planning in Victoria. While the power to change or even veto a development application represented a theoretically powerful shift in authority, in reality all of the essential decisions that mediated the size of the impact of urban development on cultural heritage had actually been made long before, in an entirely different planning forum. This was especially evident in Melbourne's designated growth areas, which came under the jurisdiction of the Growth Areas Authority (GAA). The GAA, as outlined in Chapter 4, had only a brief life: established in 2006 under the *Growth Areas Authority Act*, to coordinate and manage development in (then) seven designated periurban growth corridors, and then rolled into a larger remit that also included urban renewal areas, as the

Metropolitan Planning Authority (MPA) in 2013. At the time of this research, though, the GAA was in full operation, and in relation to its obligations under the AHA, was operating only at minimal legislative compliance. What this meant in practice was that it was in the third tier of strategic planning – site-based plans – where the AHA was triggered. Site plans expressed the specific building and design layout of a new residential development. Situated below two higher scales of planning – Corridor Plans and Precinct Structure Plans – site plans were the masterplan of a given development.

The GAA did not engage with Wurundjeri Council at either corridor or precinct planning stage. This meant that all of the key decisions impacting Wurundjeri cultural heritage interests had already been made at the corridor and precinct planning scales, leading Wurundjeri Council to feel that 'Aboriginal heritage was left at the end again' (pers. comm. 11 July 2011). Moreover, Wurundjeri Council felt that the GAA showed disregard for even a minimal compliance with legislative responsibilities, as they sent CHMPs for site development plans very late in the process. As a consequence, Wurundjeri Council refused to approve a number of early CHMPs sent by the Authority. RAP status provided the Council with a useful 'stick' to force the GAA to reconsider their approach. Yet it was only the commitment of the staff and Elders to relationship building that enabled what then unfolded. Wurundjeri Council's attempts to develop a formal relationship with the GAA, and work at the higher scale of corridor planning emerged as a fraught but insightful story of the possibilities and seductions of planning contact zones.

On realizing the implications of getting CHMPs refused by Wurundjeri Council, the GAA implemented a project of developing a 'predictive model' (pers. comm. 12 July 2011) of cultural heritage sensitivities that would overlay corridor plans and provide an early indication of potential impacts on Wurundjeri cultural heritage. The idea was to then develop CHMPs at the precinct level, to be implemented by proponents at the site scale. An archaeological consultant was appointed to begin mapping registered cultural heritage areas from the OAAV database and then plug in a series of assumptions about where the highest sensitivity areas were likely to be – such as around waterways. This model then created maps, graded into different colours (based on landforms and terrain units, geology, vegetation cover and so on) to predict levels of sensitivity in precise planning areas. Both OAAV and GAA at the time saw the predictive model as an efficient way to get lots of CHMPs done quickly for less cost and to know well in advance at the corridor planning scale where the impacts would be.

But this was not a process that built trust and engagement with the Wurundjeri people or the Council. The GAA was aware of this, reflecting afterward that they realized Wurundjeri were:

> ... fairly down about what this would be used for, mainly because it's taking
> a very kind of scientific approach which they were pretty uncomfortable with.
> They understood it intellectually, but I think they were just thinking well you

know it's basically using a big black box model to put a bunch of variables in. (pers. comm. 12 July 2011)

And indeed it was. Thus, in an attempt to engage Wurundjeri and enable their input into the model, the GAA and the consultants funded a series of eight bus tours around the growth corridors for Elders and council staff. The Elders involved talked about this experience as an important, if often emotional, one, because it brought to the surface stories of dispossession and marginalization that were painful to recall. On the bus tours, Elders were asked to fill in surveys and provide information from their knowledge of each area. Much of that information was very sensitive, and was carefully edited by Council staff before being sent to the GAA and their consultants. The GAA considered that they did not get the information they had expected to, and in a form that could be appropriately plugged into the model (pers. comm. 12 July 2011). This response was received by Wurundjeri as extremely disrespectful of Elders time, expertise and knowledge. The whole process was seen as 'grossly inadequate' (pers. comm. 12 July 2011) by all parties.

The GAA quietly shelved the model after this disastrous outcome and sought to return to a focus at the site scale. But Wurundjeri Council maintained their position that the strategic level of planning was much more important for their engagement as it was here that all of the key decisions were made:

> … the layout of the housing is already locked in so you can only move the parts around. So that broader level of planning you know like this is a water we really should have a massive buffer here or this part of the waterway should have a big park, has to be done right at the early stages. (pers.comm., 11 July 2011)

GAA staff broadly agreed, noting that '[w]e don't really want to find out that there's a 5 hectare site in the middle of the development when the precinct structure plan assumes that land can be developed' (pers. comm. 12 July 2011).

Yet the regulatory framework of the AHA does not easily lend itself to including cultural heritage interests at the more strategic planning scales. In part, this is because the legislation requires the cost of implementing a CHMP to be borne by the developer. Thus, any decision taken by the GAA in negotiation with Wurundjeri at the precinct scale, would have to be imposed as a development cost on the proponent, and the GAA was at the time quick to reject that trajectory, reasoning that this imposed an unacceptable level of uncertainty and cost.

Yet Wurundjeri Council persisted in their negotiations to ensure their interests could be protected at the precinct scale. Their practices in this regard have more recently enabled a very significant outcome to establish a partnership agreement with the now Metropolitan Planning Authority (MPA). In February 2015, the Council signed a Memorandum of Understanding (MoU) with the MPA, the aim of is to collaboratively manage cultural heritage to achieve successful outcomes for both Wurundjeri people and the MPA (pers.comm. 18 August 2015). The MoU sets out the protocols and principles for consultation to enable the Wurundjeri

Council to exercise both statutory and cultural responsibilities at the earliest stages of planning, particularly at the precinct structure plan scale. The agreement also sets out the process for communication and engagement between the partners, and the heritage advisory services that will be provided by the Wurundjeri Council.

Public Lands and Water Management: Spaces of Opportunity and Partnership

Actively seeking relationships with agencies responsible for public land and water management has been one of Wurundjeri Council's most successful strategies over the past 10 years. It is a strategy that arises from Wurundjeri lore, a sense of identity and an urgent need to somehow carve out access to a land base in a rapidly developing metropolis, for cultural survival and revitalization:

> Our old people's responsibility was caring for country, caring for family, and we still feel like that we've got the same role that's been passed down even though it was very nearly cut off. So for us to be able to care for country and water we want to get involved with these managers ... but it's basically making country come back to where it was, keeping it healthy, cleaning it up ... and working with them to do that. (pers. comm. 12 July 2011)

The capacity to seek and develop such relationships was possible because the very existence of the Council provided Wurundjeri the base to capitalize on shifts toward a more consultative approach. Staff at the Council realized an opportunity was knocking when the number of requests from agencies and organizations to have Wurundjeri involvement in all manner of programs and projects began to intensify.

While the Council was pleased at the interaction, the increase in requests raised some challenges. Capacity to respond was limited, and staff at Council felt they were always in a position of reacting, rather than initiating, projects and plans. Their response was to negotiate with individual government agencies to fund liaison positions held by Wurundjeri people but who then stayed as employees at the Wurundjeri Council. The State agency with the most long-standing relationship with Wurundjeri Council is Parks Victoria. Over the past 15 years, a close relationship has developed between Wurundjeri Council and Parks Victoria, facilitated through partnership on projects such as a food and fibre garden, a canoe tree project, support for a funding application to build a cultural education facility, and ongoing negotiations about naming, layout, facilities, trails and signage throughout the extensive protected area network on Wurundjeri country. For some years, Parks Victoria also funded a staff position at Wurundjeri Council, to be the dedicated liaison between the two organizations. Perhaps due to its quite progressive and open approach, Parks Victoria is considered an ally by

Wurundjeri Council staff: 'they have the same outlook protecting the natural and cultural values of the place, that's exactly what the Wurundjeri want to do' (pers. comm. 11 July 2011).

Melbourne Water is the government agency responsible for management of the waterways across the Port Phillip and Westernport catchment areas. This agency also has a relationship with the Wurundjeri Council, arising out of the preparation in 2007 of its Regional River Health Strategy. This strategic document explicitly recognized the importance of waterways for Aboriginal cultural heritage and the continuing connections Aboriginal people have with places along waterways. Council used this to broker a more lasting partnership with the authority through a Memorandum of Understanding. Melbourne Water also co-funded a position at Wurundjeri Council, and partnered with the Council to undertake a cultural values mapping and assessment project along the Merri Creek.

It was also through partnerships that brokered internal capacity for Wurundjeri to prepare a strategic plan for country. It is to that initiative that we turn in the final section of this chapter.

Wurundjeri Narrap: Planning for Country in Metropolitan Melbourne

Augmenting this array of procedural and relationship-building efforts of Wurundjeri Council to be present and visible in decision making about land use and management in Melbourne, has been the development by Wurundjeri Council of the Narrap Country Plan. Plans for country are now widely used by Indigenous organizations across Australia and beyond, as they provide a way to articulate Indigenous lore, culture, identity and land management techniques in a form more immediately recognizable to settler states. Very few, however, have been prepared in heavily urbanized contexts and for that reason Wurundjeri's Narrap Country Plan is a practice that has transformative possibilities for urban planning contact zones.

The Narrap Plan articulates quite clearly the aspirations of the Wurundjeri people for 'new ways to take a greater degree of responsibility to care for Country' (Wurundjeri Tribe Land and Cultural Heritage Compensation Council 2012, 1). It does so by focusing on the public and private tenures that now structure Wurundjeri country and imagines a variety of mechanisms through which Wurundjeri Council will seek to exercise that greater control. This includes seeking further opportunities for Wurundjeri Council to own freehold title to land outright, as well as ways in which they can partner with land management and planning agencies to increase their access to a land base. The Wurundjeri Council now has a Narrap land management team that is focused on the 'protection, management and enhancement of environmentally and culturally significant places on Wurundjeri country' (Wurundjeri Tribe Land and Cultural Heritage Compensation Council Incorporated 2015, np).

Conclusion

Melbourne as a city makes manifest the dispossession that enables it to exist every day, but in entirely unrecognized ways. That present history of dispossession tends to thwart the possibilities of a major restitution of title for the Wurundjeri people. Wurundjeri relationships with urban planning, then, are conducted in a context of non-recognition. Yet, despite that context, Wurundjeri have managed to prise open niches within the planning and urban development system governing Melbourne where their voices are increasingly urgent and important. Using cultural heritage as a catalyst, the Wurundjeri people have worked cleverly to make a partial, highly limited system work more in their interests.

In this chapter we have looked at the ways in which the Wurundjeri Council have achieved this remarkable outcome through persistence in engagement even when the regulatory environment appears to render them invisible, and through leadership and clever capacity-building. The story also shows how the Wurundjeri turned the discourses of certainty in planning to their own ends, thus creating a slightly wider space for engagement on urban developments that concern them. Developing a strategic country plan is a further statement of the visionary capacity of the Wurundjeri people, as they seek to use the planning system to access a meaningful land base. These crucially important forms of agency and the detailed attention the Wurundjeri people have paid to the terms of the struggle they have been engaged in can teach us important lessons about these conditions, as we will discuss in Chapter 9.

While these struggles have achieved the remarkable in a context of non-recognition, the underlying presumption of political authority and development impetus in Melbourne has not shifted. All of the changes achieved to date are framed within existing presumptions about urban development and the ultimate legitimacy of the settler state as the final arbiter on urban matters. Those powerful tropes about who is recognizably Aboriginal, and where Aboriginal interests can legitimately become part of a planning conversation, persist. These critically important bounding mechanisms, which we discuss in more detail in Chapter 10, construct a highly limited and partial contact zone. In this chapter we showed how the regulatory and legislative regime that constructs the contact zone in Melbourne comes to ground and operationalizes the persistent dispossession of the Wurundjeri people from control of their lands and waters.

Chapter 6

Negotiating Bounded Recognition: Seeking Co-management on the River Red Gum Flood Plains

Introduction

A long-standing dispute over logging in a small forest in north-west Victoria has led to significant changes in public land classification and kindled a movement towards co-management of parks and public lands in the region. One of the Aboriginal nations at the forefront of that struggle is the Wadi Wadi people. Their main fight through the 1990s and 2000s was to stop logging in the Nyah and Vinifera State Forests, of immense cultural, spiritual and economic significance in Wadi Wadi law. Their struggle unsettled the presumptions for timber harvesting and forest classification, and continues to defy the impulse in public land planning in Victoria to recognize Aboriginal interests only when they are archaeologically recordable (Porter 2010).

These actions have gradually widened the planning contact zone on the river red gum flood plains of northern Victoria. An alliance of Aboriginal nations and environmental campaign groups, along with an independent commission that investigated the management of public lands, has successfully achieved important legislative changes. Co-management of public lands and reserves is now possible – albeit as yet unrealized – for the Wadi Wadi people, and the reclassification of public lands has significantly enhanced the opportunities for recognition of Wadi Wadi country.

But as this chapter will show, the recontextualization of native title proof tests intersecting with planning's will to certainty persistently works to resettle planning and management activities as rightfully the purview of the settler state. Just as the Wadi Wadi and other Aboriginal nations manage to widen the contact zone, so too do the entrenched colonial relations of power work to close it down. This chapter charts the complex twists and turns of the Wadi Wadi people's struggle for recognition on the river red gum flood plains of north-west Victoria, highlighting both the possibility and the fragility of negotiated agreements.

Wadi Wadi Country, Governance and Planning Struggles: The Context

Wadi Wadi country straddles the Murray River and is therefore located in the two states of Victoria and New South Wales. On the Victorian side, their country lies just north of the rural centre of Swan Hill, extending westwards toward Ouyen and northwards to just south of Robinvale. The riverine red gum flood plains of the Murray River have long been a significant cultural and economic environment for Aboriginal and non-Aboriginal people in Victoria. Prior to British settlement, the river (Milloo, in the language of the Wadi Wadi people) was densely settled along its full extent – a rich source for life and economy, and one of enormous spiritual significance. Colonial settlement spread rapidly along the Murray, as the river provided support for a strong agricultural and trade economy. More recently, because of its economic and cultural significance, the Murray River and its catchment have been the source of considerable policy debate about irrigation and water rights and the focus of struggle for Aboriginal people.

The number of people now recognized by the Wadi Wadi people themselves as connected to the nation has grown over time, with 11 principal family groups linked through key apical ancestors and more family and kinship ties being discovered as groups piece back together the family connections that colonialism disrupted. As this (internally) recognized group expanded, new challenges around governance and decision making emerged. In order to address these, cultural protocols were put in place alongside an agreed-upon governance system. This established the principle that each family group recognized by the Wadi Wadi Nation could send two representatives to regular meetings, where the focus is principally on native title and co-management negotiations.

Decisions are made through consensus among all the families with two key negotiators, consulting with family representatives and feeding information back and forth. Much of the workload of negotiation meetings falls to these negotiators, of whom have families and jobs outside of this work. They regularly report back to the family governance structure. Talking, meeting and being on country are seen as intrinsically important to the process for coming to consensus decisions among the families.

Most of this activity takes place at Tyntyndyer, a historic homestead built by the first white settlers of the region in 1846. Tyntyndyer, purchased by the Wadi Wadi through the assistance of the Indigenous Land Corporation, is now a significant base and focus for Wadi Wadi activities. The homestead is used as a meeting place, and there are future aspirations for a cultural centre with associated opportunities for economic development and employment. In one Elder's words, Tyntyndyer is 'our own solid ground' (pers. comm. 13 July 2011).

The Wadi Wadi people are engaged in an ongoing (and very drawn-out) native title claim over their country. They first lodged a claim, in 1997, which included what were then the separate Nyah and Vinifera State Forests. In 2002, that claim was amended to become a joint claim over an expanded territory with two neighbouring nations (Barapa Barapa and Wamba Wamba). This joint claim (as yet unresolved) does not include Nyah-Vinifera Park. The exclusion of the park becomes significant later in the story about the Wadi Wadi struggle for recognition through co-management. Outside of native title, co-management is seen as a 'step forward', as one Elder said, toward proper recognition because it means becoming 'equal partners' with public land management agencies and is seen as a way to 'take control back … that should never [have] been taken away' (pers. comm. 25 May 2011).

Nyah-Vinifera Park is close by to Tyntyndyer homestead and is a culturally significant place rich in ancient and contemporary heritage, including ancestral remains and burial sites, and sacred areas. It is an interconnected landscape of living, sentient beings and ancestral spirits and is therefore a place of deep importance for the Wadi Wadi people, who continue to express their connections to the area through cultural, social and economic practices. It is this significance that drives the Wadi Wadi people's engagement with the Victorian State Government and its public land management agencies – to negotiate meaningful and effective power and authority in the management of the park. This includes the full range of park management activities, including park planning, cultural heritage management, visitor management, interpretation, employment, flora and fauna conservation, and management of fire and water.

The struggle for recognition of the Wadi Wadi people's rights to this small but significant forest in Victoria's north-west is the focus of the story in this chapter. The story dates back to the 1990s, when key leaders took action against logging in Nyah and Vinifera, which were then classified as state forests and therefore open to resource extraction (for more detail, see Porter 2006a; Porter 2007; Porter 2010). Nyah Forest in particular had been intensively harvested for red gum timber since colonization and during a planning process in 1996 had been earmarked for further logging in three harvest coupes. In the summer of 1997, graders entered the northern end of the forest to widen tracks for logging activities. As they did so, they bulldozed through a burial mound. At the time, a senior Wadi Wadi spokesperson also happened to be a registered cultural heritage inspector under the previous cultural heritage management laws (the *Aboriginal and Torres Strait Islander Heritage Protection Act 1983 [Cwth]*, now replaced by the *Aboriginal Heritage Act 2006 [Vic]*). Registered inspectors had powers to place injunctions over logging or other activity that threatened cultural heritage, and it was this power that was utilized to bring logging to a halt in Nyah and Vinifera.

Subsequent community activism by the Wadi Wadi Nation and allies, including the Friends of Nyah-Vinifera Forest (a local campaign group of Aboriginal and non-Aboriginal people), continued to interrupt plans for logging in the forest through the late 1990s and 2000s. At the same time, action was being taken further upriver by the Yorta Yorta Nation with regard to logging in Barmah-Millewa Forest. A successful sit-in protest at Yorta Yorta's Dharnya Cultural Centre in 1998 led to the formation of two key networked alliances: the Barmah-Millewa Collective, an alliance between Yorta Yorta and Friends of the Earth; and the Murray Lower Darling River Indigenous Network (MLDRIN).

Both alliances were lobbying for greater conservation protection for the river red gum flood plains and much wider recognition of Aboriginal rights and title. A broader regional planning process underway during that period, covering all of the flood plain state forests of the region, continued to list Nyah-Vinifera as available for timber harvesting. Due to the pressure brought about by the Wadi Wadi and their allies, timber licences in Nyah-Vinifera were finally revoked in 2002. Moreover, those actions helped catalyze the River Red Gum Forests Investigation by the Victorian Environmental Assessment Council (VEAC), with significant outcomes for the shape of the contact zone. This process, and the outcomes it catalyzed for the contact zone, is the subject of the next section.

Widening the Contact Zone: The VEAC Investigation

It was in this landscape of contested values and deep historical and traditional connection that the VEAC was tasked in 2005 by the Victorian Minister for Environment to 'identify and evaluate the extent, condition, values, management, resources and uses of riverine red gum forests' and make recommendations as to their conservation, based on principles of ecologically sustainable development (Victorian Environmental Assessment 2008). Specifically included in the terms of reference was the consideration of options for joint or co-management of public lands in the riverine red gum region.

The VEAC was established through the *Victorian Environmental Assessment Council Act 2001 (Vic)* to conduct investigations at the request of the Victorian Government relating to the protection and sustainable management of public lands and natural resources. Two precursor organizations – the Environment Conservation Council and, before it, the Land Conservation Council – had previously fulfilled this role. Made up of five expert members, the VEAC is notionally independent of government, though it is tasked directly by government and has no power of its own to either initiate investigations or implement its recommendations. New South Wales initiated its own investigation on the north side of the Murray River at the same time to provide cross-state coordination.

As part of its remit, the VEAC was required to undertake wide consultation in the study area – which stretched along the Murray River from the South Australian border to just south of the town of Albury. Initially, the Wadi Wadi people were very skeptical of the consultation process, because there was a strong feeling (and a justified one) that the process was largely being hijacked by non-Aboriginal interests and especially by 'rednecks'. One incident in particular was important as an indication of not only the power of 'redneck interests' in the region but also the quiet insistence of the Wadi Wadi people to be heard. Having waited patiently to make their representation to what some described as the VEAC 'road show' (pers. comm. 26 May 2011), three Wadi Wadi representatives were finally given an opportunity to present their comments on the VEAC's discussion paper and to make representations about the protection of cultural heritage and proposals for joint management. But that meeting was interrupted by the intrusion of 'three hundred other people, woodcutters', 'rednecks and horsemen' who 'came and stormed in' (pers. comm. 26 May 2011). The Wadi Wadi representatives walked out of this meeting. However, as part of the later stages of the consultation process, the VEAC commissioned Indigenous consultants to run Indigenous-specific engagement in order to provide a separate space for Indigenous people to represent their views on the draft recommendations that had been published in 2007.

The Wadi Wadi utilized this additional process to make clear to the VEAC panel two important demands: first, higher levels of conservation protection for the natural and cultural values of the region, particularly the density of Wadi Wadi cultural sites in Nyah-Vinifera; and second, full joint management of Nyah-Vinifera involving a handback-leaseback arrangement of the land tenure. Such demands were mirrored across the region, and the Indigenous-specific consultations not only clearly identified the reclassification of public lands to higher conservation status and arrangements for joint or co-management as critically important but also presented a raft of suggested changes to licensing and access regulations to enable Aboriginal people to use and enjoy their lands for cultural practices. When the VEAC reported to government with its recommendations in July 2008, it was clear how influential Wadi Wadi and other traditional owner representations had been.

Yet the recommendations were certainly a tamer version of what the Wadi Wadi, along with other Aboriginal nations, were demanding. Of primary importance for the Wadi Wadi was the recommendation in the VEAC's report regarding Nyah-Vinifera Forest, which was to reclassify and combine Nyah and Vinifera together, forming a regional park (see Figure 6.1) and to establish Indigenous co-management arrangements over the park (Victorian Environmental Assessment 2008). The VEAC recognized the significant of Nyah-Vinifera for the Wadi Wadi people and recommended the reclassification of the forest as a regional park (a higher conservation status) in order to protect natural and cultural values from timber harvesting.

These recommendations were implemented by then Labor Victorian State Government, championed by then Minister for Environment and Aboriginal Affairs, Gavin Jennings. Changes were made to the legislation through the *Parks and Crown Land Legislation Amendment (River Red Gums) Act 2009* (hereafter the *Red Gum Act*) to enable co-management agreements. This moved the goalposts significantly for the Wadi Wadi Nation. Reclassifying the park with a higher conservation status removed the long-running conflicts over logging and enabled at least symbolic recognition of the park for the Wadi Wadi people – for example, through signage proclaiming the park as Wadi Wadi country (see Figure 6.2). Moreover, it gave a legislative base for the Wadi Wadi to engage with government about greater involvement in park planning and management. It was clear that there was some will in government to support working towards greater Aboriginal participation in park planning and management.

Figure 6.1   Map of Nyah-Vinifera Regional Park

Source: Map courtesy of Parks Victoria, used with permission

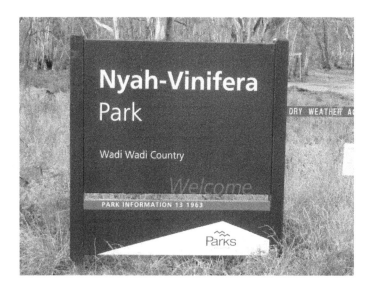

Figure 6.2   Sign in Nyah-Vinifera Park recognizing Wadi Wadi country
Source: Photo by Libby Porter

With regard to the management arrangements, however, the VEAC recommended a tamer version of Wadi Wadi demands: a co-management arrangement. This was a much more limited form of recognition, with a resultant shallower contact zone. The difference lay in the recognition of tenure. In a joint management arrangement, traditional owners are formally recognized as holders of title. Under co-management, neither title nor any specific rights to enjoy or use the land are recognized. Instead, the government and its agencies can agree with an Aboriginal group to allow that group to participate in planning and management activities. While the Wadi Wadi people were pleased that co-management had at least been recommended, their aspiration was for a more full recognition through the handback of the land:

> It's more like saying, 'Well it's been handed back for us to take care of'. [We want to] work with the other partners to get a good outcome for everybody. We need to have some control because in the end it's about our land … and we need to be acknowledged as the traditional owners, and the right people you're talking to. (pers. comm. 15 July 2011)

While some legislative teeth were co-management as a form of agreement, the legislation did not provide a minimum mandate for the powers the minister would hand over. Instead, this was to be determined at the discretion of the minister. Nor was a program put in place – as had been recommended by the Indigenous-specific consultations to the VEAC process – to improve Aboriginal nations' capacity through resourcing and administrative support, so that they could come to the negotiating table with government. As we will see, these two limitations, combined with the story that then unfolded, have not served Wadi Wadi interests well.

A Cunning Promise: Negotiating for Co-management

Much was celebrated around the time of the reclassification of Nyah-Vinifera Park and the (at least symbolic) recognition it represented of Wadi Wadi rights and interests in the park. The new park was formally opened, with a Wadi Wadi welcome and smoking ceremony and many other celebrations that are remembered as significant moments in the Wadi Wadi people's story. The then minister, Gavin Jennings, was present and had begun to build a relationship with Elders and negotiators.

Yet despite this high-level support, actually setting up and getting to a negotiating table with the Department of Sustainability and Environment (DSE) to implement a co-management agreement for the park proved difficult. This was where alliances with broader movements were instrumental. Prior to and throughout the VEAC process, the Wadi Wadi had developed a relationship with the Friends of the Earth (FoE) and, in particular, FoE's campaign at Barmah-Millewa to support the Yorta Yorta people in a full joint management handback-leaseback arrangement. The Barmah-Millewa Collective was a long-running campaign by FoE and managed to gain considerable traction and respect as a progressive alliance between a conservation activist group and an Aboriginal nation. The Wadi Wadi had begun to develop a trusting relationship with one particular campaigner at FoE, who had been involved in the negotiation of a cooperative agreement between the 10 traditional owner nations, including the Wadi Wadi, who make up the Murray Lower Darling River Indigenous Network (MLDRIN). After a long silence from the DSE on the implementation of co-management over Nyah-Vinifera, this campaigner made a telephone call to Gavin Jennings's office on behalf of the Wadi Wadi and demanded that he begin negotiations. It became clear that the DSE was planning, at that stage, to concentrate efforts on negotiating a co-management agreement with Yorta Yorta and were going to 'leave Wadi Wadi until later' (pers. comm. 3 June 2011). This was unacceptable to the Wadi Wadi, and through the FoE campaigner, they pushed hard for the DSE to come to the table with them more quickly.

In 2009, after much pushing, the DSE provided funding of $411,000 over two to three years to support the Wadi Wadi people's ability to negotiate. While the funding was reasonably limited, this was nonetheless significant. At that time the Wadi Wadi people as a collective had no organizational structure, no income stream as a nation and no paid employees or support staff. In short, it meant that resourcing for the Wadi Wadi to come to the negotiating table was provided on an entirely voluntary basis. People attended meetings outside their regular day jobs and family commitments, at their own cost, and worked in their spare time on reading materials and making responses to government. Such heavily restricted resourcing severely limited the capacity of anyone to participate in a negotiation process.

The funding, then, was recognition that the DSE had a responsibility to support the Wadi Wadi people in their efforts to get to the table. As the Wadi Wadi themselves had no formal structure or bank account through which the government could provide and distribute funds, the finances were directed through FoE, and from those funds the Wadi Wadi hired the FoE campaigner on a part-time basis to support their negotiations. The funds were also used to provide support for Elders and negotiators to attend meetings, covering travel and accommodation costs. Most meetings involving the whole Wadi Wadi group were held at Tyntyndyer, but many Elders and family representatives lived some distance from the homestead. Wadi Wadi negotiators routinely travelled to Melbourne and other regional centres for other meetings and traditional owner workshops. Getting even this level of support was frustrating and protracted. While the money was committed, it took six months to actually receive some initial funds. There were ongoing issues about late payments and the efforts required to actually receive the money committed from the DSE.

Despite these challenges, with some funds and wider support in place, a program of two-day meetings and negotiations was held through 2009 and 2010. By late 2010, the wording of a co-management agreement had been agreed upon and drafted, and was under legal review. But two unrelated events then unfolded that undermined that process. A state election was called in late November 2010, placing huge pressure on the timing for sign-off on the agreement. At the same time, the state Attorney-General, through the Department of Justice, advised that the government would not sign a co-management agreement with an unincorporated entity.

Co-management by agreement was suddenly off the table. In response to the Department of Justice's directive, the DSE initially put three options to the Wadi Wadi: 1) a full board of management over the park, 2) a Wadi Wadi advisory committee for the park and 3) the negotiation of a Memorandum of Understanding (MoU) to 'work together in good faith'. Conflict over these options, what they meant, and how they could be made real, became the next battleground.

Narrowing the Contact Zone: Re-settling Legitimate Planning for Public Lands

Option one, the full board of management, was quickly withdrawn. At the same time as the DSE was presenting these three options, the Department of Justice had, in consultation with the Traditional Owner Land Justice Group (see Chapter 4 for a detailed discussion), adopted a new principle of 'right people – right country'. Combined with the allocation, through the *Red Gum Act*, of decision-making power on joint management to the Attorney-General and the Department of Justice (rather than with the DSE), this meant that any Aboriginal group seeking agreement with government on co- or joint management would be required to achieve the same burden of proof as claimant groups under native title. Indeed, the principle went further to assert that co- or joint management could be agreed upon only with the same people as in existing native title claimant groups. This raised a significant recognition issue: an agreement could not be made with anyone who wasn't recognizable to the Department of Justice as a native title claimant and who could not pass the threshold proof test for asserting their native title.

The Wadi Wadi were left in a serious predicament. Since 2000, their native title claim had been linked with those of two other neighbouring claims. This would mean that any board of management or co-management agreement would have to recognize all three claimant groups, even though those groups and government all publicly recognized the Wadi Wadi as the traditional owners of the country on which Nyah-Vinifera Park was located. But to add an even greater complication to the story, Nyah-Vinifera Park was not included in the boundaries of that native title claim. A full Wadi Wadi board of management, then, was considered by the government to be untenable.

Two options thus remained. After considerable discussion, the Wadi Wadi refused to choose either and instead negotiated for a combination – both an MoU to work together in good faith, and an advisory committee to provide some level of power and authority over park planning and management. The DSE was unwilling to countenance a combination of the two options and confirmed that they were in fact willing to negotiate only for option 3 – a basic 'good faith MoU' which would establish 'how we play together in the sandpit', in the words of one senior government official at a negotiation meeting (pers. comm. 2 July 2011). Moreover, in the view of the DSE, the MoU meant that the Wadi Wadi would have to 'put [their] native title aspirations off through this agreement' (pers. comm. 2 July 2011). Once again, recognition of title would become a bargaining chip forced on Aboriginal owners as a kind of tradeoff for being allowed to participate.

And so when the state election in late 2010 resulted in a change of government, with no agreement signed, the opportunity for co-management was, at least momentarily, lost. Moreover, the Wadi Wadi Nation felt they had lost a key ally in Minister Gavin Jennings as well as the enormous momentum they had built around the co-management agreement. The incoming conservative government was much less enthusiastic about the commitments made to co- and joint management more generally and the agreement-based approach of the *Traditional Owner Settlement Act* specifically. The new minister proved less accessible and willing to engage, and DSE senior staff left unclear as to the government's negotiating position. Consequently, negotiations rapidly stalled, with longer breaks between meetings and a general lack of communication between the parties. Frustration and distrust mounted.

Through 2011 and 2012, negotiations toward a MoU continued sporadically. The Wadi Wadi people had decided that they had to stay at the table with the

DSE, even though what was being negotiated fell very short of their demands. Both parties communicated a willingness to negotiate a MoU in the hope that it might one day turn into a co-management agreement. At the same time, the Wadi Wadi pursued becoming an incorporated body in order that the government might eventually sign off that agreement with them. This process has proved to present new challenges, as the rules for recognizing an incorporated body do not sit easily alongside traditional kinship structures or Wadi Wadi law. The rules around incorporation are very prescriptive, requiring that internal practices around auditing and accounting, reporting structures and the like be recognizable to government.

The DSE has held closely to the requirement for the Wadi Wadi to produce proof requirements of their ancestry in order to progress to even a limited MoU. At a meeting in 2011, the DSE asked 'for its own purposes' to see a 'skeletal outline of apical ancestors and links to the past' (pers. comm. 2 July 2011). This was met with some disgust by the Wadi Wadi people, who found it insulting that they be asked to prove to a government public lands agency their right to be at a negotiating table. The DSE considers that they are merely operating under the legislative requirements, which demand that proof of connections be demonstrated before planning contact zones can be officially acknowledged. Moreover, the view of senior bureaucrats is that the provision of this proof is unproblematic because the research exists already (having been collected through the native title anthropology and genealogical research process) and that it simply needs to be shared with another agency. There is no recognition that the particular history of colonization in this part of the country renders that burden of proof the most anxiety-producing aspect of these negotiations.

While this rather messy situation was unfolding, the Wadi Wadi took a strategic decision to work in other areas and on agreements with other agencies operating in their country. This fit well with their long-standing approach of developing personal, everyday relationships with local staff in planning and land management agencies. The next section looks at how those kinds of relationships work in this planning contact zone and explores their vulnerabilities and fragilities.

Informal Agreements through Everyday Relationships: Possibilities and Vulnerabilities

Personal relationships are perceived by the Wadi Wadi people to be an essential part of their strategy to achieve greater recognition and involvement in Nyah-Vinifera Park planning. Building relationships with local staff in land management agencies enables close communication on local issues, where a telephone conversation or a fortuitous meeting in the street can help disseminate information and prompt action. Those relationships also enable conflict to be presented, aired and managed when things go wrong.

Given the fragility and deep structural problems associated with formal agreement making as outlined in the story above, at the very least the Wadi Wadi can create informal agreements with local staff operating in the park. This means that in day-to-day operations in the park – fencing, pest control, fire management, ecological surveying and so on – the Wadi Wadi can achieve much greater input into a process through those informal relationships, without having to deal with the messy bureaucracy further up the hierarchy.

To some extent, this is viewed positively by staff in the local land management agency. Parks Victoria in particular has oriented its organizational activities to partner with and engage traditional owners, regardless of native title or other recognition outcomes. Both on-the-ground staff located in the region and more senior staff in the head office of Parks Victoria consider local agreements and relationships to be a route toward more meaningful recognition of Aboriginal nations in park planning and management, as this senior executive of Parks Victoria states: 'Just because there is no claim or no settlement, VTO [Victorian Traditional Owners] still have rights to be consulted through PV [Parks Victoria] procedures and strategy as PV seeks to recognize and work in partnerships with VTOs' (pers. comm. 27 June 2011). The Wadi Wadi people spoke about a number of initiatives that exemplify this orientation of Parks Victoria to do meaningful, on-the-ground recognition, such as a program of plant species monitoring that the Wadi Wadi were negotiating to lead on, in partnership with Parks Victoria, and a regional Aboriginal sites assessment program.

Relationships at this level can also help deal with the difficult question of scale. Especially since their engagement with native title processes, the scale at which the Wadi Wadi people are trying to leverage greater authority and control in planning and land management has been a vexed issue. Wadi Wadi country, like that of most Aboriginal nations whose country is along the Murray River catchment, extends into two state jurisdictions and has a highly fragmented or 'patchwork' land-tenure pattern. Added to that is the complexity of land management actors who are operating on Wadi Wadi country at their own scales. In the context of the DSE's public lands jurisdiction, Nyah-Vinifera is a tiny place, where the planning and management will be done at a much larger regional scale to create efficiencies. Combined with the particular emphasis that the Wadi Wadi people place on Nyah-Vinifera, where the desire is really to have government recognize the Wadi Wadi as the authority on the park, the multiple scales at which the nation is working is complicated even further. One person expressed it like this:

> It's not just about the Nyah-Vinifera forest, that's only a part of our full country. And when you're talking with [local land management staff] this is what I keep saying to them, even though [the MoU agreement] is about Nyah-Vinifera, there are still other things in your department that you are doing ... They're taking [trainees] to places and blowing up rabbit warrens and a couple of the young [Wadi Wadi] boys came and told me that they found an axe head and none of them knew what happened to this axe head ... [so I say to them], 'Don't tell me

you're going to work in good faith over here in Nyah-Vinifera because we're not going to believe you if you've still got your workers over here doing stuff [without us]'. (pers. comm. 25 May 2011)

This illustrates that while relationships are positive and vital, they are just as often vulnerable and fragile. That vulnerability is clear in the discrepancy between what senior officers are committing to at negotiating tables and what is happening every day on the ground. If a planning or land management activity does not appear to impact a cultural site (and sometimes even when it does), then most local staff see no need to involve the Wadi Wadi people in that activity. Despite the many years of effort that the Wadi Wadi people have devoted to building relationships with those local staff and educate them about the issues on which they would really appreciate a telephone call and why it matters, their interests are routinely forgotten or sidelined; they are not seen as the core business of the agency. When an activity does not visibly and obviously affect a cultural site, then local agency staff perceives those interests as even less visible or relevant.

One story serves to highlight this fragmentation and its impacts. Throughout 2011, and alongside the unfolding difficulties of negotiating an agreement with the DSE, the Wadi Wadi sought partnerships with other planning and management agencies operating on their country. One of these was the Mallee Catchment Management Authority (MCMA), with responsibility for ecologically sustainable management programs for lands and water across its 4-million-hectare jurisdiction in Victoria's north-west. Nyah-Vinifera Park and much of Wadi Wadi country falls into this region.

As part of its healthy rivers strategy, the MCMA was developing a number of initiatives to restore catchment health. One of these was a 'mock flood' of the Parne Milloo Creek, a seasonal tributary of the Murray River running through Nyah-Vinifera Forest. Parne Milloo is a Wadi Wadi word, and the creek is a significant feature of the forest for the Wadi Wadi, partly because of the intensity of cultural sites along its banks. Mostly the creek is dry, running only during flood season. Nyah-Vinifera is a flood plain, normally flooding every two to three years, changing the entire landscape. Floods are of critical importance to Wadi Wadi culture and economy because they restore health to the forest and are part of a cosmic cycle of change and renewal.

Flood cycles have been seriously interrupted in the region for decades now, due to extended drought coupled with the siphoning off, over generations, of water from the Murray-Darling basin for agricultural irrigation. There had not been a flood in Nyah-Vinifera for many years, and so the Parne-Milloo had been dry a long time. As part of its strategy to restore catchment health, the MCMA initiated a mock flood event, pushing water through the Parne Milloo system. But they did so without either discussing the idea with the Wadi Wadi people or involving them in its implementation. While the Wadi Wadi people were supportive in principle of an initiative to restore catchment health and provide the flood plains with some much-needed water, they expressed a deep sense of insult from the lack of consultation.

Aside from the insult, two further concerns were also expressed. The implementation of the flood event – the placement of infrastructure, direction of the water flow and so on – had impacts on cultural sites and places. Without consultation, the MCMA had little way of knowing the likely impact. In response to this concern, the MCMA reported it had discharged its duty effectively because prior to undertaking the mock flood it had checked Aboriginal Affairs Victoria's register of cultural sites. However, it is well known and acknowledged by many in the region (including in the VEAC report) that only a few cultural sites in Nyah-Vinifera are registered and that very many places are unrecorded in archaeological terms. A second major concern for the Wadi Wadi people was the missed opportunity to shape the direction and location of the water for cultural purposes. The MCMA had used its bioregional datasets to determine where water would be best directed for ecological outcomes, but 'cultural water' was not a priority in its water planning (indeed, wasn't even recognizable as a value in water). It was only due to Wadi Wadi presence and practice in the park that a major problem of the flood was noticed and the alarm raised: the flood had enabled black water to leak into the river system, adding further anxiety and layers of mistrust to the Wadi Wadis' relationship with the MCMA.

Attitudes of local staff are clearly critical to determining whether informal relationships as planning contact zones are meaningful and effective. For some, the idea of partnering in a joint or co-management arrangement with Aboriginal people is not what land management is all about; or at least, they feel, it shouldn't have much impact on their regular activities. For one senior staff member in the MCMA, there was a strong sense that the possibility of a co-management agreement with the Wadi Wadi over Nyah-Vinifera Park would not change very much for the operations of the authority. He stated, 'If we wanted to we could just go along and be doing our own thing without taking that into account' (pers. comm. 6 July 2011). This is at some remove from the spirit and intent of co-management, not to mention Wadi Wadi perceptions of what co-management might mean.

The Politics of Recognition over Nyah-Vinifera Park

This is the messy, conflictual context, then, in which the Wadi Wadi people have sought to widen and deepen a very shallow planning contact zone for Nyah-Vinifera Park. It is clear that for the government agencies operating in this contact zone, recognition itself is not really the main focus. Indeed, senior bureaucrats involved in the co-management negotiations regarded recognition as the 'easy' part, merely the 'stroke of a pen' (pers. comm. 24 June 2011). The discourse about Wadi Wadi recognition here is telling in its exemplification of monological recognition. For the pen, and the ability to make its stroke, belongs to the recognizing authority, in this case the Victorian State Government, which will ultimately decide (or not) to recognize Wadi Wadi claims. The only recourse for the Wadi Wadi is to make a claim that is legitimate in the eyes of the recognizing authority support with the kind of evidence and proof demanded by the legislative regime that the settler state has enacted and that performs sufficiently like a Western organization.

At times, the gap between Wadi Wadi claims and aspirations, and planning and land management agencies perspectives is a veritable crevasse. Much of the work that the Wadi Wadi and their representatives do in the contact zone, then, is to try to translate their perspective into something that government can recognize, as one Wadi Wadi representative describes:

> They say one thing, we say something [else] and it's just like trying to meet in the middle between two worlds. Because the way we see it, they don't want [because of] legislation and all that. They just want to do what they have to by their legal obligations ... We just do it the way we know and what we've been taught traditionally. And it's trying to find that middle ground between the two – that's where we have a lot of struggles sometimes. (pers. comm. 26 May 2011)

Yet for government, the critical question is one of balancing Wadi Wadi interests, that 'other world' in the quotation above, with the demands of others and the 'balance' that the legislative framework requires. One of the MCMA water planners put the same conflict described above, in these terms:

> We deal with the Indigenous community [over] the concern about cultural values and you know just trying to get them to understand that there's also other balances that need to be achieved, you know environmental, economic values that have to be all worked in. That's probably one of the greater challenges, getting [traditional owners] to understand the bigger picture. (pers. comm. 6 July 2011)

There is a significant difference, then, between how government planners and land managers conceive of the places in their jurisdiction, and how Aboriginal people perceive them. Not surprisingly, this contributes to a pervasive sense that the Wadi Wadi people are misunderstood, their knowledge marginalized and their perspective seen as troublesome because it doesn't 'fit' with the imperative for 'balancing the bigger picture' towards which planning is persistently oriented.

Conclusion

This story is in part about the intersection of the micro-politics of particular settings and personalities with the macro-operation of wider discursive norms. The Wadi Wadi Nation has, with the help of key allies and supporters, successfully achieved very significant changes that support their interests, changes that resonate with those in the case studies we will address in Chapter 9. Commencing their action more than two decades ago with legal action and then a long cross-community struggle, the Wadi Wadi people have successfully pressed for the reclassification of Nyah-Vinifera to a higher conservation status. This opened up all sorts of possibilities that had simply not been available under earlier land-use classifications. The confluence of shifts in public perception about Indigenous recognition, the more widespread acceptance of co- or joint management within planning and land management professions, and the influential investigation by the VEAC were instrumental to those changes. There is much to be learned here from the quiet insistence of the Wadi Wadi people to be present at the table, to be heard, and through a variety of strategies make not only their own interests but also those of their country visible and present. A strategy of special importance for this story is the strong use of alliances with key organizations that could facilitate the kind of institutional capacity that the Wadi Wadi did not have available. Finding allies, building personal relationships and networks within both Indigenous and non-Indigenous communities has been a key strategy in the Wadi Wadi struggle, and was instrumentally important in getting themselves to the planning table.

Yet this story is also a disheartening one, when seen from the perspective we take in this book of discerning what kinds of conditions are required to create more transformative and socially just forms of Indigenous recognition through planning systems. What is clear in this story is the difficulty that Indigenous peoples face in puncturing colonial relations of power. Even at the most apparently mundane or practical level – resourcing and capacity for instance – it is clear just how embedded and persistent are the relations of power that mediate Indigenous–settler state relationships in planning contact zones. There is no level playing field here.

Those persistent colonial relations of power are also present at multiple scales of operation, and work to bind and constrain the scope and possibility of the politics of recognition for the Wadi Wadi Nation. In this chapter, we have seen the powerful role that monological forms of recognition play in discursively mediating the shape of planning contact zones. Requiring final, certain closure on who is being recognized with regards to what and where, as demanded by the recognition regime in Victorian law and policy, has heavily constrained the Wadi Wadi Nation in securing their demands. Indeed, the planning system in this case has been actively used to recontextualize that monological formulation of recognition, deploying its own discursive strategies around certainty, the public interest and standardization to limit the claims of the Wadi Wadi people. In Chapter 10 we pick up these themes again to demonstrate further the crucial point that when planning systems are deliberately structured to realize only monological forms of recognition, the resulting injustice is stark.

Chapter 7
Neighbour-to-Neighbour Planning Relations along Vancouver's North Shore

Introduction

Like the Victorian context, the recognition of Indigenous rights and title in British Columbian urban planning is much more constrained when compared to planning initiatives for public lands and protected areas. As discussed in Chapter 4, the statutory framework that guides municipal planning actually says very little about Indigenous peoples and is entirely unclear as to whether Indigenous peoples participate as stakeholders or as the holders of constitutionally protected rights. The goal of this chapter is to provide an empirical account of some of the ways in which Indigenous peoples are (mis)recognized in urban planning processes. We will do this with reference to the neighbour-to-neighbour planning relations that are beginning to emerge in metropolitan Vancouver. This growing metropolis, Canada's third largest metropolitan area, is composed of 25 local authorities that cooperatively pursue various regional governance activities (including regional planning and growth management) under the auspices of a regional governance body known as Metro Vancouver. Although there are numerous First Nations with traditional territories that overlap and underlay what is now metropolitan Vancouver and who are engaged in some kind of planning contact zone with both the member municipalities and the regional governance body (see Metro Vancouver Aboriginal Relations Legal and Legislative Services 2015), this chapter will focus on the experiences of just one: the Tsleil-Waututh Nation.

The Tsleil-Waututh Nation, or 'the People of the Inlet', is a Coast Salish Nation that has inhabited the lands and waters around Burrard Inlet since time immemorial. 'As the original Coast Salish inhabitants of Burrard Inlet, Tsleil-Waututh has a 10,000 year history of use and occupancy within the traditional territory stretching from the vicinity of Mt. Garibaldi in the north to the 49th parallel and beyond in the south, Gibsons in the west, and Coquitlam Lake in the east' (pers. comm., 26 June, 2015). The 'heart' of Tsleil-Waututh's community is on the Burrard Inlet, where they have their primary reserve. The Tsleil-Waututh Nation is a relatively small First Nation, with approximately 500 members. As per the provisions of the *Indian Act*, it is governed by an elected Chief and Council. Although the elected (or 'Band') Council is the formal decision-making body, it works closely with the nation's Traditional Council: a family-based system of representation that includes all nine family groups and provides purpose, direction and advice to the elected leaders. The Band Council also oversees the work of five administrative

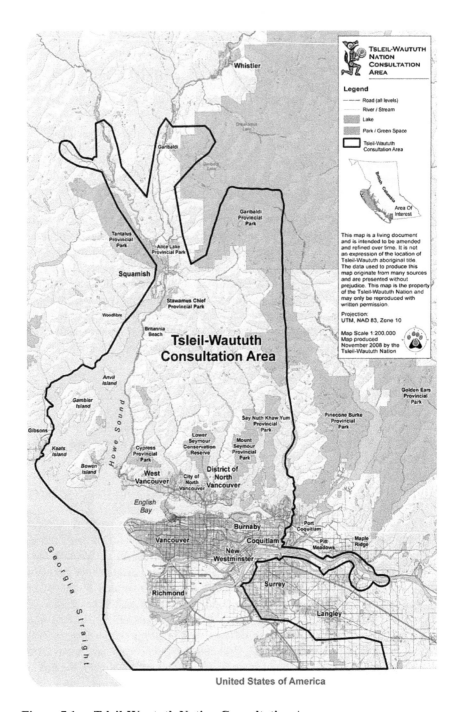

Figure 7.1 Tsleil-Waututh Nation Consultation Area

Source: Map courtesy of Tsleil-Waututh Nation, used with permission

departments (Administration and Public Works; Property Taxation; Treaty, Lands and Resources; Community Development; and Economic Development).

As will be discussed, the Treaty, Lands and Resources (TLR) Department has a substantial history with land-use planning and has worked to develop its in-house planning capacity, drawing on the expertise of both Indigenous and non-Indigenous professionals. As with the elected Council, provisions have been put in place to ensure that Tsleil-Waututh interests, law (or *snewyel*), and responsibilities and obligations (*shXalmes*) are properly represented. All of the decisions of the TLR Department are made by consensus, using a caucus approach. The TLR Department describes the Caucus as

> 'an advisory body that can be comprised of TLR staff, Tsleil-Waututh elders, youth, the TWN [Tsleil-Waututh Nation] Council, and representatives from other departments as well as members from Traditional Council, depending upon the issue. The Caucus is an inclusive organization and is also often attended by advisors and community members. Caucus meetings are held as required and are used to gather advice, formulate and refine strategies' (Tsleil-Waututh Nation, Treaty Lands and Resources Department, 2012, 3).

Much of the work of the TLR Department and Caucus over the last number of years has focused on planning for the broader traditional territory and for lands not encompassed by metropolitan Vancouver's urban footprint. For example, the Tsleil-Waututh Nation entered into agreements with the BC government in 1998 and 2005 to collaboratively develop the Say-Nuth-Khaw-Yum/Indian Arm Provincial Park Plan and the Indian River Watershed Integrated Stewardship Plan.

However, the Treaty, Lands and Resources Department and Caucus are not solely concerned with natural resource and environmental planning issues. The TLR Department has been mandated to address and engage in negotiations

Figure 7.2   Burrard Inlet
Source: Photo by Janice Barry

around a wide range of Aboriginal rights and title issues, including those within urban and urbanizing environments. As a result, it aims to engage in the land-use planning activities of the 17 different municipalities and one regional authority operating within Tsleil-Waututh territory. In 2009, the TLR Department and Caucus also released a new *Stewardship Policy*, which outlined the Tsleil-Waututh Nation's expectations around the duty to consult (see Chapter 4) and mapped the core area of Tsleil-Waututh territory to which this duty is owed (Figure 7.1). A significant portion of this core area is within metropolitan Vancouver's existing urban footprint, which has drawn attention to and (as we will see) created tension over how First Nations ought to be engaged in the long-term development of the individual municipalities, as well as the region as a whole.

This chapter will focus on the 15-year-plus planning relationship with just one of the municipalities operating in Tsleil-Waututh territory: the District of North Vancouver (DNV). The DNV is one of four municipalities on the north shore of the Burrard Inlet, with a population of approximately 85,000 (Statistics Canada 2012) and a projected growth of 40,000 additional residents by 2030 (District of North Vancouver 2011). The District is characterized by an abundance of mountainous natural parkland (all of which is in the Tsleil-Waututh Nation's designated consultation area) and four mixed-use town centres. DNV lands almost completely surround the Tsleil-Waututh Nation's home reserve, with significant residential development immediately north and west of the reserve and a smaller residential area adjacent to the southeast corner of the reserve. The District also includes Cates Park/Whey-ah-Wichen, which is an area of great cultural significance to the Tsleil-Waututh Nation, and one that led to a more cooperative planning relationship. Yet, as this chapter will illustrate, these encouraging beginnings were tested during the preparation of a new Official Community Plan (OCP), in which the desire to protect public amenities came into direct conflict with the recognition of Indigenous rights, title and governance systems. This chapter will trace the emergence of the planning contact zone between the Tsleil-Waututh Nation and the District of North Vancouver, highlighting major catalytic forces as well as key moments where the contours of the contact zone were conceived, enacted and contested. In doing so, the chapter will highlight key themes and issues that will be analyzed in greater detail in subsequent chapters.

Putting Tsleil-Waututh's Face Back on Tsleil-Waututh Territory

The BC Treaty Process represents one of the first and most obvious shifts that led to a reconsideration of the relationship between the Tsleil-Waututh Nation and the District of North Vancouver. The Tsleil-Waututh Nation entered the treaty process in early 1994, with the submission of its Statement of Intent, and was declared negotiation 'ready' in August 1995. As per the requirements of the six-step BC Treaty Process, the Tsleil-Waututh Nation, the Government of Canada and the Government of British Columbia also signed off on an 'Openness Protocol' in

February 1996. That protocol included provisions that would allow a member of the Lower Mainland Treaty Advisory Committee to participate in main and/or side table discussions to advise on local government (municipal and regional district) issues. The Openness Protocol also acknowledged the importance of a 'strong, and positive relationship between the Tsleil Waututh Nation (sic), and the municipalities and regional districts within the Tsleil Waututh (sic) traditional territory ... and recognize the need to begin to define and to formalize that relationship during the treaty process' (1996, 2). As part of this process of relationship building, DNV staff, councillors and citizens began to be educated about the implications of the treaty process, with representatives of the Ministry of Aboriginal Affairs and Lower Mainland Treaty Advisory Committee making a formal presentation to council in early 1999. DNV's mayor also became very active in treaty discussions, which further heightened awareness of the potential benefits of developing a productive governance relationship with First Nations.

From the perspective of the Tsleil-Waututh, their involvement in the BC Treaty Process provided the impetus for a broader conversation about how to put 'the Tsleil-Waututh face' back on their territory outside of the reserve boundary (pers. comm., 13 June 2011). For although the BC Treaty Process creates opportunities for specific parcels of public land to be transferred back to the First Nation, the level of urban development and land privatization in Waututh territory meant that there would be less opportunity to acquire new lands. The Tsleil-Waututh Nation had to find other ways to pursue their land-use interests, increase their visibility and become a more integral player in what was going on around them. They recognized that, while they had no intention of going anywhere, neither did the 2 million people who now called metropolitan Vancouver home. Partnership arrangements were seen as an effective avenue to address their concerns and to pursue their community development goals. It was through their involvement in this process that the Tsleil-Waututh Nation began to articulate and act toward the development of an integrated community development strategy – with joint planning as one of the prongs.

But before they could fully contemplate the kinds of partnership they might want to pursue, the Tsleil-Waututh needed to develop a better handle on the contemporary and historical land management and development activities in their territory. Mapping was recognized as an effective way to tell their 'story' (Tsleil-Waututh Nation 2015) and the Treaty, Lands and Resources Department embarked on extensive data collection and digitization exercise. A local planning practitioner, with expertise in bioregional mapping, was brought on board and started to work with another Treaty, Lands and Resources staff member, who was also a community member and had a wealth of knowledge on cultural use. Together, they began compiling a bioregional atlas that combined the biophysical (forest cover, geology, wildlife, plants) and cultural elements of Tsleil-Waututh Nation territory and that made use of extensive oral history work with Elders and others in the community. They also began to map the various jurisdictional and administrative boundaries within Tsleil-Waututh territory (e.g., local governments and regional district boundaries, as well as provincial forest management area and water management districts). This 'dual process' (pers. comm. 15 June 2011) of presenting traditional knowledge alongside other secondary datasets helped the Tsleil-Waututh Nation visualize key aspects of their territory. In recent years, the Tsleil-Waututh Nation has also been mapping the primary data generated through its own ecological monitoring work.

The Emergence of a Joint Planning Arrangement for Cates Park/Whey-ah-Wichen

From the mid- to late-1990s, Tsleil-Waututh Nation was actively working on their bioregional atlas and was beginning to develop planning partnerships with the provincial government (though, in the case of the Say-Nuth-Khaw-Yum Heritage Park, not without the threat of legal action). However, there were not yet any clear mechanisms for using that knowledge as a foundation for the formation of new planning partnerships with local governments. The BC Treaty Process was still relatively new, and municipalities (including the District of North Vancouver) were still coming to grips with how it affected their relationship with First Nations. In addition, the duty to consult Indigenous peoples had not yet been clearly articulated by the Supreme Court of Canada (see Chapter 4).

In fact, the Tsleil-Waututh Nation's first major planning partnership grew out of the conflict over the desecration of a Tsleil-Waututh archaeological site at Cates Park/Whey-ah-Wichen – an incident that seems to have arisen out of a complete lapse in consultation. As recalled by a Tsleil-Waututh community member who was directly involved in the Treaty, Lands and Resources Department at the time, the non-Indigenous practitioner that the Tsleil-Waututh Nation had hired to support their bioregional mapping project had noticed some digging while on an informal visit to the park in spring 1999. Community members and Elders were informed of the activities and returned to the park to investigate further and lodge a complaint. That complaint precipitated a meeting with District of North Vancouver Parks Department and eventually led to the initiation of an archaeological study of the area and ultimately to the development of the 2001 *Cates Park/Whey-ah-Wichen Protocol/Cultural Agreement*.

That agreement began by stating the parties' desire for an open and cooperative working relationship and by asserting 'Cates Park/Whey-ah-Wichen is a place of aboriginal cultural and spiritual significance to the Tsleil Waututh (sic), cultural significance to the District, and a place of historical and recreational significance to both Parties' (District of North Vancouver and Tsleil Waututh Nation 2001, 1). Both parties went on to express their desire to protect and enhance the natural and cultural features of the park through the joint planning, management and operation of Cates Park/Whey-ah-Wichen. The protocol agreement also committed to the establishment of a joint committee, with equal representation from each party. Its duties would include initiating and overseeing cultural heritage and master planning. The work of the joint planning committee did not, however, get underway until 2005. Neither the Tsleil-Waututh Nation nor the District of North Vancouver had any previous experience with cooperative park planning and, as a result, the formation of this new relationship required a great deal of time and resources – a constraint that was largely overcome through Tsleil-Waututh involvement in the BC Treaty Process. A significant amount of the financial resources needed to get the joint park planning process off the ground was provided by Tsleil-Waututh through their 'Treaty-related Measure' fund (pers. comm. 7 June 2011). Treaty-related measures are an interim step, intended to help resolve potentially contentious issues while treaty negotiations are underway (Indian and Northern Affairs Canada 2010).

Early on in the process, Tsleil-Waututh Nation and the District of North Vancouver jointly hired a team of consultants that included planners, landscape architects, an architect and a graphic designer. Environmental and archaeological consultants were also brought in to work on particular areas of concern. Although many First Nations are hesitant to rely on outside expertise and often prefer to find ways to build their in-house planning capacity, the consultants' role in gathering information and day-to-day process management was not particularly contentious. The difficulties arose when the consultants submitted their draft plan. Both the Tsleil-Waututh Nation and the DNV acknowledge that the plan required a substantial number of rewrites to ensure that it appropriately acknowledged Tsleil-Waututh interests and culture. District of North Vancouver representatives note

Figure 7.3   Tsleil-Waututh Canoe in Whey-ah-Wichen
Source: Photo by Janice Barry

that the Tsleil-Waututh Nation was much more careful about the specific language that was used in the plan than they would ever have been. For the Tsleil-Waututh, it was not simply a question of language and protecting themselves against misinterpretation; it was about asserting who they are as a people, including their connections to and responsibilities for their territory. This assertion of Tsleil-Waututh interests also necessitated changing the very way the planning process was conceived. The *Cates Park/Whey-ah-Wichen Protocol/Cultural Agreement* had originally described the Cultural Resources Interpretation Management Plan (CRIMP) and Master Plan as two separate documents, though it was acknowledged that the Master Plan would need to integrate at least some elements of the CRIMP. Once they got into the planning process, the Tsleil-Waututh Nation pushed for a single planning document.

The final plan was approved by both Tsleil-Waututh Nation and District of North Vancouver Councils in June 2006. The *Cates Park/Whey-ah-Wichen Park Master Plan and Cultural Resources Interpretation Management Plan* included various strategies to protect and improve native forests and sensitive riparian areas, as well as various physical planning interventions to improve circulation and the public amenities that were available at the park. It also provided design templates and outlined the key messages that would be included in new interpretative panels, with a particular focus on Tsleil-Waututh's ongoing connection to the site. Through the plan, the DNV expressed its commitment to ensure that all new structures 'have a unified "Coast Salish" design expression that addresses the place, its history, landscape, and traditional uses, with a contemporary and metaphorical design approach' (2006, 12). To Tsleil-Waututh's disappointment, many of these structures (including a culturally important feasthouse) have not been built, due to a lack of funding. However, as the next section will show, the plan did play an important role in triggering further discussions of the possibilities for a long-term planning relationship between the two forms of government. In fact, the possibility of creating a broader protocol to guide the relationship between the Tsleil-Waututh Nation and the District of North Vancouver was first raised at a treaty negotiation session a mere month after the formal approval of the joint park plan – though it does need to be acknowledged that there were other factors driving these discussions.

The Development of the Cooperation Protocol: A Coalescence of Multiple Factors

By the mid-1990s, the Tsleil-Waututh Nation had established a partnership with well-known Vancouver property developers (Sligo Holdings) to create multi-family townhouse and apartment-style homes that would be primarily marketed to non-Tsleil-Waututh members. The Tsleil-Waututh Nation became a majority owner of Takaya Development, which also includes Sligo Holdings and NSI Strategic Investments – described as an investment firm that was founded to create 'top-quality real estate developments in partnership with First Nations Bands' (Raven Woods 2014, 1*)*. Takaya development has built almost 900 homes in the last 20 years (Raven Woods 2014, 1). These kinds of on-reserve development projects usually require a Servicing Agreement with the adjacent municipality to provide the necessary infrastructure (e.g., sewer, water, fire, social services). The first Service Agreement between the Tsleil-Waututh Nation and the District of North Vancouver was signed in 2000 and was up for renewal in 2005, which further underscored the need for a more coordinated approach to development. During that same period, the Tsleil-Waututh Nation was taking additional steps to enact their long-term vision for the economic and physical development of their reserve lands. In 2003, the Tsleil-Waututh Nation was also added to the *Framework Agreement on First Nation Land Management*, which would allow them to begin to develop their own Land Code and ultimately extricate themselves from the cumbersome land-related sections of the federal *Indian Act*. The Tsleil-Waututh Nation's Land Code came into affect in 2007.

Around that same time, the Federal Government was working to develop the *First Nations Commercial and Industrial Development Act (FNCIDA)*, an entirely new piece of legislation that was in direct response to increasingly complex on-reserve development projects. Although the Act was catalyzed by development projects being pursued by five other First Nations (Aboriginal Affairs and Northern Development Canada 2012), as opposed to the work of Takaya development, there is a connection. FNCIDA prompted a great deal of debate and consternation among the members of the Lower Mainland Treaty Advisory Committee (see, for example, Lower Mainland Treaty Advisory Committee 2011). Servicing was a major point of contention, with serious concerns raised about whether the existing infrastructure could support the potential scale of development. One of the other major issues concerned how on-reserve development would take into account the Official Community Plans of the neighbouring municipalities, as well as the Regional Growth Strategy for the entire regional district.

As we discussed in Chapter 4, the British Columbian urban planning system includes several provisions to ensure that adjacent municipalities are in regular conversations about how land-use planning can be better coordinated at both the local and regional scale. For many municipalities, including the District of North Vancouver, it simply makes good sense to try to develop a similar planning relationship with First Nations. This would offer a way to avoid incompatible development projects on either side of the municipal/First Nation reserve boundary and to try to formulate common goals around potentially contentious issues like growth management targets. However, as we will discuss in the next section and then again in Chapter 10, this way of framing municipal relationships and responsibilities towards First Nations advanced a rather weak recognition of the Aboriginal rights and title that exist beyond the official boundaries of the First Nation reserve.

In 2007, the Tsleil-Waututh Nation and the District of North Vancouver took a significant step towards their shared desire for a more cooperative and coordinated approach by signing a new *Cooperation Protocol* that expressed their desire for a strong working relationship, while still protecting each other's areas of authority. Although not exclusively focused on planning, the protocol between the Tsleil-Waututh Nation and the District of North Vancouver laid some of the groundwork in terms of future planning relationships. It began by stating that the 'Tsleil-Waututh Nation asserts aboriginal rights and title to its traditional territory' and that the 'District of North Vancouver is a municipality with governance authorities as set out in Provincial legislation'. Both parties were described as having 'mutual interests and shared objectives' and an interest in furthering a 'working relationship based on mutual respect and trust'. It went on to establish an official Steering Committee to implement the protocol, with equal representation from both parties and an aim to meet quarterly. These staff-to-staff discussions would be supported by an annual Council-to-Council meeting, to provide the Steering Committee with its overall 'vision, policy and strategic direction' (Tsleil-Waututh Nation and District of North Vancouver 2007, 1).

In more substantive terms, the protocol committed the parties to provide written notice of any proposed land-use developments that might impact each other's Aboriginal and municipal interests. Given that the District of North Vancouver must also hold formal public hearings on certain land-use decisions (as per the requirements of the *Local Government Act*), it agreed to ensure that the Tsleil-Waututh Nation was given adequate notice of the time, location and purposes of the hearing and that it received a copy of any proposed by-law. In addition, the Steering Committee was to develop a consultation procedure 'for decisions, public works or by-laws that the District proposes, that may infringe an aboriginal right of TWN [Tsleil-Waututh Nation]'. As described by one senior DNV staff member, the district hoped to use the *Cooperation Protocol* not only to receive feedback on their draft policies but also to 'hear more about [the Tsleil-Waututh Nation's] community planning and specific interests in the future' (pers. comm. 9 June 2011). Overall, the development of the *Cooperation Protocol* suggests that, although the planning relationship between the district and the Tsleil-Waututh Nation began as a targeted and strategic response to conflict, it has now progressed into a long-term governance arrangement. In fact, senior DNV staff describe the protocol and the processes it has put in place as a relationship 'by choice', one that grows out of a recognition that 'we are neighbours planning with neighbours' (pers. comm. 14 June 2011). At the same time, this relationship cannot be interpreted solely as a product of the actions of individual governments as it also sits against the backdrop of changing legal and political conceptions of appropriate relationships between Indigenous and settler governments.

As discussed in Chapter 4, there is a real lack of legislative, policy or procedural direction regarding how First Nations should be involved in municipal planning decisions. Unlike the relationship that exists between Aboriginal people and the Crown (federal and provincial governments), municipalities' responsibilities towards Indigenous peoples are much less certain and have been the subject of several recent court cases. From Tsleil-Waututh's perspective, this uncertainty has resulted in an 'awkward' and at times 'uncomfortable' relationship with local government, particularly when it comes to the question of whether the consultation provisions in the *Cooperation Protocol* arise out of a desire for neighbourly planning relationships or the legal duty to consult and accommodate First Nations. In Chapter 4, we discussed the fact that there is still ongoing legal uncertainty as to whether this duty applies to municipalities, which (as one Tsleil-Waututh advisor suggests) has been particularly challenging to many First Nations:

> ... the big question that remains unanswered is: To what degree do the Crown's legal obligations track to statutory creatures of the Crown (local governments, regional governments and so on)? From a First Nations perspective, if it quacks like a duck and looks like a duck than it's probably a duck. (pers. comm. 7 June 2011)

Despite these competing perspectives over whether municipalities possess the duty to consult, the two other levels of government that the Tsleil-Waututh Nation's Treaty, Lands and Resources Department liaise with on a regular basis through their marine and terrestrial monitoring and conservation projects most certainly do. In fact, the 2004 *Haida* court decision (see Chapter 4) is described by some the Tsleil-Waututh Nation staff as having had a 'tsunami effect' (pers. comm. 7 June 2011) in terms of the number of 'referrals' received by their TLR Department. While the bioregional atlas provides a relatively efficient tool to determine the nature and scope of potential impacts, the fact remained that Tsleil-Waututh Nation had no operational funding to support the current volume of consultation requests. The Tsleil-Waututh Nation's policy response to this situation came in 2009 when it released its *Stewardship Policy*, which was described as 'a mechanism to further the growth of the relationships that we have built in recent years' and as 'an invitation to work together with the full, up front and transparent knowledge of our needs and expectations'.

Under the *Stewardship Policy*, consultation with Tsleil-Waututh Nation would need to entail timely notice of the matter to be decided; the provision of the financial resources needed to allow the nation to be effective participants; sufficient information on the nature of matter and its potential impacts; sufficient timeframe for the nation to develop and present its views, and for the proponent to respond to and accommodate Tsleil-Waututh rights and title; and a process to resolve issues. The policy also included a clear articulation that the Tsleil-Waututh Nation is not currently funded to dialogue or consult with governments and individual proponents, as well as a summary of the nation's new referral fee structure. The Tsleil-Waututh Nation has since hired a Stewardship Coordinator to help implement the policy, though not all proponents and governments in their territory are conforming to the requirements of this new policy. Several local governments, as well as the Lower Mainland Treaty Advisory Committee, were particularly vocal in their opposition to the new fee structure. Several went on to suggest that they simply would not pay for these kinds of services, framing the provision of comments of another government's planning documents as part of the regular business of regional governance.

At this point in our narrative, it is worth underscoring that two rather different ways of understanding the relationship between the District of North Vancouver and the Tsleil-Waututh Nation emerged in the years following the Cates Park/ Whey-ah-Wichen plan. The first, which is most clearly connected to the 2007 *Cooperation Protocol*, appears as an extension of existing approaches to regional governance. However, this neighbour-to-neighbour approach offers only partial recognition of First Nations' unique governance status, in that it frames First Nations as an adjacent government. As will become apparent in the next section, this way of seeing Indigenous-municipal relations sits uncomfortably with the reality of Indigenous rights and title that extend beyond the official boundaries of the First Nation reserve. And although the *Cooperation Protocol* acknowledges the potential for DNV plans and policies to infringe upon those rights and title, it provides little guidance on how the district ought to respond to those conflicts or how the Tsleil-Waututh could be supported to assess the impact of such potential infringements. In many respects, the 2009 *Stewardship Policy* (the second way of framing Indigenous-municipal relations that emerged during this period) was a direct response to many of these omissions. It begins by asserting that the Tsleil-Waututh Nation has an ongoing role in the stewardship of its entire territory, including areas that have been incorporated as municipalities. In doing so, it suggests that the District of North Vancouver and the Tsleil-Waututh Nation are not just neighbours, but that they also have overlapping and concurrent coexisting spheres of responsibility. As the previous discussion has already shown, this way of seeing Indigenous-municipal relations was difficult for many local governments. However, it was not until DNV launched a major strategic planning initiative that these conflicting views were really brought to the fore.

Tsleil-Waututh Nation Engagement in Municipal Planning: Testing the Relationship

Although the establishment of a clear process for Aboriginal referrals had previously been identified as one of the major topics of discussion under the *Cooperation Protocol,* it was not until the District of North Vancouver was about to embark on a major update to its Official Community Plan (OCP) that the parties began to seriously consider the terms of their relationship. In fact, it was during one staff-to-staff discussion initiated under the *Cooperation Protocol* that the DNV first began to discuss its upcoming OCP process and the possibility of developing Terms of Reference to guide Tsleil-Waututh involvement in this process. These discussions continued right through the official launch of the OCP process in June 2009, and the terms of Tsleil-Waututh involvement were not yet decided when the DNV held its 'Official Community Planning Visioning Summit' in November 2009 to determine the overall planning principles and goals. Given that these discussions were occurring after the release of the Tsleil-Waututh Nation's *Stewardship Policy*, a great deal of attention was paid to whether and how Tsleil-Waututh participation might be funded. Meetings tended to be long and relatively open-ended, though they became much more focused in autumn 2010 as the District of North Vancouver approached its November deadline for an initial OCP draft.

As discussed in Chapter 4, an Official Community Plan is a statutory requirement of the *Local Government Act* and is the primary strategic planning document for BC municipalities. For the District of North Vancouver, the OCP process provided an opportunity to create an Integrated Community Sustainability Plan as well. Given that these sustainability plans often go beyond the existing statutory requirements, the DNV sought additional funding for this more elaborate planning process through the Canadian Federation of Municipalities' Green Municipal Fund. Part of DNV's funding bid for that additional funding was focused on securing the resources needed to explore new and innovative mechanisms for public consultation. Ultimately, DNV was able to use some of its $350,000 from Green Municipal Funding to support Tsleil-Waututh involvement in the OCP, and attention shifted to gathering Tsleil-Waututh input on the OCP draft.

Although the Tsleil-Waututh were invited to all of the visioning sessions and public engagement events that were built into the OCP process, their role ended up taking the form of more a traditional consultation or referral process. After engaging in its own internal caucus processes, the Tsleil-Waututh Nation submitted its written comments in March 2011. By this time, the District of North Vancouver was already working on incorporating its stakeholders' feedback on the second draft, in the lead-up to the public hearing (a formal requirement under the *Local Government Act*) that was scheduled for May 2011. The DNV was able to integrate some of Tsleil-Waututh's feedback. For example, the Tsleil-Waututh objected to the way they had been characterized in relation to other levels of government. They were particularly concerned with the phrase 'senior levels of government, adjacent municipalities and First Nations', as they see themselves at the same level as senior government. The DNV changed the language used in the plan, which no longer makes an explicit differentiation between First Nation and 'senior' government. However, many of the more contentious issues proved less easy to address.

For example, the Tsleil-Waututh Nation was particularly concerned with plans to increase public access to the marine shore by opening up street ends. These tidal areas have been a traditional food source and are already heavily polluted. The Tsleil-Waututh Nation saw increased public access as yet another threat to their ability to rehabilitate these areas to the point that they could once again exercise their Aboriginal right to collect these culturally significant resources. The proposal to open up the street ends was very favourably received by the District of North Vancouver's stakeholders, who had asserted very early on in the OCP process that 'public access to the waterfront needed to be secured' (District of North Vancouver 2009). The Tsleil-Waututh Nation interpreted the DNV's unwillingness to change or reconsider its plan for open street ends as a privileging of stakeholder views over their Aboriginal rights and title.

Somewhat similarly, the Tsleil-Waututh Nation saw the District of North Vancouver's refusal to exempt First Nations from the urban containment boundary as a substantial infringement on their Aboriginal rights and title, one that might prevent them from developing any lands they might obtain through the BC Treaty Process. In the minds of the Tsleil-Waututh, this growth management tool was completely insensitive to the ongoing inequities created by the urbanization of Tsleil-Waututh territory:

> [The urban containment boundary] was basically, 'On this side of the line, we're going to do urban development and on the other side we are going to keep the forest undeveloped.' Great idea – it makes sense. But, from an Aboriginal rights and title point of view (and particularly from a Nation that is seeing development go on all around it) to be subjected to a policy that says 'by the way, we're kind of done; we've done what we want to do, so we're going to protect all the rest now; so, if you have lands up in that area or have other opportunities up in that area, you're not allowed to [develop] them now' – it is not something TWN [Tsleil-Waututh Nation] can support without further discussion. (pers. comm. 13 June 2011)

The District of North Vancouver saw the following statement, which was included in the first few pages of the OCP, as offering sufficient protection to current and future Aboriginal land interests: 'The Plan has been written without prejudice to First Nations' assertions of aboriginal rights and title to their traditional territories' (Tsleil-Waututh Nation and District of North Vancouver 2007). The Tsleil-Waututh Nation was clearly unconvinced and continued to forcefully assert its rights, title and authority within its entire territory in the final OCP staff-to-staff meetings. Such assertions were not always seen as an opportunity to find creative means to accommodate coexisting sources of authority. In Tsleil-Waututh's mind, their nation's refusal to accept any potential infringements on their rights and title was an invitation for additional discussions – discussions that would need to find ways to reconcile these competing sources of authority.

There has been some indication that the District of North Vancouver hopes to address some of these outstanding concerns when it progresses to more localized or area-specific planning (e.g., town and village centre implementation plans). In fact, Tsleil-Waututh Nation staff and caucus members quite strategically positioned these concerns as 'go-forwards', language that very purposefully underscored the need for and their ongoing commitment to a long-term planning relationship. But these area-specific planning processes were not initiated before the plan progressed to the next stage of the OCP process. The Tsleil-Waututh Nation, therefore, felt unable to endorse DNV's Official Community Plan. The OCP by-law received two formal readings at DNV Council Meetings in April and May 2011 before undergoing a formal public hearing in May 2011. Council considered the results of that hearing before giving the OCP by-law its third and final reading on June 20, 2011. It was formally adopted on June 27, 2011.

Conclusion

Given its many limitations and ongoing points of contention, it is difficult to see Tsleil-Waututh's involvement in the District of North Vancouver's Official Community Plan process as a 'successful' planning relationship that resulted in noticeable changes to the underlying planning system as it sought to recognize and accommodate Aboriginal rights, title and governance systems. Not all of the Tsleil-Waututh Nation's concerns were addressed, and existing DNV planning principles and ways of framing the jurisdictional boundaries of the relationship tended to take precedence. Even DNV acknowledges that, in order to meet its deadlines, its response to the Tsleil-Waututh Nation's comments was rushed. At the same time, DNV's commitment to try to address outstanding Aboriginal concerns in future, and to more localized, planning processes is indicative of the potential for future change.

In fact, the very language of 'go-forwards' was not only seen as an effective negotiation approach on the part of the Tsleil-Waututh Nation; it also underscores the ongoing and iterative nature of the planning relationship between the Tsleil-Waututh Nation and the District of North Vancouver. All of these future relationships will be supported by what is now becoming a relatively long history of municipal–First Nation cooperation, one that was catalyzed by the Tsleil-Waututh Nation's participation in the BC Treaty Process and by both parties' response to the conflict over the lack of consultation regarding Cates Park/Whey-ah-Wichen. While there are ongoing issues with respect to finding the necessary financial resources to fully implement the plan, the relative success of the *Cates Park/Whey-ah-Wichen Master Plan and Cultural Resources Interpretation Management Plan* helped chart a course for the development of a different kind of planning relationship. The core principles of this relationship were reflected in a formal *Cooperation Protocol.* Yet this chapter has also shown that these kinds of relationships cannot be understood solely through the lens of formal protocol agreements. They are also the result of years of community visioning, tireless advocacy, and very strategic acts of institutional capacity development. We will return to these themes in Chapter 9.

When looking at the planning relationship between the Tsleil-Waututh Nation and the District of North Vancouver as a whole, it is clear that physical and social connections between these two communities allowed both parties to turn the conflict over Cates Park/Whey-ah-Wichen into an opportunity for greater communication and cooperation. At the same time, the Tsleil-Waututh Nation's ongoing planning relationship with DNV is situated within a urban planning system and a local government structure that has not yet fulfilled the British Columbia government's vision for a 'new relationship' that recognizes Aboriginal rights and title in its 'full form' (British Columbia 2005). DNV's conceptual framing of the relationship as one that is grounded in the idea of being a 'good neighbour' (pers. comm.9 June, 2011 tends to limit the conversation to issues that arise out of the fact that the District of North Vancouver and the Tsleil-Waututh Nation's primary reserve share a geographic boundary. As we will elaborate upon in Chapter 10, this way of seeing the relationship, along with the persistent uncertainty as to whether the Crown's duty to consult and accommodate Aboriginal peoples applies to municipalities, does not seem to be very conducive to addressing coexisting title and coexisting authority: two factors that clearly are at the heart of the Tsleil-Waututh Nation's long-term vision.

Chapter 8

Planning for Wilp Sustainability in the Nass and Skeena River Watersheds

Introduction

As discussed in the opening chapter, the Gitanyow Huwilp's involvement in the long-term planning and management of the Nass and Skeena River watershed provides an opportunity to examine the lived experience of the planning contact zones that exist between Indigenous and settler governments in the Province of British Columbia. As in the Wadi Wadi case presented in Chapter 6, the Gitanyow Huwilp's planning concerns centred not on the built environment but rather on the ability of the Gitanyow to sustain deep cultural connections to their traditional territories. These territories include approximately 6,200 square kilometres (Gitanyow Hereditary Chiefs 2006) in the area from the 9-mile post near the Kitwanga River in the south, north to the Bell One Bridge on the Bell-Irving River, and from Kinskuch Lake in the west to Bonney Lake in the east. The Gitanyow's main reserve is situated on Highway 37, approximately 20 kilometres north of Kitwanga Junction. It represents an extremely small portion of Gitanyow territory.

These traditional territories have been subject to increasing pressure from development, with industrial forestry as one of the greatest threats. As outlined in a 2006 planning document (Philpot Forestry Services 2006), decades of clear-cut timber harvesting, dating back to the mid-1950s (Sterritt et al. 1998), have resulted in the loss or damage of many traditional harvesting sites as well as significant changes to the forest ecosystem. Mature, old-growth forests have been converted to young, structurally simple stands, and this has promoted ongoing concern about habitat loss and potential impacts on the plants, birds, animals and fish that the Gitanyow depend on for food and medicine. Not only have Gitanyow territories been clear-cut, but there have also been significant problems with companies not fulfilling their silvicultural obligation to replant (*Gitxsan and other First Nations v. British Columbia [Minister of Forests]* 2002 BCSC 1701). As per the findings of a Gitanyow-commissioned report, forest harvesting has also resulted in the mapping of over 3,400 km of roads (ForTech Consulting and Magellan Digital Mapping 2007), which has allowed other recreational users and harvesters to access Gitanyow territory and has deepened concern about the security of their food and medicine sources. As will be discussed, land-use planning provided a way for the Gitanyow to begin to address these and other more substantive concerns about the management of their traditional territory. Perhaps more importantly, though, planning provided an additional mechanism for the Gitanyow to express their rights, title and long-term vision for their Wilp territories – one that is based in traditional laws and governance structures that continue to inform the work of the Gitanyow Huwilp.

The Gitanyow Huwilp refers to the two clans (or pdeek), comprised of eight houses (or wilp), that make up the Gitanyow Nation: the Lax Gibuu consists of Wilps Gwass Hlaam, Wii'Litsxw, Malii and Haizimsque; and the Lax Ganeda consists of Wilps Gamlakyeltxw, Gwinuu, Luuxhon and Watakhayetsxw. Each Wilp has a defined territory (or *Lax'yip*), which includes all of the 'lands, waters, land forms, and life forms within the boundaries of a specific Wilp Lax'yip including plants, animals, birds, and fish resources which make the Wilp Lax'yip

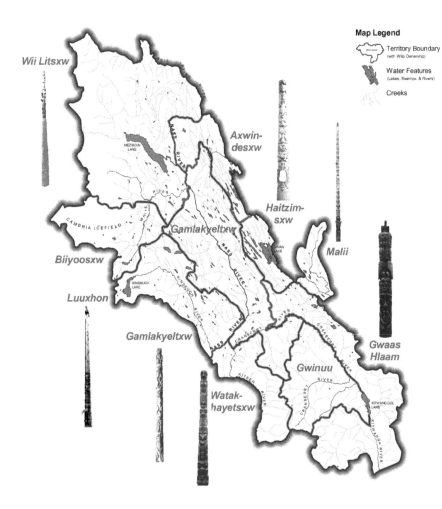

Figure 8.1   Gitanyow *Lax'yip*

Source: Map courtesy of Gitanyow Hereditary Chiefs Office, used with permission

home permanently or periodically' (Gitanyow Nation 2009). Each Wilp also has a Chief (or *Simogyet*) and a Chief Matriarch (or *Sigidim hak*), as well as a wing- or sub-chief and other name holders. These names and leadership roles, which are decided through a matrilineal system and are affirmed at a feast (or *Li'ligit*), come with specific responsibilities – all of which are related to maintaining the integrity of Gitanyow law and Gitanyow territories. Feasts are also opportunities to explain and pass on oral traditional knowledge of how to appropriately use and protect Wilp resources and to help ensure that the understanding of Wilp boundaries is 'respectful and clear' (per. comm. 23 April 2012).

Figure 8.2   Wilp Luuxhon *Git'amgan* (totempole)

Source: Photo by Sk'a'nism Tsa 'Win'Giit (Joel Starlund), Gitanyow Wilp Member, used with permission

One of the key priorities for the Gitanyow is

'maintaining and protecting the integrity of both the wilp as well as the
relationship among the Gitanyow and their continuing relationship to their
Adawaak [ancient histories passed down by the oral tradition], Ayuuks [Wilp
crests that show the identity of a Wilp and its members, and convey the sacred
connection to their *Lax'yip*]' (Gitanyow Nation 2009, 4).

At the same time, the Gitanyow have 'agreed to co-exist with other Canadians'
(Gitanyow Nation 2009, 3) and are generally willing to work with external
governments, particularly with regards to land and resource management planning.
The preparation of what is often referred to as the Gitanyow Wilp Sustainability
Plan was facilitated through the establishment of a formal planning relationship
between the Gitanyow and the BC Government, which included Gitanyow
involvement in the discussions surrounding the preparation of two different
strategic land-use plans. As this chapter will show, the planning relationship with
the province was a long and complicated one, running from approximately 2004 to
2012. The formation of this contact zone was catalyzed and then further punctuated
by legal action, as well as an ongoing provincial desire to facilitate additional
resource development through the construction of a new power-transmission line.

Although the Gitanyow Wilp Sustainability Plan needs to be understood as a
mode of expressing Gitanyow customary law and the Gitanyow Huwilp's vision for
the sustainable use of *Lax'yip* lands and resources, it also has clear (though often
contested) connections to the land-use planning tools, approaches and processes
that exist within the provincial government. Although the formation of a land-use
planning relationship with the BC Government created a forum and provided some
of the resources needed to advance the Wilp Sustainability Plan, it also meant that,
at certain stages in the process, the Wilp Sustainability Plan was framed in terms
of provincial planning language and according to provincial planning tools. As a
result, the remainder of this chapter refers to both the Wilp Sustainability Plan and
the names and terminology that were used in the two provincial planning processes.

As discussed in Chapter 4, these provincial plans are not guided by a single
statute but rather numerous acts that concern specific elements of lands management,
including the *Forest and Range Practices Act* and the *Land Act*. Within these statutes,
there is no formal requirement for the completion of large-scale land-use plans.
However, the BC Government's substantial history with regard to strategic land
and natural resource planning has resulted in the creation of numerous provincial
policies and guidance notes that express both the desired process and the outcomes
of strategic natural resource planning. These policies and guidance notes continued
to evolve over BC's over-20-year history with strategic natural resource planning,
often in direct response to the introduction of new legal precedents regarding
government responsibilities to uphold Aboriginal rights and title. In recounting the
development of the planning contact zone between the Gitanyow Huwilp and the
Province of British Columbia, this chapter will begin to illustrate how both sets of

texts (those specifically related to the practice of planning and those that concern the more general processes of Indigenous recognition) powerfully shape the depth, breadth and overall contours of the contact zone. Yet, as this chapter will also show, the planning contact zone that has evolved in the Nass River watershed is also very much a product of its local context: its history, as well as the unique makeup of the involved group of Indigenous and non-Indigenous actors.

As in the previous three chapters, the goal of this final story of (post)colonial planning is to explore the evolution of this contact zone and identify some of the planning results that have been achieved thus far. In doing so, the chapter will also highlight specific moments of contestation: instances when the goals and aspirations of the Gitanyow Huwilp came in conflict with the norms and discourses present within British Columbian natural resource planning policy and procedure, as well as instances when those norms and discourses were challenged and changed through the strategic action of both Indigenous and non-Indigenous actors, resulting in a more robust recognition of Aboriginal rights and title. The chapter concludes with an analysis of the resultant Gitanyow Wilp Sustainability Plan and begins to raise questions about the possibilities for coexistence.

Early Foundations of Gitanyow Land-Use Planning

Achieving outside recognition of the Gitanyow Wilp system has been a longstanding struggle – one that dates back to the arrival of some of the earliest government surveyors and resource developers. Throughout this period, the Gitanyow have fiercely defended their territory and have long resisted government-imposed reserves. In the early twentieth century, European farmers attempting to settle in their territories were chased away, barricades were established on forestry access roads and Gitanyow Chiefs were jailed for confiscating government surveying equipment (Sterritt et al. 1998). Alongside these more direct acts of resistance, the Gitanyow Huwilp have long been laying the foundation for their own system of land-use planning – from the hand-drawn maps and ownership statements presented to Indian Agents as early as 1910 to the detailed fieldwork, inventorying and mapping that began in the late 1970s (Sterritt et al. 1998) – and continue to do so to the present day. Much of the present work is conducted through the Hereditary Chiefs Office, an organization set up to facilitate work on common issues among the Huwilp. Questions of rights and title are still handled by the individual Wilp; the Chiefs Office simply provides a structure for the Wilp to come together and to develop relationships with other governments and resource developers.

Although it has been a long-standing area of interest for the Gitanyow Hereditary Chiefs Office, this focus on developing relationships with external parties was particularly catalyzed by the BC Treaty Process. Although the Gitanyow Huwilp have not progressed beyond their 1996 Framework Agreement (Stage 3 of the six-stage BC Treaty Process), the provincial government had identified them as one of six possible 'breakthrough [treaty negotiation] tables' in 2001 (ILMB and

Gitanyow Hereditary Chiefs Office 2005). Given the Gitanyow people's ongoing concern with forest management practices in their traditional territory, this designation led to several years of discussion between the Gitanyow Hereditary Chiefs Office, the Province of British Columbia's Treaty Negotiations Office (now the Ministry of Aboriginal Relations and Reconciliation), the Ministry of Forests and the Ministry of Sustainable Resource Management (a precursor to the Integrated Land Management Bureau [ILMB], which oversaw the development of strategic natural resource plans but was absorbed by the newly created Ministry of Forests, Lands and Natural Resource Operations in 2010). Land-use planning featured prominently in those discussions, especially in light of their participation in the Kalum and Kispiox Land and Resource Management Plans (LRMPs) in the 1990s and early 2000. Although the Gitanyow saw these plans as being heavily biased toward economic interests, they remained committed to the idea of land-use planning – so much so that they effectively abandoned their treaty negotiations, which had been at an impasse for over 10 years In fact, the Gitanyow chief negotiator has described the treaty as a 'bad deal': 'It's basically a model of extinguishment [of land title] by B.C. and Canada' (as quoted in Pollon 2012).

Legal Action and the Formal Initiation of a Contemporary Planning Contact Zone

Although the idea of engaging in strategic land-use planning and the possibility of a Gitanyow Wilp Sustainability Plan appear to have had a much longer history within the work of the Gitanyow Hereditary Chiefs Office, the origins of their more recent planning relationships with the provincial government lie in a court case launched by the Gitanyow and some of the neighbouring First Nations. The 2002 case, *Gitxsan and other First Nations v. British Columbia (Ministry of Forests)*, centred on whether the province had met its duty to consult and accommodate Aboriginal rights and title as part of a decision to transfer the control of some of the forestry tenures in Gitanyow territory. BC Supreme Court Justice Tysoe found that each of the petitioning First Nations (including the Gitanyow) 'has a good *prima facie* claim of aboriginal title and a strong *prima facie* claim of aboriginal rights with respect to at least part of the areas claimed by them' (*Gitxsan and other First Nations v. British Columbia [Minister of Forests]* 2002 BCSC 1701, para. 72). He also rejected the province's argument that a change in the control of existing forest tenures had no impact on those claims and found that the Crown had not yet fulfilled its duty to consult and accommodate Aboriginal rights and title. Yet Justice Tysoe was unwilling to quash the transfer and directed the parties to attempt to 'undertake a proper process of consultation and accommodation' (*Gitxsan*, para. 106) with longer timelines and greater attention to the nature of the consultation process itself. If the parties were unsuccessful in their efforts, the matter could be brought back to the courts.

Unsatisfied with the province's attempts to fulfil its consultation and accommodation duties, the Gitanyow went back to court in 2004 with Justice Tysoe presiding over their case for a second time. While many of the Gitanyow Huwilp's issues centred on the province's attempt to employ the standardized accommodation measures and revenue-sharing formula used in the Forest and Range Agreements being developed across BC, the Hereditary Chiefs Office had also requested joint strategic land-use planning. Although the original hearing had been scheduled for April 2004, it was delayed several times – both to allow more time for the parties to attempt to reach agreement and to await the Supreme Court of Canada's decision on *Haida* and *Taku River* (see Chapter 4). During those delays, the provincial government changed its position on the possibility of engaging in strategic land-use planning with the Gitanyow Hereditary Chiefs. Their original position had been that joint planning could proceed only if funding could be provided through a treaty-related measure. By early November, they had invited the Gitanyow to engage in forest management planning, and by January 2005 a joint planning process with the local Ministry of Forests office was underway.

Initial Experimentation with Joint Land-Use Planning

While the 2002 and 2004 court cases had clear implications in terms of challenging the status quo, the joint planning initiative of the Gitanyow Hereditary Chiefs and the Ministry of Forests (MoF) also appears to have been a product of more localized changes to the forest planning and management system. A reorganization of MoF boundaries meant that portions of Gitanyow territory were now within the Skeena Stikine Forest District. That district had already done some experimentation with landscape unit planning in the Bulkley Valley, southeast of Gitanyow territory. The Skeena Stikine district manager was also viewed as a bit of an innovator and as someone who was willing to question the shortcomings of the current system. She recognized that Aboriginal consultation in her district had become strained, with long and often confrontational meetings over specific logging proposals. Landscape-scale planning was seen as a more 'proactive approach' (Lloyd-Smith 2009), as it would allow for Aboriginal input at a more strategic level and over a much larger geographic area.

The Gitanyow Hereditary Chiefs Office had also been questioning the efficiency and effectiveness of providing comment on operational-level forestry decisions. They had also been involved in very early attempts at strategic natural resource planning and had been frustrated by the lack of attention shown to the protection of their interests. Caught between an onerous and time-consuming model of commenting on individual cutblocks and a strategic land-use planning model that seemed to be more oriented toward economic interests than the recognition of Aboriginal rights and title, the Gitanyow Hereditary Chiefs – and their chief negotiator, in particular – began to consider alternative planning approaches. Their efforts were aided by a professional forester with over 25 years of experience in the area, including previous work with neighbouring First Nations. Although he had initially been tasked with reviewing individual development plans and rendering opinions about how the proposed forestry operations might affect Gitanyow interests, he started to work with the Chiefs Office to formulate their own vision for strategic land-use planning. That vision was internally piloted in Wii'litsxw territory before progressing to a wider planning initiative with the MoF.

This planning relationship with the MoF was somewhat unusual, in that strategic planning was one of the responsibilities of the now defunct Integrated Land Management Bureau (ILMB). The local ILMB office did not have the funds to support a new planning initiative and, as a result, the local MoF office took the lead on this new initiative and committed the funds to support it. This plan was originally conceived to sit somewhere in between the high-order strategic plans produced by the ILMB and the operational cutblock plans produced by individual forest licensees. The plan aimed at producing a landscape-scale for Gitanyow territories in the Cranberry and Kispiox Timber Supply Area (TSA) and was developed according to the old MoF *Landscape Unit Planning Guide* as well as the existing Landscape Unit Plan (LUP) within the Skeena Stikine Forest District. Although it is officially known as the *Landscape Unit Plan for all Gitanyow Territories within the Kispiox and Cranberry Timber Supply Areas,* this chapter will refer to it as the Cranberry-Kispiox LUP.

The plan was described as the result of a 'co-operative consultation and planning process with Gitanyow, the Ministry of Forests, and Forest Licensees' (Philpot Forestry Services 2006). In reality, the Gitanyow's forestry consultant completed the majority of the work. Although the MoF retained him, he saw himself as 'working for the Gitanyow' (per. comm. 10 June 2011). He proceeded to organize a series of workshops and meetings with Chiefs and interested members from each of the houses that had territories within the Cranberry-Kispiox timber supply area (TSA). Those meetings were relatively unstructured and were designed to allow the Wilp members to identify resource management issues and potential solutions before attempting to translate their concerns into the more technical language that is used in LUPs to articulate resource management objectives and strategies. Once the consultant had formulated the objectives and strategies, the draft LUP was brought back to the Gitanyow for review and to ensure that their 'interests, values and desires' (Philpot Forestry Services 2006, 7) had been accurately conveyed. The MoF was kept informed of the progress of the planning process and was sent a copy of the draft objectives and strategies but was otherwise uninvolved in its inner workings. The remainder of the planning process proceeded in much the same fashion, with back-and-forth meetings as the consultant worked to translate Gitanyow interests into the established LUP format. Alongside all of this work, the consultant was using his 40 years of experience as a professional forester to identify and map areas suitable for timber harvesting as well as the forest ecosystem networks, high-value wildlife patches and wildlife corridors needed to protect other biodiversity and cultural values. Both the maps and the written planning direction were reviewed again by the Gitanyow Hereditary Chiefs Office before the draft Gitanyow LUP was sent to the MoF for review.

Although the Gitanyow and MoF had reached agreement on the LUP, there was 'real sensitivity' within government (per. comm. 12 May 2011) about calling it an actual land-use plan. It had not been developed in the same way as other provincial plans and had not undergone the same kinds of public review processes. As a result, forest licensees were encouraged to voluntarily comply with the LUP, but it would not be afforded the same weight as Strategic Resource Management Plans (SRMPs) and other types of strategic land-use plans, which are subjected to a formal period of public consultation before being sent for Cabinet approval.

Linking Initial Planning Innovations to Broader Provincial Planning Initiatives

Although the Gitanyow Huwilp's planning relationship with the provincial government began as an initiative with the MoF, the second phase was under the direction of the ILMB. Not only did the provincial agency change but the new Nass South SRMP was conducted within a different policy context and used different resource management tools. This change in underlying policy context and preferred planning approaches, tools and expectations did have an impact on the Gitanyow Huwilp's planning relationship with the provincial government and also had the potential to limit the recognition of Gitanyow rights, title and governance systems. As will be discussed below, the constraints and expectations created by provincial policy and organizational norms were not insurmountable, and the Gitanyow were able to 'drag the province along' (per. comm. 23 April 2012) to a more meaningful mode of recognition.

Initiated in November 2005, the Nass South SRMP was developed within the context of British Columbia's over-20-year history with strategic land and natural resource management planning. Although the statutory direction for this kind of collaborative land-use planning is virtually non-existent, and many of the manuals and procedural guidelines are no longer considered to be current provincial policy, there is a strong and persistent set of expectations among government planners regarding the desired processes and outcomes of strategic land-use planning. The preparation of these plans is seen by government as an exercise in shared decision making, in that a range of actors strive to reach consensus on the allocation of lands and resource management objectives for both commercial and conservation purposes. At the same time, land-use planning has long been conceived of as a way to afford 'certainty' to the forest industry by providing a clearer understanding of the size of the timber-harvesting land base and the overall resource management direction. The shift to the new *Forest and Range Practice Act* (FRPA) further underscored the need to provide concrete resource management objectives, as the results-based approach used in the new Act demanded the articulation of clear, measureable targets that industry would be able to implement on the ground.

At the same time, BC strategic land-use planning is increasingly being cast as a tool for addressing Aboriginal interests. Planners, including those heavily involved in the establishment of the Nass South SRMP, explicitly state that these processes are not to address Aboriginal rights and title, but rather 'the interests that are associated with the rights and title' (per. comm. 12 May 2011). Strategic land-use planning is also increasingly seen by government as a tool for improving the ease and efficiency of consulting on potential infringements on Aboriginal rights and title. Plans are often seen as a way to articulate and spatially represent areas of Aboriginal interest. They are seen to help all parties – Indigenous, government and resource development proponents – contextualize the identified Indigenous interests and to define how they ought to be addressed. Planning processes are also increasingly being framed as opportunities to determine how the legal obligations of consultation and accommodation might be fulfilled in future decision-making processes.

The provincial government's apparent struggle to attend equally to both the new resource management culture created by FRPA and the interests that underlie unresolved Aboriginal rights and title is evident in the initial Terms of Reference for the Nass South SRMP. Although the development of the Nass South SRMP was clearly seen as a 'partnership' with the Gitanyow, the actual terms made little to no reference to the Gitanyow Huwilp's specific planning vision or interests. Instead, it was strongly framed by provincial policy and provincial priorities – not the least of which was to avoid further legal challenges. In an era of limited government resources to support land-use planning, the Nass South SRMP was justified by the province on the basis of its potential to avoid further legal action from the Gitanyow and help 'streamline' future consultation efforts (ILMB and Gitanyow Hereditary Chiefs Office 2005, 5). Planning was also seen as a 'critical short term need for the District Manager of Forests' (6), as strategic planning processes are often seen as the means for developing and reaching consensus on the specific resource management objectives needed to direct commercial forestry practices. The kinds of 'values' that strategic planning can address are largely laid out in *Forest and Range Practice Act*, which allows for the creation of legally enforceable objectives concerning species at risk, regionally important wildlife (for example, grizzly bears), fish habitat, community water sources, overall biodiversity, visual quality and cultural heritage.

Because these values do not always match Indigenous interests and aspirations, Gitanyow Hereditary Chiefs have often had to act strategically in order to frame their interests in ways that carried weight with the provincial forest management system. Part of this work involved building informal relationships with key decision makers and knowledge holders within the provincial government. For example, the Gitanyow were able to develop a particularly productive relationship with the MoE representative, who (given the mandate of his ministry and his own personal orientation) was also looking to achieve increased environmental protection. He had also worked with the Gitanyow Huwilp's forestry consultant in the past and described their overall outlook on

Figure 8.3   Gitanyow Lake

Source: Photo by Sk'a'nism Tsa 'Win'Giit (Joel Starlund), Gitanyow Wilp Member, used with permission

planning as being 'the same peas in the same pod' (per. comm. 12 May 2011). Ultimately, the Gitanyow were able to see the MoE representative as an ally within government: someone 'who understood that these concerns ... affected all British Columbians and not just the Gitanyow' (per. comm.,6 June 2011) and who could help them frame their concerns in the language of conservation science. As the Gitanyow Hereditary Chiefs Office asserts, their involvement in planning processes was about combining their traditional knowledge with 'good, sound science' (per. comm. 16 May 2011).

Yet, the MoE representative was not the Gitanyow Huwilp's only source of ecological data. In addition to their longstanding relationship with their forestry consultant, they also used the consulting services of two professional ecologists, who helped them articulate the long-term ecological risks to the Wilp territories. The Gitanyow also worked with a local archaeologist, who helped them develop their Cultural Heritage Strategy: a Gitanyow-specific policy that is now sent to all resource developers operating within Gitanyow territory. In many respects, these relationships with both consultants and provincial officials can be seen as a response to the technical and scientific nature of both the LUP and SRMP. It was a way for the Gitanyow to access new sources of information and to draw on very particular skills that may not have been well represented among the existing staff of the Hereditary Chiefs Office.

Although positive working relationships were being formed and progress was being made in terms of developing the substance of the Nass South SRMP, there was still the unresolved issue of how agreements reached during the previous Cranberry-Kispiox LUP would gain legal force. The lack of legal force given to the plan was one of several issues raised in the Gitanyow Huwilp's third appearance before the BC Supreme Court. Like the previous cases heard before Justice Tysoe in 2002 and 2004, the 2008 case, *Wii'litswx v. British Columbia (Minister of Forests)* was concerned with whether the Crown had adequately performed its consultation and accommodation duties. The judge ultimately decided that she did not have sufficient information about the legislative underpinning of the LUP to make a determination as to whether its voluntary nature represented an insufficient form of accommodation. Madam Justice Neilson's decision did, however, reiterate the importance of the Wilp (and Wilp territories) as 'an integral and defining feature of Gitanyow society' (BCSC 1139, para. 222). Interpreting and implementing this declaration arguably presented one of the largest challenges for the local ILMB planners – one that became particularly contentious as they tried to consider the overlapping claims and interests of other Indigenous groups.

The Gitanyow were afforded a significant role in the Nass South SRMP, in that they co-authored the original Terms of References and played a direct and sustained role in all the deliberations over the long-term future of the Nass River Watershed. The Nass South SRMP process primarily involved the Gitanyow chief negotiator and the ILMB, with representation from other BC ministries and other Gitanyow Chiefs and Wilp representatives. Given that so many of the issues were forestry based, it was also agreed that licensees should be invited to participate in the planning meetings. However, the ILMB were also insistent that the process would need to involve the neighbouring Nisga'a Nation, with whom the province had signed the first modern land claims agreement in 2000. One of the results of that treaty had been the creation of the Nass Wildlife Area, a designated area for joint wildlife management. Given that this area has been the source of a longstanding and intense post-contact dispute between these two Aboriginal groups (for a discussion of pre-contact relations, see Sterritt et al. 1998), the ILMB decided that it would be counterproductive to have both groups at the same planning meetings and opted instead to engage in an exercise in 'shuttle diplomacy' (per. comm. provincial planner, 12 May 2011). The Gitanyow were not pleased with the arrangement and its incursion on their planning relationship with the province, but they were able to live with it. However, they could not accept the constant references to the neighbouring Nisga'a in the draft plan. In their mind, the plan needed to be a reflection of a bilateral relationship. As one provincial representative recalls, the dominant sentiment within the Gitanyow appeared to be that 'if [Nisga'a] have the treaty, we have the plan' (per. comm. 12 May 2011). In the ILMB's mind, the Nass South SRMP needed to uphold the rigorous, though largely unwritten, standards of any other strategic land-use planning and needed to demonstrate that it had addressed the interests of a wide range of actors, including all of the affected First Nations.

The ILMB proceeded to develop an almost-150-page plan that summarized both the overall planning context and the draft land-use zones and resource management objectives. In describing the planning context, that document made consistent reference to both the history and specific land-use interests of both the Nisga'a and the Gitanyow. The expectation was that both groups would sign off on the plan before it was subjected to a 45-day public review process and subsequent revisions. At this point it would be sent for Cabinet approval – just like any other strategic land-use plan. However, the Gitanyow were completely unwilling to give their formal approval to a document that they saw as legitimizing Nisga'a authority within Gitanyow territory. The process had reached an impasse, which could be solved only by essentially separating the approval of the particular planning objectives and zones from the approval of the actual land-use plan. It was agreed that the Gitanyow would be asked to sign off only on the maps and resource management objectives, and the plan would simply become a tool for public consultation and for Cabinet approval.

Creating a Single, Legally Binding Expression of Gitanyow Law

Although the Gitanyow Huwilp's involvement in the Nass South SRMP effectively come to a close in March 2009, when the draft plan was sent for public review, their struggle to use land-use planning to assert and uphold their Aboriginal rights, title and governance systems was not yet over. For as important as both the Nass South SRMP and the previous LUP for Gitanyow territories within the Cranberry-Kispiox TSA were, they did not address all of Gitanyow territory and were prepared under two entirely different planning frameworks. The Gitanyow began to push the provincial government to consolidate and address any inconsistencies between the Nass South SRMP and the Cranberry-Kispiox LUP, as well as a few small portions of Gitanyow territory that were under the direction of the much older Kispiox LRMP. Having kept a keen eye on what was happening elsewhere in the province, the Gitanyow began to focus on the development of a comprehensive and legally binding land-use agreement with the province. The BC Government has begun to negotiate similar agreements across the province. Given that these agreements were developed on the heels of the 2005 *New Relationship Policy Statement* (a document that grew out of the 2004 *Haida* and *Taku* rulings – see Chapter 4), they included not only clear land and resource management objectives (that would be given legal force under the *Forest and Range Practices Act*) but also a clear protocol for including and consulting the First Nation signatories on all future land-use decisions – and, in many cases, for revenue sharing. The Gitanyow Huwilp's vision for their eventual *Recognition and Reconciliation Agreement* went one step further; they saw it as an opportunity to demand recognition of key customary laws and principles related to the cultural and ecological integrity of each Wilp Lax'yip.

The proposed construction of a new energy transmission line (that would service major mineral operations north-east of Gitanyow territory) strengthened the Gitanyow Huwilp's case for the creation of a *single* legally binding land-use plan that both presented a clear vision for the long-term sustainability of each of the eight Wilp territories and was reflection of Gitanyow customary law. Although the Gitanyow had first expressed their concern over the Northwest Transmission Line (NTL) in November 2007 during its pre-review, their concerns escalated as it became more apparent that the line would completely bisect their traditional territories. Although the province has a clear desire to support revenue and job-generating natural resource development projects, the NTL simply could not go ahead without substantial consultation and accommodation – a reality that bolstered the Gitanyow Huwilp's negotiating power and allowed them to demand adherence to the land-use plan that they were putting together for their entire traditional territory and the incorporation of the plan into a legally binding agreement. For the next two years, the negotiations surrounding these two agreements (the *Impact Benefit Agreement* for NTL and the broader *Recognition and Reconciliation Agreement* that would give force to the Gitanyow Huwilp's own land-use plan) were held tightly together, with one informing the other. In the words of the Gitanyow chief negotiator, the Gitanyow were keenly aware of the strategic advantage of 'hooking' their desire for a comprehensive land-use plan into the province's economic agenda and 'using that to advance all the things that we have' (per. comm. 17 May 2011).

The Gitanyow Wilp Sustainability Plan (officially referred to as the *Gitanyow Lax'yip Land Use Plan*) represented a consolidation of all of the land-use plans the Gitanyow had been engaged in since the mid-1990s. Getting BC Hydro (the proponent of the NTL) to recognize and uphold the recommended land-use designations in this plan took several years of tense negotiations. At issue was the proposed protected area for the Hanna and Tintina watersheds, which are 'known to the Gitanyow as Xsi' anhahlye'e and Nihl nihlt'ina' and considered to be 'sacred lands ... due to the high cultural values of salmon, wildlife, food and medicinal resources and the rich cultural history of occupancy and extensive use through time' (Gitanyow Hereditary Chiefs et al. 2010, i). After over a year of negotiation, the Gitanyow walked away from the process in April 2011 but eventually returned to the negotiation table when the transmission line was routed away from these sensitive watersheds.

The *Recognition and Reconciliation Agreement* between the Province of British Columbia and the Gitanyow Hereditary Chiefs was signed on 28 March 2012, though the province did not issue the official press release until September of that year – presumably so that the press release could also announce the resolution of the issues surrounding the NTL (see Ministry of Aboriginal Relations and Reconciliation 2012). The March 2012 agreement includes all of the written management objectives and mapped resource management zones from both the

Cranberry and Nass South SRMPs, as well as the relevant portions of the earlier Kalum and Kispiox LRMPs. The Gitanyow Huwilp see this combination of maps and written directives as providing the backbone of their own Wilp Sustainability Plan. Unlike the individual land-use plans, this *Recognition and Reconciliation Agreement* includes provisions for ongoing economic development and revenue sharing, the application of a shared decision-making approach and the creation of a Joint Resources Governance Forum. Recognition of the Gitanyow traditional governance system is also a key feature of the agreement. Individual Wilp territorial boundaries are an integral part of all of the land-use planning maps included in this agreement. It also includes explicit references to the importance of maintaining ecological function and sociocultural well-being for each Wilp.

Conclusion

The Gitanyow Wilp Sustainability Plan, as well as the broader *Recognition and Reconciliation Agreement* that it is embedded within it, represent a significant departure from the BC Government's preferred approach to Strategic Resource Management Planning. Provincial policy and procedure – including their level of recognition of Aboriginal rights, title and governance systems – were actively challenged and changed at key stages in the development of the Gitanyow Wilp Sustainability Plan. These changes were often the result of the strategic actions of various people involved. For example, relationships were built with consultants and other allied people within government. The Gitanyow also bolstered their reputation for tough negotiation and demonstrated their willingness to turn to the courts when necessary. As a result, the Gitanyow have consistently shown themselves to be unafraid to say 'we simply cannot accept this' and to use all of the tools of Western government, including the judicial system, when advocating for an alternative approach.

Yet, the Gitanyow Huwilp's relationship with the BC Government was not simply a litigious and adversarial one; a number of formal and informal relationships were built with provincial government officials and external consultants who shared Gitanyow concerns. These relationships can be seen as a response to the technical and scientific nature of both the LUP and SRMP. It was a way for the Gitanyow to access new sources of information and to draw on very particular skills that may not have been well represented among the existing staff of the Hereditary Chiefs Office. However, it was not simply about acquiring new skills; the Gitanyow were using these relationships to 'translate' their concerns into the language of provincial planning – a key strategy that we will return to in Chapter 9. The Gitanyow Huwilp's willingness to learn and strategically respond to existing government policy extended beyond specific forest management tools and zoning approaches. They were also keeping a keen eye on the BC Government's response to other First Nations' demands for increased recognition in land-use and natural resource management, an awareness that ultimately led to their *Recognition and Reconciliation Agreement*.

The development of the Wilp Sustainability Plan is also illustrative of ongoing tensions between Indigenous demands for increased recognition and the rules and expectations created by the existing planning system, a theme that we will return to in Chapter 10. The Gitanyow encountered a planning system that had been forced to acknowledge the strength of their claim to Aboriginal rights and title and was willing to explore opportunities for partnership and collaboration. But that system ultimately sought to develop mechanisms to 'streamline' its consultation and accommodation duties. It was also a planning system with a strong statutory need to develop concrete resource management objectives in order to direct the actions of individual forest licensees. While there was not a great deal of formal government policy to direct the process used to develop these objectives, the Gitanyow came up against some strong organizational norms and expectations about what a strategic land-use plan should look like, who needed to be involved, and how it would be approved. These expectations were not always in line with Gitanyow traditional law, planning vision or understanding of the nature of their planning relationship with the provincial government. While there is certainly no set formula for finding a way through the constraints of the existing land-use planning system, the Gitanyow experience highlights the importance of relationship building, the strategic use of the courts and the conscientious use and adaptation of Western science.

PART III
Conceptualizing Coexistence in Planning Theory and Practice

Chapter 9

Negotiating, Contesting, Reframing:
Indigenous Agency in the Contact Zone

Introduction

The case studies presented in Part II are all stories of Indigenous struggle within and against a system that continually seeks to marginalize, oppress and dominate Indigenous lives – even as it purports to include and accommodate their culture, laws/lores, customs and spirituality. Understanding the different dimensions and expressions of this struggle is critical and demands a close look at how Indigenous agency is articulated in specific socio-historic circumstances. In this chapter we look at how these contact zones were 'hailed into being' (Butler 1999, see Chapter 3) through the agency of the Wurundjeri, Wadi Wadi, Gitanyow and Tsleil-Waututh Nations. We pay attention to how the confluence of systems of planning and recognition discussed in Chapter 4 provided a political opportunity structure that Indigenous leaders could use to make their concerns visible to state-based planning agencies, often using language and tools that already existed within the planning system. We also look at the softer, less tangible dynamics of action within the contact zone, where Indigenous people strategically mobilized the possibilities that hybrid spaces like this might offer. Capacity, leadership, allies and champions – all are important in different ways and all contribute to a deeper understanding of how these four visionary Indigenous nations negotiated, contested, and reframed the practice of state-based planning.

Despite these commonalities, there is no particular type of event, structure or action that calls planning contact zones into being, nor a recipe to follow for transforming everyday planning practice. What the stories offer is a spectrum of possibilities, each with distinct limitations and conditions. Each provides insight into how recognition in planning became possible under different kinds of conditions. In examining these stories, we must also remember that for many Indigenous peoples this impulse to use state-based planning tools and processes to defend, reconstitute and reclaim the lands and waters within their traditional territories is informed by specific socio-ecological and cultural relations. As Indigenous peoples often articulate, their *responsibility* toward their traditional territory is deeply rooted in their own laws/lores, customs and spirituality. Their efforts to hail contact zones into being can be understood as one way of upholding these responsibilities.

As we will see, Indigenous socio-ecological and cultural perspectives are also reflected in their careful and transformative use of existing planning approaches and tools. As we discussed in Chapter 3, the colonial power relations that surround these acts of cross-cultural negotiation, contestation and transformation run deep. But planning contact zones can still be understood as hybrid, third space (following Bhabha 1994), with Indigenous customary law/lore increasingly brought to the fore. The chapter begins, then, with this important wellspring of Indigenous agency, as articulated by the peoples of the Wurundjeri, Wadi Wadi, Gitanyow and Tsleil-Waututh Nations.

Indigenous Customary Law and the Planning 'Impulse'

The four nations whose stories we have told in this book all share very similar concerns and motivations in relation to planning. All are concerned with the impacts of development on their rights, title and political authority, as well as the cultural, economic and ecological integrity of their lands and waters.

For the Wurundjeri people, the struggle over the terms and nature of recognition is set within the responsibility to continue the practices of countless generations of ancestors, in whom Wurundjeri people express pride and respect. One Wurundjeri Elder described it like this:

> Our old people's responsibility was caring for country, caring for family, and we still feel like we've got the same role that's been passed down even though it was very nearly cut off. So for us to be able to care for country and water we want to get involved with these managers … [helping] country come back to where it was, keeping it healthy, cleaning it up … and working with them to do that. (pers. comm. 18 July 2011)

As this quote expresses, the impact of colonization is profoundly felt in everyday life, where the struggle to practise that responsibility is persistently and sharply curtailed. Wurundjeri people seek ways to express that responsibility under these colonial conditions, and their work has led to a focus on cultural heritage management as well as language reclamation, ceremony and dance. They also work to develop new places for the practice of Wurundjeri culture, such as at the former mission station at Coranderrk. Their practice of responsibility also leads to the finding and linking of relatives previously lost to Wurundjeri families and to the educat of non-Indigenous people.

Wadi Wadi people describe the central importance of Nyah-Vinifera Park to their practices, law and relations on an everyday basis. Nyah-Vinifera is sometimes talked about by Wadi Wadi Elders as a 'centre ground', or a 'spiritual base' from which Wadi Wadi responsibilities to ancestors and country can be practised. A significant element of that practice in recent years has been the fight to protect and assert responsibility for Nyah-Vinifera Park and other areas of Wadi Wadi country. As one Elder put it, 'What I want is for us to be acknowledged and recognized' (pers. comm. 6 July, 2011), and this assertion is deeply linked with the country itself.

Tsleil-Waututh people describe their relationship with their lands and waters as having existed 'since time out of mind'. Renewing and maintaining that relationship on an everyday basis arises from responsibilities and obligations (*shXalmes*), which demands a responsibility to 'speak for', protect and rehabilitate lands and waters. Under law (*snewyel*), this demands holistic practices, reflected in contemporary Tsleil-Waututh governance practices where the work of governing territory is done in circles and through consensus-based caucus arrangements. For Tsleil-Waututh, the aim is to 'put the Tsleil-Waututh face' back on their territory outside of the reserve boundaries (pers. comm. 13 June, 2011).

Gitanyow law (*Ayookxw*) forms the foundation of the Gitanyow Huwilp's engagement with the BC planning system, as it expresses their inherent right to be a self-governing people. That law expresses their relations to each other and to their traditional territories, and articulates the structure of their institutions and governance practices (Gitanyow Nation 2009). As stated in their constitution,

> We live by and are required to pass along to future generations, our inherited Ayookxw [law], Lax'yip [territory], the eight historic Wilp [group or unit] and our respective Ayuuks [crests], Adawaak [record of Wilp history], and Git'mgan [carved poles], the Simalgyax language, and the practice of the Li'ligit [institutions of Wilp authority and governance]. (Gitanyow Nation 2009, 3)

This constitutional expression is one way Gitanyow people express their rights and responsibilities through the territory and authority of each Wilp and its respective *Lax'yip*.

These quotes demonstrate that the impulse to engage in planning arises from a much wider set of cultural responsibilities that are governed by the laws/lores of each of these four communities. Engaging with planning is seen as offering one mechanism through which better control of land-use and development might be achieved. This engagement is articulated through the responsibilities that Indigenous peoples hold toward their lands and waters as well as toward all the beings (human and non-human) that call these places home.

Hailing Contact Zones into Being through Indigenous Agency

Contact zones do not magically appear. In many cases they are the result of generations of struggle across multiple fronts, with sophisticated, strategic and often highly variable expressions of Indigenous agency. As discussed in Chapter 4, the systems of planning in Victoria and British Columbia are starting to address the legal discourses around Indigenous rights and title that circulate within the Australian and Canadian states' approach to Indigenous recognition. However, as our case studies clearly show, such high-level recognition may not readily translate into the formation of planning contact zones. Contact zones are conceptually constructed through the confluence of state-based systems of planning and recognition, but they must also be 'hailed into being' (Butler 1999) through the co-constitutive performance of structure and agency (Bourdieu 1977). As we will see, the ongoing struggle and action of Indigenous peoples in this regard is deeply tied to the presence of appropriate political opportunity structures (Tarrow 1994) – for example, the legal decisions and statutory powers that make Indigenous interests visible to state-based planning agencies. The contact zones in these stories, then, are thoroughly hybrid places: the products of knowledgeable, strategic, visionary Indigenous agents, whose actions draw upon and often transform broader political and legal structures, as well as planning norms and techniques.

Legal Action and the Demand to Become Party to State-Based Planning Initiatives

The long backstory that is common to our four cases is the rise of a land-use or development conflict. Such conflicts do not arise out of nowhere and should be read as one dimension of the violent histories of colonial dispossession and the struggles that Indigenous people have always fought to retain their lands, political authority, cultures and languages. In our cases, direct conflict over particular instances of the abrogation of rights and title was an intrinsic part of how contact zone came to be. The Tsleil-Waututh Nation disputed actions by the District of North Vancouver that led to destruction of their cultural heritage at Whey-ah-Wichen (Cates Park). Wadi Wadi people waged a 15-year anti-logging campaign focused on Nyah-Vinifera Park. The Gitanyow Huwilp took court action to stop the transfer of a timber licence that would affect their rights and title. Wurundjeri peoples had long been in quiet conflict with developers and local councils over the cultural impacts of urban development. Each of these disputes is part of a broader political and legal landscape that continues to shift on questions of Indigenous recognition. Sometimes the common law or statutory impulse to engage Indigenous peoples is not direct or overt, but these shifts nonetheless trigger different expectations and norms about the extent to which planning now has to 'deal with' Indigenous peoples.

It is worth briefly recounting key elements of this shifting landscape, as they bring into sharp relief the importance of these wider conditions. Settler governments in both Canada and Australia have recognized the possible existence of Aboriginal title, and state responsibilities toward it. In Australia, native title established a new and highly limited framework within which we can read Indigenous struggles. Neither the Wadi Wadi nor the Wurundjeri peoples' struggles with planning were catalyzed in a straightforward way by native title. The Wurundjeri are neither claimants nor holders of native title, and the Nyah-Vinifera Park is actually outside the Wadi Wadi people's native title claim area. However, the broad socio-political shifts that the native title regime catalyzed are important parts of both stories, and Victoria's *Traditional Owner Settlement Act* (TOSA) enables Aboriginal peoples to become a party to planning in ways not possible before. While BC's approach to Aboriginal title is quite different, and similarly heavily criticized (see Woolford 2005), the BC Treaty Process did bring First Nation concerns to the attention of nearby municipalities. It was through their involvement in the treaty process that the District of North Vancouver came to appreciate the importance of establishing a cooperative planning relationship with First Nations – an understanding that ultimately triggered the district's relationship with the Tsleil-Waututh Nation during the development of its Official Community Plan.

The common law is a more directly causal part of the Gitanyow Huwilp's planning contact zone with the provincial government. Gitanyow Huwilp launched two legal challenges against the transfer of a forest licence on their territory. This work was made possible by the Hereditary Chiefs Office, an organization that is grounded in traditional Gitanyow governance structure but draws on the expertise of a Vancouver-based lawyer who has worked with the Gitanyow for decades. These court decisions effectively ordered the provincial government to return to the negotiating table to meaningfully address Gitanyow rights and title. Although specific to Gitanyow interests and culture, these court cases also need to be understood within the context of other legal precedents. The *Haida* case was particularly significant, as it triggered a more widespread use of the language of 'government-to-government' relationships – language that ultimately increased the Gitanyow Huwilp's standing in both the Landscape Unit Plan and the Nass South SRMP.

Threat of court action has been similarly effective in forcing settler-state agencies to get to the table with each of these nations or to stay at that table in good faith. For example, the District of North Vancouver's willingness to undertake the joint planning initiative at Cates Park/Whey-ah-Wichen was partially triggered by concerns that the Tsleil-Waututh might pursue some kind of action to highlight the destruction of the site that DNV works had caused. However, the threat of a court or direct action does not emerge from nowhere – and it certainly requires strategic human agency. The Tsleil-Waututh Nation's response to the DNV's actions at Whey-ah-Wichen needs to be understood within the context of their broader organizational history. The Tsleil-Waututh had developed a strong governance framework that included both their elected Band Council and traditional Council and that expressed a clear vision for how they would work with their hired staff and trusted advisors (both Indigenous and non-Indigenous). It would not be a stretch to suggest that it was this framework that allowed a quick and decisive response to the conflict over Cates Park/Whey-ah-Wichen, a response that ultimately led to their first planning contact zone with the District of North Vancouver.

The Wadi Wadi Nation's use of a legal injunction to stop timber harvesting in what was then Nyah State Forest brought open conflict into a dispute that had been simmering for years and catalyzed an entirely different planning outcome: a higher conservation status to protect the lands and values in Nyah-Vinifera Park. Unlike the Tsleil-Waututh, the Wadi Wadi had no formal institutional capacity, but they nonetheless managed to push a contact zone into being through sheer tenacity and hard work. This was supported by important alliances, including the locally based Friends of Nyah-Vinifera Forest and, ultimately, the Friends of the Earth (FoE).

At the request of the Wadi Wadi, one activist from FoE came to play a central role in the negotiations for a co-management agreement with the State Government.

No threat of court action is possible without a legal framework supporting the possibility of recognition, even if that legal framework does not at that stage overtly recognize the differently positioned actors making claims upon the settler state. Other legislative and policy changes are similarly important. The Wurundjeri people also used the legal framework then in place to protect cultural heritage in order to gain minimal recognition of their rights to own and control their own heritage values. The visionary leadership by Wurundjeri leaders to establish the initial in 1985 was possible in part because of the existence of the then legislative framework. The Wurundjeri people, through what is now the Wurundjeri Council continue to use the current legislative framework extremely effectively, creating possibilities out of very limited statutory powers, as will be discussed later in this chapter.

Finding Openings within the Planning System

The planning system itself can yield surprising possibilities for Indigenous action and for the creation of sites where meaningful recognition and relationships can be built. For the Gitanyow Huwilp, the Landscape Unit Plan marked a real shift away from early efforts to engage Indigenous peoples, efforts that have been described by Gitanyow members as 'empty and meaningless' (per. comm. 6 May 2011). This was partly a response to the long history of disputes and partly a response to visionary leadership – in terms of both the Gitanyow Hereditary Chiefs Office and the provincial government itself. The president of the Gitanyow Chiefs Office was a long-time advocate for protection of lands and, along with other key leaders, came to the view that the best way to achieve this was through land-use planning. In his words, 'people just say it's a land-use plan and for us it's protection; it's a lot of protection, recognition and protection – and entrenching that into the land-use agreements … and leaving that in place for future generations … ' (pers. comm. 16 May 2011).

It had become clear that responding to, and sometimes being directly confrontational about, individual cutblocks was insufficient. Strategic action was seen to afford better recognition, and better protection of Gitanyow values. Gitanyow calls for planning were met by the district manager for the (then) Ministry of Forests, someone whom Gitanyow leaders describe as very progressive and who was supportive of their action to use planning to open up a space for greater recognition. It was this officer who enabled the initial Landscape Unit Plan. Although this process required additional funding and represented a significant departure from planning norms and procedures, it could be easily justified through the use of concepts and discourses that were already emerging within the provincial planning system. As discussed in Chapter 4, the province was beginning to frame planning as a means of creating efficiency and certainty in a climate of potentially risky legal proceedings. Planning was a tool through which all the stakeholders could articulate their interests, while the final plans provided proof that the province was fulfilling its legal obligations around consultation and accommodation.

BC's urban planning system can also catalyze a contact zone with Indigenous peoples, as in the case of the District of North Vancouver (DNV) and the process that unfolded with the Tsleil-Waututh Nation with regards to their Official Community Plan (OCP). Under BC's *Local Government Act (1996)*, the DNV is legislatively responsible for undertaking long-range planning – and is strongly encouraged to develop appropriate measures for consulting First Nations on these matters. However, it was the Tsleil-Waututh Nation's strategic actions and long-term economic vision that prompted the DNV to consider a more involved approach to fulfilling this basic requirement. The Tsleil-Waututh Nation had become a much larger player in the development of the North Shore, both through the approval of its own Land Code and through more than ten years' experience with building market housing on its reserve. The DNV's uncertainty over how the Tsleil-Waututh Nation's development plans might impact its own growth and development became a strategic opportunity to broaden the Tsleil-Waututh Nation's involvement in the OCP.

In each of these stories, the catalyzing of new contact zones was not simply the result of a legal or political shift; it was about mobilizing these new-found resources and finding the *capacity* to act. In some cases, it was a person with vision and leadership who could make things happen and inspire others to follow. In others, this capacity was about establishing a base from which to organize – an office or a small team of staff as well as some tiny pockets of funding to buy in some additional technical help or expertise. In fact, it was a variety of combinations and permutations of these kinds of dimensions and actions by Indigenous peoples that brought contact zones into being. In addition, Indigenous peoples strategically utilized established legal orders, regulations and precedents to support these actions, which forced state-based planning agencies to take notice and to make Indigenous peoples a party to their decision-making processes.

While this was a marked achievement, Indigenous struggles are about being more than a 'party' – a visitor received politely into a world where all the rules remain unchanged. Once contact zones are created, much more work has to be done by Indigenous peoples, and their allies, to unsettle and reimagine the possibilities for coexistence. It is to those everyday practices at work inside the contact zone that we now turn.

Everyday Practices inside the Contact Zone

Small changes can trigger much more significant shifts. Such is the case in the four types of contact zone we are discussing in this book. Participants across BC and Victoria, particularly in government, talked (sometimes with incredulity) about how much had changed. For some, it was about practice – the sense that 10 years ago joint management, for example, was given little thought and was even less possible to practise. For others, it was about what current practices signalled in a more symbolic way: a greater recognition that planning with Indigenous peoples was not only necessary but, in fact, an improvement on past practices.

These changes represent what might be identifiable as system-transforming practices. Yet, as we will discuss more in Chapter 10, the myriad practices, structures and agencies at work in planning contact zones often seek to constrain this potential. As these four case studies show, Indigenous people make huge efforts to counteract these tendencies and to hold open the possibility of system-transforming moments. These efforts are visible in the everyday practice of actors within those contact zones – what they do, when they do it, how they operate, and where they decide to invest their energy and resources. One of the Wadi Wadi negotiators describes this as trying to push government agencies beyond 'minimum compliance' with legislation:

> They just want to do what they have to by their legal obligations ... We just do it the way we know and what we've been taught traditionally. And it's trying to find that middle ground between the two – that's where we have a lot of struggles sometimes. (pers. comm. 26 May 2011)

We might also think of these practices as the 'arts of the contact zone' (Pratt 1991, see Chapter 3). In this section we take a closer look at these arts, paying close attention to four principal dimensions, some of which have already been foregrounded in the previous section: developing institutional capacity, building relationships and using allies, using the tools and norms of planning systems themselves to 'speak back' and using cultural heritage powers strategically. While none of these on its own is necessarily 'system transforming', together they build the foundation for practising the arts of the contact zone, which widens the space of potential for transformation.

Developing Institutional Capacity

Capacity is a word heard frequently in and about planning contact zones, and one that can be understood in many ways – institutional, financial, political and cultural. Government agencies routinely wield the charge of 'lack of capacity' within Indigenous groups like a grand excuse, masking their own inactivity and unwillingness to shift systemic injustice. Chapter 11 will advance a more critical reading of this debate about capacity, turning it on its head so that we can draw attention to a second (and much less talked-about) dimension: the enormous capacity deficit that exists within settler-state planning agencies when it comes to questions of coexistence. For now, we focus on the range of practices that Indigenous people have pursued to build capacity within their own peoples and institutions. For it is clear that the less tangible – but undoubtedly material and profound – violence done by colonization has been to strip capacity from Indigenous peoples. Population dispersion and loss, dispossession and the subsequent erosion of economic and cultural sustainability, and the socio-economic disadvantage that many Indigenous peoples face in comparison to non-Indigenous citizens all factor in any discussion of capacity.

Efforts to rebuild capacity of various kinds are clear in all four of the stories we are presenting here. As discussed in the previous section, three of the nations we worked with in this research had established formal institutions as a means of building this capacity (the Gitanyow Huwilp Chiefs Office; the Tsleil-Waututh Nation's elected and traditional councils, with supportive administrative departments; and Wurundjeri Council). At the time of the research, the Wadi Wadi Nation was working toward setting up a formal organization to support its work. While no formal institution exists at the time of writing, the Wadi Wadi have nonetheless adopted practices that mirror formal institutional processes, while respecting their own governance system. Why are Indigenous institutions so important in the contact zone? A large part of an answer to that question is their ability to concentrate and build capacity – in terms of finances, knowledge, technology, translation, culture and employment. Because settler states and other stakeholders with interests on Indigenous territory recognize formal organizations more immediately, nations bringing such organizational forms to the contact zone can leverage greater control and authority. Indeed, in the case of the Wadi Wadi Nation, the Victorian Government will not sign an agreement with the nation until it is incorporated into a formal, legally recognized organizational entity.

If capacity is measured in terms of organizational size, scope and income, then it is clear that the four case studies here represent a highly differentiated range of circumstances. The Wurundjeri Council is a significant institutional structure, having grown from just a handful of people in the early days to a staff of around 35 in 2012 and grown again to a staff of around 55 in 2015. The two BC cases are also relatively well resourced in terms of staff numbers, organizational finances and scope of work. The Tsleil-Waututh Nation's organizational structure is spread across a number of departments, including the Treaty, Lands and Resources Department. Initially it had a staff of just three, and focused primarily on the treaty negotiations; by 2011, the department had more than 40 GIS, stewardship, natural resource planning and field staff. Although their staff complement is much smaller, the Gitanyow engage in similar areas of work. Both the Gitanyow Huwilp and the Tsleil-Waututh Nation have also made occasional use of external consultants to build their capacity and to access a particular professional skill. Lawyers and other high-level policy advisors have also been important, giving counsel on legal issues around environmental planning and land use.

Our case studies also highlight how Indigenous peoples strategically respond to the increasingly intense problem of draining consultation and engagement demands, including research projects such as this one. After having spent significant time and money on engagements that never returned any benefits to the organization, the Tsleil-Waututh Nation developed their *Stewardship Policy*. This policy sets a fee structure for engaging with the nation on almost any matter that will demand staff resources and time (including this research project), which sends an important message to all of the agencies operating in the Tsleil-Waututh Nation's designated consultation area about the distribution of costs. In this way the *Stewardship Policy* takes significant steps toward correcting a deeply unequal contact zone that saw the Tsleil-Waututh Nation shouldering all the cost for little of the gain. The Wurundjeri Council's process for managing engagement with CHMP proponents is similar in this regard. They also found that the increasing level of engagement sought from government agencies, archaeologists and developers was demanding a huge amount from an already stretched resource, and they too developed a fee structure to recoup some of those costs.

The situation for the Wadi Wadi is very different. Although they have a strong and culturally grounded governance approach, there is no formal organizational structure or source of funds to support their activities. This had a huge impact and was discussed time and again during the research. The Friends of the Earth campaigner was the only person paid (on a part-time, short-term basis), and her remuneration came from funds provided by the Department of Sustainability and Environment (DSE) to facilitate an agreement toward co-management. All of the other work was voluntary – a massive input for a small and, in socio-economic terms, relatively disadvantaged population. People spoke about the impacts that working all weekend and most evenings during the week (all while caring for families and holding down regular, paid jobs) had on individuals and the community. Because of the demands of everyday life, it was often hard to get representation from all of the family groups at meetings. The Wadi Wadi had no income stream, no paid human resources, no funding for external consultants, and no dedicated information and communications technology to support their work. What they had was culture, spirit and law – plus the extraordinary effort, dedication and skill of their people. They also had the Tyntyndyer Homestead as a meeting place, the support of FoE, and the small funding from the DSE to cover the costs of Elders attending meetings. In addition, they were committed to learning from the process; as one of the lead negotiators at the time expressed it, 'If we say, "No, we don't think that's right", and it turns out to be that we made the wrong decision, then we want to be part of that mistake' (per. comm. 25 May 2011).

Building Relationships and Finding Allies

As the Wadi Wadi experience suggests, establishing strong relationships and alliances with external agencies (both governmental and non-governmental) can be not only a way to address noticeable capacity gaps but also a way to learn and jointly strategize about possible ways forward. These relationships can also be a very pragmatic response to a Canadian Supreme Court Justice's oft-cited comment, 'We are here to stay' (*Delgamuukw [1997]*, para. 186). This was certainly the case for the Tsleil-Waututh, who were faced with a dizzying array of overlapping jurisdictions within their territory: federal, provincial and local governments (including the District of North Vancouver), as well as the multiple agencies, private landowners, quasi-governmental organizations, port authorities and others that operate on their land. The Tsleil-Waututh Nation very intentionally sought out partnerships as a way to navigate this complexity and ensure that its presence and action in its traditional territory was known and respected.

The Wurundjeri have encountered a similarly complex set of interests and jurisdictions that operate on their country with little to no recognition that it is an Indigenous place. They have also used partnerships and agreements, with all levels of government, to achieve basic practical outcomes of 'caring for country' and to fulfill their living, ancestral responsibilities in a large and rapidly growing city. They have a particularly strong and long-standing relationship with Parks Victoria, who have partnered with the Wurundjeri to carry out a number of projects that recognize traditional ownership on public lands under Parks Victoria's jurisdiction. High-level agreements with local councils about engagement, cross-cultural education, and high-level input into strategic activities have also been areas of significant activity for the Wurundjeri. Some agreements, including those with Parks Victoria, VicRoads and Melbourne Water, have funded positions within Wurundjeri Council to develop capacity and deepen those relationships further.

Agreement making is at the heart of Victoria's *Traditional Owner Settlement Act* (TOSA), and so the impulse for making agreements is also a legislative one. For the Wadi Wadi, however, the agreement they are trying to achieve with Department of Sustainability and Environment (DSE) sits right at the edge of the legislative requirement of that Act. The relationship with government keeps that agreement-making impulse alive and working, though it also needs to be acknowledged that agreement making is a long-standing, core element of the Wadi Wadi's overall strategy. They have long been aware that solid personal relationships with on-ground staff and operators are one of the best ways to be engaged, and relationships have also been important for them during points of deep conflict. The role that Friends of the Earth played in the Wadi Wadi story demonstrates how a practice of seeking allies in other places can support a strategic initiative. FoE's position as external to the Wadi Wadi Nation (but appointed by the nation and supportive of it) allowed their appointed facilitator to make a series of strategic, active moves that would have been much harder for the Wadi Wadi themselves to practise – what she called 'raising the scoundrel card' (per. comm. 3 June 2011).

The Gitanyow were also able to develop supportive alliances. One of their more significant and long-standing relationships was with a forestry consultant, who had worked in the region for over 25 years. His involvement allowed the Gitanyow to capitalize on an entire generation of knowledge and professional networks – which augmented their negotiating capacity at an early stage in the process – and also helped solidify the relationship with the Ministry of Forests, as he could help express Gitanyow values according to myriad provincial forestry regulations. Relationships, however, can be fragile, and the Gitanyow have always sought to have legally binding force sitting behind their relationships.

Speaking Back: Using the Tools of the System

While planning knowledge and procedures are thoroughly Western and deeply implicated in colonial dispossession (Porter 2010), they nonetheless provide a malleable and strategically useful domain in which Indigenous peoples can 'speak back' to the system – as the experience of using forest management regulations begins to suggest. These acts of 'speaking back' often use and then creatively expand the tools, processes and discourses of the system to create new opportunities for recognition. The presumption of citizen participation and consultation is one such planning tool. While by no means sufficient and, as we discussed in Chapter 2, deeply implicated in the cunning politics of recognition that plays out in settler states, the initial moment of consultation can become a strategic moment for Indigenous agency. In both Canada and Australia, the premises of wide consultation proffers the opportunity of using participation to wedge open a wider recognition space, with often interesting results.

The Wurundjeri story draws attention to how some rather traditional and narrowly defined planning discourses can be used as a strategic resource in the struggle for coexistence. The Wurundjeri have successfully promoted their interests and agenda through careful use of the discourse of 'certainty' that is so strong in Western planning and is particularly prevalent in a development-pressured city such as Melbourne. Being authorized as a Registered Aboriginal Party (RAP) gave the Wurundjeri Council not only a place but also significant powers at the planning-decision-making table. However, it also became clear to the Wurundjeri Council that the *Aboriginal Heritage Act (2006)* (AHA) worked in such a way as to reduce certainty for development proponents, because it created an additional layer against which development applications would be assessed. It also threatened to cause RAP organizations to be seen as anti-development. Their response was to take that certainty discourse and use it to reimagine a process that involves proponents and sponsors of developments and CHMPs engaging early and throughout the CHMP-development process with Elders and Council staff, to create a forum for early discussions about the development plans. This process 'creates certainty', since proponents have much greater access to the Wurundjeri Council and Elders, have a better sense of what their values are and have an earlier gauge on what will be approved and what will not.

This kind of action speaks to the more quiet forms of agency around agenda setting and process design, which can be extremely potent dimensions of everyday practice in the contact zone. For the Wadi Wadi, agenda setting and process design are two of the very few dimensions where the nation has been able to exert control. While all parties jointly agree on meeting agendas, the Wadi Wadi lead that process, and it was the Wadi Wadi–appointed facilitator who organized, chaired and facilitated those meetings. The Wadi Wadi people were therefore in control of how the meetings ran, whose voices were dominant and how much time was spent on particular agenda items. The timing of meetings (and especially the time taken to communicate between meetings) was a source of ongoing conflict between the Wadi Wadi and the Department of Sustainability and Environment. Again, the Wadi Wadi exerted some influence over this by designing and pursuing a cultural protocol of building consensus, sharing information and practising a structure of governance arising from Wadi Wadi law and values. This was one quite significant way in which the nation could exert some process control. The location of negotiation meetings was also important and, by holding most of them at Tyntyndyer Homestead, Wadi Wadi country was made more present. As expressed by the Wadi Wadi people, country is a sentient, living presence; holding meetings 'on country' is therefore vitally important.

Shifting the dynamic in order to regain control of the agenda was also a strategic practice of the Gitanyow. After the original Landscape Unit Plan process had been managed and run mostly internally by Gitanyow in a highly unusual process, control of the agenda shifted back to the province as the Nass South Strategic Resource Management Plan (SRMP) process got underway and as a different arm of the provincial government began to exert its influence. A planner from the Integrated Land Management Bureau (ILMB) chaired this second process and set the agenda for each meeting. While the Gitanyow provided input into the terms of reference and could review individual meeting agendas, they did not agree to the final plan itself. That lack of agreement did not quell the Gitanyow people's sense that planning was the most effective forum through which to give material effect to their rights of self-government and control of their territory. Instead, they shifted the focus to the negotiation of an agreement (rather than a plan), using the planning proposals in both the Nass South SRMP and the Cranberry-Kispiox LUP. The scope changed again when the Gitanyow learned of the protocol being developed by the Haida Nation with the province, and so they began to push the province in that direction instead, which culminated in the signing of the *Recognition and Reconciliation Agreement* in 2012.

The Tsleil-Waututh have also long expressed the importance of controlling the agenda and of 'holding the pen' (per. comm. 8 June 2011) during major acts of strategic planning in their traditional territory. As discussed in Chapter 7, the entire Cates Park/Whey-ah-Wichen planning process was guided and jointly approved by both parties, even though the actual document was largely written by outside consultants. The Official Community Plan process was quite different, with the District of North Vancouver controlling planning agenda and timeline. We will return to the shortcomings of this particular planning process in the next chapter. Here we want to draw attention to the Tsleil-Waututh Nation's success with 'controlling the agenda' in other ways, often by blending GIS and other spatial technologies with the cultural knowledge and expertise of Tsleil-Waututh members.

While maps and the practices of cartography have long been critiqued as a source of colonial power, privileging a scientific knowledge base and a white 'view' of space, maps have also been used in these four cases to great strategic effect. Bioregional mapping helped the Tsleil-Waututh visualize key aspects of their territory. For example, it quite starkly illustrated the degree of overlapping jurisdiction (per. comm. 13 June 2011), which allowed them to identify additional sources of data about their territory and other opportunities for partnership. Their maps have been instrumental in joint planning initiatives and the Tsleil-Waututh Nation's response to individual development referrals. Indeed, the Tsleil-Waututh consider their maps to be 'the most powerful tool' they have:

> We are able to put a map on the table and say exactly where our land is, what we are responsible for, and what resources were there, what is there currently, what probably affected the resources that aren't there any longer. We know more than three different levels of government and that's empowering for the nation. (per. comm. 13 June 2011)

As the Tsleil-Waututh story clearly shows, mapping can be a very effective tool and can often be used to 'change the position of the nation' (per. comm. 15 June 2011) in its negotiations with settler governments. The map is an intrinsically important part of planning practice and knowledge, though one that often operates in entirely unseen and unreflexive ways. Maps work to visualize space according to a certain viewpoint, rendering a host of other people-place relationships invisible. As the literature on cultural use and occupancy mapping shows (Tobias 2009, 2000), maps can also be appropriated for other purposes and provide specification of the location and nature of Indigenous rights, title and interests in a way that is difficult for planning systems to ignore.

The Gitanyow Huwilp have used maps to present values that had been marginalized, if not completely invisible, in previous planning processes. They worked to present knowledge generated from cultural practices right alongside knowledge generated from scientific practices. This was a deliberate and strategic choice: the Gitanyow were acutely aware that in the preparation of evidence to support planning decisions, scientific knowledge was valued much more highly than cultural factors. Provincial planners, even those seen as progressive and supportive, initially had difficulty appreciating cultural knowledge. For example, conceiving of berries as more than an economic or food resource, but as intrinsic to a particular Wilp's way of life, was no easy thing to communicate. The Gitanyow's cultural inventory work used knowledge about trails, food, gathering sites alongside more codified knowledge such as archaeological sites. As the Gitanyow Hereditary Chiefs Office's cultural heritage specialist explains, this work was about 'articulating cultural values in a way that Western institutions [could] understand' (per. comm. 6 May 2011). In presenting both, neither as more important than the other, the Gitanyow have managed to achieve recognition and a certain level of respect for different kinds of knowledge.

The Gitanyow Huwilp have taken the idea of cultural and ecological mapping a step further, in that their maps offer a powerful visual expression of their inherited law (*Ayookxw*) as well as the territory (*Lax'yip*) of the eight Wilp. These maps have been used to communicate the importance of planning with these cultural boundaries in mind, so that the ecological and cultural sustainability of each individual Wilp is taken into account. By using maps as the communication medium, the Gitanyow were able to catalyze greater recognition of their traditional governance structure. The land-use zones and buffer areas indicated on these maps were given legal force through the *Recognition and Reconciliation Agreement* and are now being used by forest licensees. The Wilp Sustainability Plan, therefore, represents a particularly fascinating example of using the tools of a system in practices that seek to transform that system.

For the Wurundjeri and Wadi Wadi, the use of maps has not been such a prominent and important part of their story. When maps did appear, they were used in deeply political, system-maintaining ways by government agencies. Such was the case for the Wurundjeri with the attempts of the Growth Areas Authority (GAA) to build a map-based model that would predict the likelihood of culturally sensitive areas being located in urban development corridors. As outlined in Chapter 5, the GAA attempted to collect information from Wurundjeri Elders about culturally important places and ongoing connections but was dismissive of the data that was eventually returned. That data did not conform to the GAA's expectation of the production of a database of places, names and times that could be easily incorporated into their spatial model. Indigenous knowledge is labelled 'cultural' and as such is seen to have less force and value, particularly when it is incompatible with the universalizing standpoint assumed by Western scientific knowledge production.

Strategic Essentialisms: Using Cultural Heritage as a Source of Power

The material objects, ancestral remains and significant places that are part of the constitution of living cultures are of tremendous contemporary importance to Indigenous peoples in settler states. The sordid histories of colonial theft, grave robbing and the desecration of cultural materials are ever present in the debates about cultural heritage in contemporary Canada and Australia and have given rise to about the ownership and protection of sites, artefacts and places. The management of Aboriginal cultural heritage has afforded a certain level of protection for these materials, though often from a paternalistic position privileging the colonial notion that cultures leave 'artefacts' from past times, which can be used to understand and interrogate social and economic lives. This line of thinking is, of course, informed by the discipline of archaeology. As in any discipline, the theory and practice of archaeology is subject to many lines of debate – including long debates over the politics of cultural heritage (see Smith 2004).

Perhaps because of its temporally and physically bounded modality, cultural heritage management is one dimension of Indigenous lives that has been more or less seamlessly accommodated into planning and public policy. It has also long been a focus of Indigenous struggle, particularly in terms of wresting control and ownership of cultural heritage from mostly white archaeologists. Cultural heritage management represents a strong material boundary (see Chapter 10) – an object around which Indigenous recognition in planning can be rendered legitimate. Nonetheless, the everyday practice of archaeology and its enrolment into planning and land management do not necessarily value the living culture of those objects and places; indeed they demand 'preservation' by non-use, in direct contravention of the living cultures that Indigenous peoples express. The version of 'culture' that is given space in planning is the material artefacts that represent a much safer, tamer past culture. In Chapter 10 we will return to these more critical and limiting aspects of cultural heritage as a way of regressively managing Indigenous interests within planning systems. Here, our focus is on how the agency of Indigenous people in all four of our stories use cultural heritage as a vitally important wedge to open up a greater recognition space.

For Wurundjeri people in Melbourne – where there has been a profound and lasting silence on Wurundjeri rights, title, presence and interests – cultural heritage presented the best opportunity, and really the only recourse, to be heard. Even under the previous regulatory regime governing cultural heritage identification and management, the Wurundjeri people managed to create an institutional space that could apply pressure and maintain a presence in the city on these matters. Largely relegated to 'riding on the front of bulldozers checking for artefacts,' as the son of one of the Wurundjeri Council's founding members fondly recalls (per. comm. 3 June 2011), those practices positioned the Wurundjeri well for the legislative changes that arrived in 2006 in the form of the *Aboriginal Heritage Act.* Wurundjeri Council have harnessed their status as a RAP to create a much larger zone of influence on matters that affect their country. All of the non-archaeological work that the council does (the education programs, language revitalization, family reunion, welcomes to country, partnerships and the Narrap Country Plan) are possible because of the respect and visibility that the Wurundjeri people have created through their efforts in the only space available to them in the tightly bounded confines of recognition in an Australian city – cultural heritage management.

This sense of being able to use cultural heritage as a strategic source of power and control was also evident in the Wadi Wadi and Tsleil-Waututh stories, which both began with conflicts over damage to cultural heritage. The legal powers available to each of those nations, such as injunctions or court orders through cultural heritage management regimes, enabled each of them to get to a particular kind of planning table and open out a negotiation with the settler state. The Gitanyow also used widespread policy acceptance of the importance of protecting cultural artefacts to ensure that their land-use interests were appropriately addressed in provincial land-use plans.

In fact, the protection of distinct cultural sites was a relatively easy issue to address, as these areas could be inventoried, mapped and excluded for the timber-harvesting land base. Achieving an adequate level of protection for other instances of living Gitanyow cultures proved much more difficult to achieve, often as a result of the regulatory focus on certain distinct categories for ecological conservation (an issue we will return to in the next chapter). Although many Indigenous peoples do not subscribe to the compartmentalization of 'nature' and 'culture' demanded by many systems of resource management (Nadasdy 2003; Porter 2010), the

Gitanyow recognized the strategic importance of framing their interests according to these categories. They also referenced habitat protection tools already present in the provincial forest management system. For example, the Gitanyow realized that many of their important medicinal plants grew in riparian areas (one of the provincial categories for conservation). They were able to use that knowledge to build a case for an entire ecosystem network, a well-established concept in ecological planning (see Perlman and Milder 2005). Buffers were established around all major streams and rivers, acting like long linear protection corridors throughout Gitanyow territory and becoming an important cornerstone of the Gitanyow Huwilp's overall planning vision – one that is seen as highly compatible with traditional law:

> If you take a look at the land-use plan and how the plan is laid out, the Gitanyow
> law, the cultural system and our traditional system is reflected in the plan [...]
> If you look at the land-use plan, you will see our maps that show our ecosystem
> network: an ecosystem network that has always been in place for Gitanyow.
> [...] It will cover everything important to Gitanyow, meaning it has wildlife
> corridors, medicinal plants and berries. (per. comm. 6 June 2011)

Notably, the cultural significance of this ecosystem network is only vaguely referenced in the land-use plan that was embedded in the final *Recognition and Reconciliation Agreement*. Acknowledges that the network exists to 'maintain opportunities for traditional uses of the land' (Gitanyow Hereditary Chiefs and Government of British Columbia 2012, 31), but also positions it as part of the plan's broader biodiversity goals. This way of framing the ecosystem network points to a different kind of 'strategic essentialism' (Spivak 1990), one that seeks to articulate complex socio-cultural relationships to Indigenous lands and territories according to the language of ecological science rather than the artefact-based approach that continues to dominate the archaeological sciences. Both essentialisms create challenges (as we will discuss in Chapter 10), but both serve to hold open the possibility of system-transforming practices.

Encountering the Limits of Indigenous Agency: Impacts and Outcomes to Date

As with any research of this nature, we present here only one moment, one snapshot in time, of what are long-standing and enduring processes. In that sense, it is difficult to speak about the 'outcomes' of these practices and struggles, as these will continue to unfold. It is possible and useful, however, to look at the closing point of our snapshot in time and examine what happened or was beginning to happen as our formal research interaction with these four nations drew to a close. As established earlier, all of the nations involved in this study sought and continue to seek overt, formal recognition of their country, their governance structures and processes, laws/lores, cultures and societies, as well as their right to be more than a 'party' to state-based planning processes. The nuances are sometimes different, but the impulse to decolonize planning is remarkably similar. There are, however, some striking differences in the current position of each.

The most significant shifts appear to have occurred in the case of the Gitanyow Huwilp. Participants reflected on a marked difference between the province's planning practices in the 1990s and today, in that engaging First Nations early on in the process is now a matter of course. Here, there are currently two strategic natural resource plans in draft form, both the outcome of a negotiated, co-productive process shared by the Gitanyow and the province. Moreover, through those joint planning initiatives and the subsequent recognition of their Wilp Sustainability Plan, the Gitanyow have achieved recognition of their traditional governance structure, territory, knowledge and cultural values, in a way that transfers significant planning and decision-making authority to Gitanyow people. While there are, of course, ongoing conflicts and disagreements, and remaining concerns about implementation and monitoring, the Gitanyow case represents quite significant changes in this planning system; the shifting of political boundaries highlights the importance of practices that focus on that particular mode of recognition. The province's language away from 'decision making' toward 'decision making' was decisive in that it compels a much more overt recognition of the government-to-government nature of the negotiations.

The case of the Wurundjeri people in Melbourne also provides evidence of some significant shifts but in entirely different fields and mediated in highly varying ways. The Wurundjeri Council has been able to take up actual decision-making powers provided under an amended cultural heritage management regime and in doing so leverage authority in planning and land-use decision making. Wurundjeri can ask developers to 'move their houses or redesign their planning' (per. comm. 12 July 2011) in response to cultural heritage requirements. The position comes with authority and the power to change outcomes. Using this as a springboard, they have been able to build much wider alliances with government agencies and other stakeholders, develop institutional capacity, and expand the spatial extent of their influence of control through cultural heritage protection. Moreover, their Country Plan initiative, while under-realized at the moment, retains huge potential.

In the case of the Tsleil-Waututh Nation, the outcomes of the two planning contact zones we have discussed in this book have been quite divergent. For Cates Park/Whey-ah-Wichen, a new plan has been developed with a greater sense of partnership and understanding of the cultural and spiritual significance of the area. New agreements and protocols have also been established, paving the way for future planning work. In regard to the preparation of the Official Community Plan, the boundaries have been harder to shift, with a more limited consultative process and less satisfactory outcome. However, the Tsleil-Waututh Nation's careful exercise of authority over their reserve lands and the ongoing implementation of their *Stewardship Policy*, combined with the *Cooperation Protocol* with the DNV, hold open the possibility for expanding the current level of recognition.

For the Wadi Wadi, the outcomes are not (at least yet) indicative of major shifts. The Victorian Environmental Assessment Council (VEAC) recommendations and the subsequent change of legislation to declare Nyah-Vinifera as a higher conservation status park were an enormous achievement and catalyzed a whole range of new possibilities that had not existed before. But those new possibilities have not yet given rise to movement in this tightly constrained contact zone. The Wadi Wadi have no decision-making power, no specific planning outcome, no institutional capacity or sustainable financial position, no recognition of country or governance structure, not even (yet) an agreement about joint planning. There is much hope within these as-yet-unrealized demands – hope for a cultural centre, hope for co-management, hope for formal recognition of ownership and title, hope for sustainable futures for young people with employment and cultural opportunities. One Wadi Wadi negotiator expresses this as the aspiration to manage the park 'as equal partners, instead of just ticking the box' and with the strong belief that 'we can teach [Parks managers] and make them more aware and maybe we'll be able to look after it better in the future' (per. comm. 26 May 2011).

Conclusion

In this chapter we have looked closely at the agency and practices of Indigenous peoples within different planning contexts, where the outcomes are neither guaranteed nor stable. The four contact zones being presented in this book were hailed into being through the co-constitutive performance of Indigenous agency and the textual confluence of the systems of recognition and planning. We saw how Indigenous leaders made use of and worked to expand opportunities that arose through state-based attempts to recognize and enact their responsibilities toward Indigenous title, resorting to other forms of legal and direct action when necessary. We also saw how Indigenous groups found openings within the planning system itself, through which they were able to assert control over key aspects of process, develop capacity, and build significant alliances and other networks of support. Perhaps most significantly, we saw how Indigenous people were able to 'speak back' by carefully and strategically translating their concerns into a language and presentation format that the systems of planning could not easily ignore. These are some of the 'arts of the contact zone' through which Indigenous people struggle for coexistence.

Yet, as was foreshadowed in Part I of this book, contact zones are not spaces of endless possibility, and the outcomes and results they generate are neither guaranteed nor stable. The cases we have presented here show the huge variation in the moves that settler states might make, as well as the huge differential in the opportunities that are open to Indigenous peoples. There are some quite tangible and overt limitations, with obvious examples of the ways in which Indigenous peoples have been systematically marginalized – sometimes through lack of access to the processes and tools that dominate Western approaches to land-use planning, and sometimes through limited opportunities to generate the level of financial and staff resources needed to build these capacities. However, as this chapter also began to suggest, many of these limitations are more covert and, arguably, less easily resolved. Indigenous agency could often only be expressed in certain spaces, over certain planning issues, under certain conditions, and at certain points in the process. For as much as structures and discourses present within the systems of recognition and planning create a political opportunity structure that can be used by Indigenous people, these same structures and discourses also work contain the unsettling effects of Indigenous agency. It is to these (re)settling dynamics that we now turn.

Chapter 10

Bounded Recognition: How Planning Resettles Indigenous Claims

Introduction

The struggles and everyday agency that Indigenous people and their allies practise are aimed at a system that continues to largely fail to provide redress for their claims. Chapter 4 provided an analysis of that system, showing how the circulation of certain powerful discursive tropes in the fields of both planning and recognition mediate and shape the politics of recognition in the contact zone. Points of profound institutional inertia, structural discrimination and entrenched power are real. Far more than being merely 'barriers to better recognition', they work to *resettle* the challenge Indigenous claims present, in system-maintaining ways. Each of our cases points to the myriad different ways this tendency manifests itself in the day-to-day politics of recognition in planning. In order to understand how this occurs and why the outcomes we presented in the last few chapters look as they do, it is necessary to return to the discursive formulations that mediate and shape the way 'planning' and 'recognition' are performed together.

In this chapter we take the broad discursively structural performance of planning and recognition that we provided in Chapter 4 and show how it actively works on the ground, in real everyday life for Indigenous people interacting with settler-state planning systems. The operationalization of these discourses creates what we call 'bounded recognition' (see also Porter and Barry 2015) in three inter-related ways – around where recognition can be located (spatial), who can be recognized (political) and what that recognition is about (object). The purpose of this chapter is to show how these boundaries work to contain and limit Indigenous recognition in planning, but also to highlight where efforts to further unsettle them might be productive. We use our comparative case study approach to identify how each of these boundaries operationalizes the nodal discourses of planning and recognition.

Dimensions of Bounded Recognition

Three types of boundaries – spatial, political and object – operate at different points and work to settle and resettle planning authority and settler spaces in varying ways. Boundaries make the discursive tropes of planning and recognition operational in planning contact zones and show how and where the politics of recognition in planning comes to ground. *Spatial* boundaries construct an uneven spatiality of recognition and confines the spaces where the politics of recognition can play out. *Political* boundaries work to legitimize who can be recognized and through what procedures. *Object* boundaries mediate the politics of recognition around certain highly limited materials or concepts. Together, these boundaries work to contain, mediate and resettle the challenge Indigenous recognition claims bring to planning systems. Boundaries, of course, have to be made real and have to be continuously remade through the ceaseless negotiation of colonial power relations in the contact zone. A variety of functions perform and practise this bounding work. From the planning domain these mechanisms include zoning, mapping, categorization and regulation. In the recognition domain, these mechanisms include extinguishment regimes, consultation and accommodation, agreements, consent determinations and treaties. Before we look at how these actually work in our four case studies, some further general explication of these boundary dimensions and how they inter-relate is necessary.

There is a distinctly uneven geography to Indigenous recognition in settler states. Indigenous recognition is more possible in some places, such as conservation zones far from metropolitan areas, and much less tenable in other kinds of places, such as in urban centres. This uneven geography is a form of spatial bounding – determining a highly uneven spatiality of Indigenous recognition. Spatial boundaries are produced and maintained through the seamless interlocking of the allocation of Western property rights (where the demands for certainty and security are intense) with racialized presumptions about Indigenous identity. Property and development rights such as titles, deeds, licenses and leases constrain the spatial extent of Indigenous recognition. Extinguishment and non-recognition is spatially intense especially in built-up areas where Western private property rights are protected, whereas a sharpening of Indigenous recognition is possible at significant geographical remove from major population and economic centres and on public land, where a coexistence of titles is tenable.

Yet even within the category of public lands, there is a differentiated spatiality of Indigenous recognition, produced through the use designation of specific parcels of public land. Where public lands are classified for conservation purposes, Indigenous claims and rights appear to be easier for planning to see. In places classified for uses such as resource extraction, and where other overlapping property rights such as forestry or mining leases and licenses exist, Indigenous claims are deemed less legitimate by Western planning systems. A racialized trope of 'cultures that are closer to nature' renders Indigenous interests easily aligned with ecological values and consequently more legitimate in places where ecological and conservation values have been prioritized. Built-up, industrialized places are considered too modern, and too modified, for Indigenous culture, law, rights and interests to have survived colonization. A persistent rendering of Western cultures as modern, fluid, progressive and forward-looking, and of Indigenous cultures as traditional, located in the past, static and unchanging underpins this spatial bounding work. Put crudely, Indigenes belong 'out there' in the (supposedly untouched) wilderness, not 'in here' in the modern city.

If spatial boundaries work to fix and locate recognition by limiting Indigenous rights and interests to certain kinds of places, then political boundaries work to resettle the authority of the settler state over its territorial jurisdiction and limit Indigenous claims to political authority. This is first, then, a question of how planning sees, and conceives the position of, Indigenous people vis-à-vis settler-state systems of government. Are Indigenous people made visible to planning merely as one group of an undifferentiated public, as a particular kind of 'stakeholder', or as a political authority in their own right with coexisting jurisdiction? Indigenous people have been insistent and urgent in identifying the essential link between recognition of their rights to territory, with recognition of their political authority to make decisions about that territory. Each is a relatively empty form of recognition unless accompanied by the other – sovereign authority demands a territory over which to exert authority, and rights in land are made real through political authority. Smaller, quieter political boundaries also operate in the everyday practices of the contact zone, by setting and constraining the agenda through process and institutional design; by legitimating and de-legitimating different kinds of knowledge; and through the politics of identity and representation.

Political authority and its spatial jurisdiction are manifestly related to the objects that make this authority real. That it is considered provocative to suggest that there might be Indigenous rights and interests in transport infrastructure, commercial office development or urban renewal projects exposes just how tightly the category 'Indigenous' is bound to a highly limited range of planning objects. One such object is cultural heritage – archaeological artefacts, sacred sites, cultural places and uses or practices that are deemed cultural or 'traditional'. Indigenous interests puncture into an undifferentiated public interest discourse principally when the object of cultural heritage, or traditionality in terms of use and practice, becomes present. Bounded to culture, as an object, Indigenous people momentarily, at that specific point in a planning process, become more than just one of many stakeholders. Seen as having a special interest, but only linked to that specific planning object, Indigenous people are brought to the planning table. Mechanisms like archaeological convention, registers of cultural sites, traditional use studies and the regulatory definition of heritage and where it can be seen to exist operationalize these discursive moves. Indigenous interests are rendered legitimate about a defined list of planning objects and illegitimate (indeed, invisible) about most others.

Separating out these three bounding mechanisms as we have done here is useful analytically. It allows closer and more precise attention to be paid to what is happening in each of them, and how each works. Yet that separation is merely an analytical construct. In reality, there is enormous overlap and inter-articulation between these bounding mechanisms. The discursive moves involved in establishing an authentically traditional cultural object articulate closely with spatial boundaries that limit the geographical scope of the contact zone, and the forms of political authority under negotiation.

In the following sections, we return to our analytical separation of these boundaries and show how each is at work in our four case studies.

Spatial Boundaries

As discussed above, land tenure articulated through the system of Western property is one powerful boundary mechanism at work in planning contact zones. The terms of Indigenous recognition by settler states are much wider on public lands than they are on lands alienated to private ownership, producing an uneven spatiality to Indigenous recognition in planning. This is apparent when we look at the different contexts between our cases.

Uneven Spatiality of Recognition between Urban and Non-Urban Areas

The territory of the Gitanyow Huwilp is located far away from major urban centres. Most of Gitanyow territory is Crown land, allocated for conservation or resource extraction. While substantive issues remain concerning recognition of title and control of lands and waters, there is nonetheless a recognition by the province in its planning processes that the Gitanyow Huwilp are another governmental party to land-use and management decisions on their territory. Wadi Wadi country in Victoria is also located at some distance from principal urban centres, and the focus of Wadi Wadi actions, in relation to planning at least, has been on a spatially contained demarcated area: the Nyah-Vinifera Park. This tiny remnant of Wadi Wadi country is also defined in settler legal terms as Crown land. Under the *Traditional Owner Settlement Act* and the protected area legislation in Victoria, this produces that space as more amenable to forms of Indigenous recognition.

By contrast, in the metropolitan areas we have studied in Vancouver and Melbourne, the situation is markedly different. In relation to key planning processes in which governments began to incorporate participation of the Tsleil-Waututh Nation, the recognition of Aboriginal rights and title is largely symbolic, with 'stock statements' about how municipal plans and policies have 'been written without prejudice' to these rights (District of North Vancouver 2011, 2). For the Wurundjeri people in Melbourne, there is no recognition of rights and title according to Wurundjeri law and custom. In both these urban cases, a much more appropriating and incorporating practice of recognition is at work, where participation through inclusion and consultation serve to manage the claims that Wurundjeri and the Tsleil-Waututh Nation make to the planning system. When struggles to create and expand a contact zone are underway in places where urban planning is dealing primarily with private lands in an already-built environment, the material reality of this context obscures and constrains the possibilities for Indigenous recognition.

The production of this spatial bounding can be traced to the presumptions of certainty for private property rights inter-articulated with a persistently strong discourse of Indigenous peoples as recognizable only in places untouched by modern society. In Australia, as we discussed in Chapter 4, native title was legally extinguished on lands with certain forms of private property, principally freehold title. Consequently, recognition is only possible over public lands (including leasehold lands). Such extinguishment through Australian land tenure systems very powerfully bounds the spatiality of Indigenous recognition. For of course, places that are now fully urbanized or settled are largely alienated to freehold tenure. Native title in Australian major cities, including Melbourne, is now proving to be extremely difficult for Aboriginal and Torres Strait Islander peoples whose country is now urbanized. Since 1992, 52 native title claims had been made over country now urbanized. As of 2015, only eight of those have resulted in positive determinations of native title. Ten have been rejected, and four remain active. The rest have been withdrawn, discontinued or dismissed. The Wurundjeri people have not, to date, sought a native title claim or outcome and instead have articulated their demands through a range of other planning and land management mechanisms.

The potential scope for recognition is arguably more spatially expansive in Canada. Unlike courts in Australia, the Canadian high courts have very clearly rejected the colonial assumption that the application of settler laws and systems of property simply extinguished Aboriginal rights and title. These court decisions catalyzed two major forms of state-based recognition of Indigenous rights and title: the duty to consult and accommodate; and the BC Treaty Process. As discussed in Chapter 4, the duty to consult and accommodate applies to all Indigenous rights and title, regardless of whether or not they have been proven. It also applies to both private and public lands, including those in urban areas, though there has been a great deal of legal uncertainty as to who – the municipality or the province – holds that duty in urban areas.

Yet the duty to consult and accommodate is not 'boundary-free', especially where it interfaces with the BC Treaty Process. Like the duty to consult and accommodate, the BC Treaty Process applies to both public ('Crown') and urban lands (the Tsawassen First Nation signed the first treaty under the BC Treaty Process, which included settlement lands within metropolitan Vancouver). There are, however, strong spatial boundaries at work in the BC Treaty Process. While it may lack the spatial and identity specificity of Australia's native title regime, a similar logic of extinguishment is nonetheless present. Notably, the official language is that the process 'modifies' (BC Treaty Commission 2003) Indigenous rights rather than completely extinguishing them (since Treaty First Nations will be able to continue to practise usufruct rights in their broader traditional territory, under the agreements and conditions laid out in their treaty). This subtlety has not thwarted vigorous criticism of the process (Woolford 2011, 2005; Alfred and Corntassel 2005). That criticism has exposed how the entire process is oriented toward creating certainty in the underlying property regime by establishing clear areas of Indigenous title in deemed acceptable to the settler state, in exchange for the relinquishment of First Nations title to large tracts of land across their territories.

The Intersection of Spatial and Political Boundaries

The Victorian framework of recognition of continuing Indigenous claims, rights and interests on Crown lands is created through the *Conservation, Forests and Lands Act*. This Act prescribes the possibility of various forms of joint or co-management of conservation areas between the Victorian Government and traditional owners. Yet that can only be achieved in certain spaces deemed 'conservation areas' under the existing land-use and classification schema in Victoria. Aboriginal recognition in and of itself does not change that primary classification. Instead, it simply inserts Aboriginal interests. For the Wadi Wadi, then, the struggle for recognition over Nyah-Vinifera has been as much about the reclassification of the land as it has been for specific recognition of Wadi Wadi rights and interests. Achieving a reclassification of the land through the Victorian Environmental Assessment Council (VEAC) process (see Chapter 6), from state forest to regional park provides two important outcomes for the Wadi Wadi. First, resource-extractive industries, particularly timber harvesting, are no longer permissible; this removes the ongoing threat of destruction those industries posed to Wadi Wadi values and heritage (note the presence here also of object boundaries). Second, the reclassification enables the possibility of negotiating toward co-management of the park, a form of political recognition that has been a central plank of the Wadi Wadi struggle and activity over many years.

   In BC, strategic natural resource planning is also heavily grounded in the assumption that 'certainty' is best achieved through the designation of high-level categories or zones that are designed to address both high-intensity resource development and the conservation of sensitive ecological values. These regional acts of 'boundary-creation' have taken on new meaning in an era of increased legal action on the part of First Nations. Under the province's *New Directions* statement (see Chapter 4), all acts of strategic planning must be predicated on the establishment of a strong 'business case'. Essentially, planning will only occur in areas where the financial risks posed by not engaging in planning are the greatest; for example, in areas where the economic stability of the region is threatened and/ or the climate for investment is poor due to conflict between different users – or where there is an outstanding legal obligation owed to First Nations people (BC ILMB 2007), as was the case with the Gitanyow and the Tysoe decisions (see Chapter 8).

   The *New Directions* statement has therefore reinforced the need to give First Nation values and interests greater standing in strategic planning, and has led provincial staff to give greater consideration to the ways they might 'marry' the 'spatial direction that comes out the land-use planning process with a new way of making decisions that involves and engages First Nations' (pers. comm. 12 May 2011). This is a significant shift, but the needs and interests of the forestry industry do continue to dominate. As we saw in Chapter 8, the land-use categories that have most relevance to this industry have primacy over all other concerns – particularly during the establishment of land-use zones and other forms of spatial policy direction. What we have here, then, is a very powerful inter-articulation of spatial and political boundary mechanisms. BC's approach to forestry also led to the rather strange bisection of Gitanyow territory, as the planning boundaries used during the Nass South Strategic Resource Management Plan (SRMP) and the Cranberry-Kispiox plan were strongly linked to the existing forest management area – a bisection that the Gitanyow actively fought.

Scaling back up to the broader question of spatial boundaries between public and private, urban and non-urban lands, we see again the refraction of these discourses about where Indigenous interests can legitimately be located and accommodated in planning. When planners working in urban municipalities or senior government bureaucrats responsible for urban development and planning policy are asked precisely the same questions about the intersection between their work, planning practice and Indigenous peoples, the response is very different. In Melbourne, strategic land-use planning is silent on Aboriginal recognition, Aboriginal interests in planning process, impact and outcome and the need for engagement with Aboriginal peoples. Urban planning is not seen by the profession as a legitimate space in which Aboriginal interests need to be heard, served or treated with. In Vancouver and more widely across other Canadian urban municipalities, the level of recognition is only extended where there is a 'neighbour-to-neighbour' relationship or where a municipality shares a boundary with a First Nation reserve.

Reserves constitute a particular form of spatial bounding in the Canadian context, and require some further brief discussion. As First Nations acquire greater authority over land management and begin to create their own land codes (see chapters 4 & 7), municipalities have begun to recognize that Band Councils can have political authority over a defined spatial area, and while they are recognizing the entity and jurisdiction of Band Councils in their willingness to negotiate, the approach simply inserts Band Councils and First Nations Governments into their existing norms and practices of dealing with a political authority on abutting lands. This was the case in the preparation of the District of North Vancouver's (DNV) Official Community Plan (OCP), where the purposes of determining housing and infrastructure future priorities required the municipality to negotiate with the Tsleil-Waututh Nation because the Tsleil-Waututh reserve abuts the DNV's municipal boundary. Yet despite clear statements from the Tsleil-Waututh Nation (see, for example, Tsleil-Waututh Nation 2009) that their interests and jurisdiction coexisted with the DNV's interests across the rest of the municipality, the DNV was unwilling and unable to countenance coexisting authority, only a 'neighbour-to-neighbour' relationship where the reserve boundaries are shared with the municipality.

Reserves in Victoria are barely comparable with the Canadian context, save for their origins in the periods of frontier violence when reserving small parcels of land to house a shrinking Aboriginal population served multiple purposes: to clear the rest of the lands of Indigenous encumbrances to settler occupation; to incarcerate Aboriginal peoples and render them largely invisible to white settlers; and to more easily implement policies of assimilation where language, customs and practices were forbidden and Indigenous peoples were 'trained' to become white. In contemporary Victoria, reserves and former mission stations are now often in the ownership, through various deeds of grant, of their Aboriginal residents. Wurundjeri people own the former mission station at Coranderrk, on Melbourne's northeast fringe. Coranderrk, a highly significant historical place for many Aboriginal people in Victoria (including the Wurundjeri), was purchased by the Indigenous Lands Corporation and returned to Wurundjeri ownership. However, any planning or development on these lands would be subject to the jurisdiction of planning authorities, just like any other parcel of leasehold or freehold land in Victoria. Aboriginal people who own former missions and reserves in Victoria do not have the level of control that Band Councils in Canada have over development, strategic planning and service provision on those lands.

This evidence across our cases highlights how spatial bounding is linked intrinsically to the political dimension of authority and sovereignty – for power to access and control the use and production of space is surely as much a question of politics as it is a question of spatiality. This brings us to focus on the second important boundary dimension: the political.

Political Boundaries

Practice norms of the public interest are triggered, operating as nodal discourses, when the difference and Otherness of Indigenous claims come to the planning table, and these norms closely bound the scope and nature of political recognition of Indigenous peoples. Having shifted from what were once critiqued as the high modernist days of planning practice (Sandercock 1998a), when an elite group of experts decided what was in the public interest, the practice and institutionalized processes of planning in contemporary times is geared very closely to stakeholders. Inclusion of stakeholders brings the 'interest' in public interest to the planning table through representation by these stakeholders of their. Participation, inclusivity, consultation and engagement have become intrinsic to the norms and expectations people have of planning systems in places like Canada and Australia, as well as the expectations planners have of their own practice. This practice norm easily extends to all sorts of differently marked Others who come to the planning table, including Indigenous peoples, such that their interests become incorporated, as one of many other stakeholder interests, to be 'engaged'. The claim for political authority, then, cannot be heard because there is no model in planning participation or consultation for those stakeholders to have a coexisting, underlying and entirely separate domain of law and authority from the state.

Acts of Incorporation in Victoria

Planning in Victoria, whether it concerns private or public lands, in either urban or environmental planning contexts, does not recognize any pre-existing political authority for Aboriginal peoples arising from specific laws and customs of individual nations. This appears to contradict the native title regime, the *Traditional Owner Settlement Act* and the right people for country principle, all of which do recognize that where traditional ownership (native title) has been claimed or proven, traditional owners assert political authority, separate from the settler state, over their recognized country. What the planning system has done to resettle the political authority of the settler government in Victoria is to *incorporate* that political recognition into the existing planning decision-making regime. In doing so, it has forced Indigenous systems, where they seek recognition in the state's terms, to partially mirror and emulate those of the settler state.

This in part arises from the heavily rule-bound, standardized, top-down system of planning in Victoria. There is little space in this system for recognition of another coexisting or underlying authority, as the entire jurisdictional space is saturated with the decision-making power of the settler state. Despite the unsettling nature of Aboriginal claims about the way that a universalized public interest in planning often actively works against Aboriginal political authority, the planning system maintains the authority of the settler government as the final arbiter on matters of public interest and private development rights. Moreover, because of its rule-bound and standardized nature, there is less space for partnership or other less formal and collaborative formulations of recognizing Aboriginal political authority.

In regard to urban planning and the management of private development rights, the act of incorporating a vaguely recognized Aboriginal political authority has been accomplished through inserting Aboriginal organizations with Registered Aboriginal Party (RAP) status into the existing decision-making schema. This act of incorporation *grants* political authority to those Aboriginal organizations through the auspices of the planning system. It does not recognize coexisting or underlying Aboriginal political authority that exists separately from the settler state. For the Wurundjeri Council, this means they can assert particular kinds of authority, such as requests to amend development plans (or even veto those plans), within a prescribed process – after a Cultural Heritage Management Plan (CHMP) has been referred to them, and under certain rules of engagement. In other words, the Wurundjeri Council has the same procedural powers as other statutory consultees in the planning system. As we outlined in Chapter 9, this in itself offers the Wurundjeri Council methods to use that political authority in other ways to further open out shallow contact zone. But it does not constitute political recognition of Wurundjeri law, governance and coexisting authority. Aboriginal heritage, in this way, becomes a planning overlay, triggering certain quite powerful procedural rights but only under heavily prescribed conditions. Jurisdiction of the Wurundjeri Council in any broader sense, such as that of a body holding traditional law, is not recognized under this system.

The *Aboriginal Heritage Act* (AHA) allows for overlapping areas – in other words for more than one Registered Aboriginal Party to have status over the same territory. However, it is clear that this can only happen when the Victorian Aboriginal Heritage Council is satisfied that overlapping authority will not 'hinder the effective operation of this Act' (*(2013)* s.153 1(b)). In other words, the Act works toward a preferred situation of certainty in terms of who is responsible for which formally designated and bounded spatial areas, with clear lines of reporting and authority. This is indeed positive from the perspective of Aboriginal organizations, such as the Wurundjeri Council, who seek their own surety from the state that their statutory powers are clearly territorialized. Yet such a system is also designed to provide certainty to development proponents and planning authorities about whom to deal with, and where, and it invites a particular politics of recognition between traditional owner groups, and with the state. These minute procedures and specific regulations bound and constrain even this minimal recognition of Indigenous cultural heritage interests within development.

The planning agenda for what is legitimately on the table for Wurundjeri intervention under this system is also tightly bound to matters of management of cultural heritage (an object boundary we will return to in the next section), and into a highly standardized procedure, operationalized through the Aboriginal Heritage Regulations. Also tightly bounded in political terms is the knowledge that informs the process of determining the impact of development on cultural heritage. While there is recognition of culturally-held knowledge and the capacity to list sites that have not been subject, for various reasons, to archaeological survey, it is clear that archaeological knowledge retains its dominant position in the politics of knowledge about cultural heritage in Victoria. The Office of Aboriginal Affairs Victoria's register and the work of the registered archaeological consultants on Cultural Heritage Management Plans and those working within RAPs are given the most weight. Traditional, customary community knowledge perhaps shared and performed by Elders and others is not part of the core regulatory functioning of this particular formulation of recognition. The conflict that this politics of knowledge can give rise to was clearly evident in the story of the Wurundjeri Council's early relationship with the Growth Areas Authority (GAA) (see Chapter 5), a story that highlights the power of Western presumptions of knowledge and the unsettling nature of Aboriginal knowledges when they interact with those presumptions. There is much potential for struggle and unsettling in this process, but the settler state, as was shown in this story, worked to powerfully resettle the legitimacy of knowledge in its own interests. Wurundjeri Council continued to pursue a different approach arising from this conflict, and have now managed to secure an important Memorandum of Understanding with the now Metropolitan Planning Authority that heralds a more positive outcome (see Chapter 5).

In the environmental planning context, the planning system will accommodate a Traditional Owner Land Management Board under the *Conservation, Forests and Lands Act* (see Chapter 4). This should be read as a board of management that is controlled by traditional owners. Such control offers those Aboriginal people granted recognition as traditional owners a level of political authority over the planning and management of the protected area. This is, ultimately, what the Wadi Wadi nation are working toward, though the negotiations for a Memorandum of Understanding with the Department of Sustainability and Environment (DSE) fell quite short of that aspiration. As outlined in Chapter 6, other political boundaries were being created and maintained that worked to limit Wadi Wadi claims for recognition. Politics around identity and representation worked to undermine the level of recognition that the Victorian government was willing to negotiate with the Wadi Wadi nation. Small everyday practices by the state such as failing to pay funds on time, or rescheduling meetings, or constraining what could be on the agenda were all forms of marking the political boundaries of recognition in this case.

In operationalizing the political recognition that comes with recognition of title to lands (or 'traditional ownership' as it is now named in Victoria), this mechanism also incorporates Aboriginal political authority into an existing settler system. The *Conservation, Forests and Lands Act* heavily codifies what Traditional Owner Land Management Boards can do, and of course the purpose of the management approach is to fulfill the requirements of Victorian conservation and environmental planning legislation. In short, this does not constitute recognition of Aboriginal political authority that coexists with, and indeed underlies, the political authority of settler government. These are acts of incorporation, and they are accomplished as we have seen through a range of discursive and textual moves. Incorporation in this manner reduces Aboriginal political authority by making it *subject to* the political authority of the settler state. This incorporation is absolutely explicit in both the legislative framework and the everyday practice of government. Traditional Owner Land Management Boards are seen as a way for Aboriginal people to be 'involved in park planning', in the words of one senior Victorian Government executive, but only insofar as that involvement produces a planning outcome that looks and acts like a park plan as legislatively required and that can be 'put up for the Minister to approve' (pers. comm. 14 July 2011).

Bounding recognition in this way is also a function of the disciplining work that operates through the state's 'recognition calculus' (Povinelli 2002): recognition is available only under certain conditions and within spatial and culturally bounded limits. Those who neither perform nor conform their identity in ways that are amenable to that recognition calculus cannot be considered recognizably traditional enough to warrant 'traditional owners'. It is for these reasons that the native title regime in Australia is now widely regarded as a kind of illusory recognition, tantalizingly (indeed, seductively) offering a redress only for the dominance of Australian settler mentalities to be re-asserted (see our discussion in Chapter 2, and also Povinelli 2002, 1998; I. Watson 2005, 2015). Recontextualized within the frame of planning, this calculus of recognition proves one of the primary boundary markers of the contact zone with planning in Victoria.

The Limits of Coexistence in BC

In BC, the lack of standardization in the planning system offers greater room for recognition of First Nations' political authority over their lands and waters. This is so in both urban and environmental planning contexts. Partly in response to the changing legal context where a succession of significant court cases has expanded the scope for recognition of First Nations' underlying and coexisting political authority, the levels of political recognition on the table for negotiation are highly differentiated and circumscribed. In the context of urban planning, the *Local Government Act* merely directs municipalities to consider First Nations as one of many possible consultees during the preparation of an Official Community Plan and is entirely unclear as to whether First Nations should be consulted as another government or as a particular kind of stakeholder (see Chapter 4). Therefore, the extent to which municipalities might engage with First Nations, on what subjects and through what level of political recognition is entirely discretionary.

In some respects, this discretionary moment offers a range of potential opportunities for recognition. But perhaps, as with most areas of discretion in regulatory systems, practice norms are developed over time and operationalized when a different and potentially competing factor, such as First Nations expression of authority, intervenes. The procedural and policy norms that have developed in BC tradition of regional coordination. This tradition has a partially legislative impulse, arising as it does from the *Local Government Act*'s requirement for municipalities and the province to work together to produce Regional Growth Strategies. Here again, First Nations are listed as one of many possible consultees. This time their engagement is mandatory the form and level of the consultancy is similarly ambiguous.

Yet it is clear from the other texts that shape and constrain practice in this field (see Chapter 4) that existing norms about regional coordination and cooperation are kicked into play and extended to First Nation Band Councils because they *appear*, in the eyes of other municipalities, to be municipal-like structures. As we discussed in the previous section, the spatiality of abutting jurisdictions, where reserve lands share their boundary with municipal boundaries, appears to trigger in the municipal planning process a willingness to treat First Nations as a municipal-like structure with planning authority constrained to their reserve lands. Planners in the District of North Vancouver, for example, conceive of their relationship with the Tsleil-Waututh Nation as something analogous to a municipality-to-municipality negotiation around coordination of housing growth and supply, infrastructure and servicing for the purposes of a Regional Growth Strategy. Planners in the District of North Vancouver will recognize the political authority of the Tsleil-Waututh Nation over planning functions on their reserve lands, but not in relation to planning functions on the Tsleil-Waututh Nation's wider territory that fall within DNV's own jurisdiction.

Consequently, the Official Community Plan process represented a reversion of practice by DNV to a safer, more familiar approach to simply 'referring' their OCP to the Tsleil-Waututh for comment. When some of the content and presumptions of that OCP were challenged by the Tsleil-Waututh Nation – such as access to the foreshore for fishing and cultural practices – DNV fell back on jurisdictional boundaries and the presumption for recognizing only *abutting* jurisdiction of the Tsleil-Waututh Nation, to limit the scope of that challenge. The municipality-to-municipality approach heavily bounds Tsleil-Waututh claim in this regard. In the planning process for Cates Park/Whey-ah-Wichen, a different set of political recognitions unfolded. Here, DNV were able to be more amenable to recognizing the political authority of Tsleil-Waututh Nation due to the conflict over the destruction of cultural sites, and the more obvious materiality of Tsleil-Waututh cultural interests in that site – showing again how the inter-articulation of political and object boundaries makes the contact zone more and more shallow.

Recognition of political authority on Crown lands managed by the province for conservation and resource extraction purposes is by contrast a greater possibility. Again, this partly arises from case law, which holds that consultation with First Nations and accommodation of their rights and title is the responsibility of the Crown. In fact, the precedent-setting Supreme Court *Haida* decision (see Chapter 4) drew specific attention to the need to consult Indigenous peoples during the strategic planning of Crown lands, since these processes set the course for all future natural resource management activities. The ruling prompted the province to pursue bilateral, government-to-government negotiations with all affected First Nations before the approval of a Strategic Resource Management Plan (Barry 2011).

The Gitanyow have taken that trajectory in case law – a trajectory that substantially opens the space for political recognition without prescribing what it looks like or how it should work – and folded it through their negotiations with the province about planning and management on their territory. As a result, the Gitanyow have achieved a level of political recognition through the planning system. The Province of BC recognizes not only the substantive content and direction of the Gitanyow Wilp Sustainability Plan and its intersection with the two strategic resource management plans for Nass South and Cranberry-Kispiox (see Chapter 8) but also the continuing political authority the Gitanyow express through their traditional law and governance system over that territory. This does not entirely translate, however, into a transfer of control and decision-making authority on that territory. Rather, the *Recognition and Reconciliation Agreement* works to establish a 'Shared Decision Making Framework' (2012, 82) that includes the establishment of a Joint Resources Governance Forum and Joint Resources Council to oversee the political and technical elements of plan implementation. Like many of the other agreements with First Nations across the province, it also included an Engagement Framework that was a very explicit attempt to create an 'efficient' (5) approach for addressing the provincial duty to consult and for 'creating land-use certainty and a stable environment for investment' (6).

The Boundary Work of 'Balance'

Planning, as a system of the settler state that has a wide public interest agenda, is charged with the responsibility of balancing these different stakeholder interests. A planner working on water planning for a government catchment management authority in Victoria expressed it in this way:

> we deal with the Indigenous community on the concern about cultural values and you know just trying to get them to understand that there's also other balances that need to be achieved – environmental, economic values, that all have to be worked in. That's probably one of the greater challenges, getting [traditional owners] to understand the bigger picture. (pers. comm. 6 July 2011)

Balance, in planning decision making, signals responsibility for a range of interests – not only 'Indigenous interests', which of course are always marked as 'cultural', thus neatly isolating them via an object boundary from ecological or economic questions. This is a profound problem for planning in the contact zone. Indigenous interests, when they are inserted into the planning system as another kind of stakeholder interest, become an anxious consideration for planning practitioners for whom the public interest is impoverished by being 'hijacked' by the interests of just one group. Other interests, so the discourse goes, also have to be acknowledged and incorporated into decision making. The that Indigenous people cannot 'see the bigger picture' because the only legitimate Indigenous interest is a 'cultural' one shows the impoverishment of the mainstream planning approach to these questions at work in settler states today.

Under a generalized neoliberal push in planning policy, this 'balance' masquerades as the trumping of economic interests in planning over all others – the 'economic' serving in these cases as a shorthand for public interest. This move is so common as to have become almost expected. What makes it particularly interesting in the contact zone is when it is used in the service of the transgression of Indigenous recognition. In its more regressive forms, it argues that recognition of Indigenous peoples threatens to 'hijack' planning to ends that only serve Indigenous peoples, rather than a broader public interest. One Victorian government national parks manager expressed it in this way: '[Parks are] not a free-for-all ... [traditional owners] have got to understand these are still the rules. Even though you [traditional owners] are a part of the mechanics, the rules are there for everyone and they are for a reason' (pers. comm. 6 July 2011). This is a powerful discursive move, and has been used in many other areas of public law and policy in the service of limiting, co-opting and constraining recognition. In its more progressive forms, a delicate shuttle diplomacy ensues. Often led by planning practitioners committed to a sensibility about Indigenous recognition in their own practice, Indigenous interests appear front and centre, as in the case of the Gitanyow, but the work of the planner is to relay and translate those interests back to other stakeholders.

One further political boundary appears to be at work in these cases, and that is the question of property and development rights. The settler states in Canada and Australia own the authority to allocate development rights to other parties – land use is nationalized and collective in this broad sense. Political recognition of Indigenous peoples' coexisting jurisdiction and title would suggest that this authority to allocate development rights to other parties would need to be transferred in some way. This is such a heavily bounded aspect of political recognition in the contact zone that it is not even on the table of any negotiation or struggle around recognition in any of our cases. It operates silently, as a political boundary assumed (at least by the settler state) as firm.

Political authority of any kind, whether it is recognized or not, is not only linked to a territory (its spatiality, as we outlined in the previous section) but is also bounded to certain kinds of objects or things. The next section addresses how this occurs.

Object Boundaries

Culture and tradition as an object boundary is doing powerful discursive and constraining work in all of the four cases we have discussed here. This boundary is most obvious when it manifests in a struggle over a space that is also a struggle over political authority and rights to a land base, but can only be registered for planning within the bounded legitimacy of cultural heritage. The Tsleil-Waututh Nation's struggle to protect cultural heritage at Cates Park/Whey-ah-Wichen; Wadi Wadi protests about logging threatening cultural heritage in Nyah-Vinifera; the move by the Wurundjeri to set up an organization mobilized around cultural heritage; and the Gitanyow people's use of cultural buffer zones as a proxy for ecological protection – all are examples of the culture and tradition object boundary at work.

This partly arises from the compartmentalizing work within and between Western scientific (and social science) disciplines. It is commonplace in planning to see different dimensions or issues flagged within plans and policies that have been categorized in order to make those issues more knowable and manageable – think of categories like biodiversity, housing, transport, recreational use, public open space, and so on. Categories of this sort are deeply embedded in ways of thinking and acting within planning professions, as this quote from a planner working in the then Growth Areas Authority in Melbourne attests in discussing how they approach planning for open space networks in those growth areas: 'we're looking at ... the various multitude of values that go with them. They've got a hydraulic function and they've got a biodiversity value, they've got a recreational function and inevitably they have cultural heritage values as well' (pers. comm. 12 July 2011). Identifying these as *different* values perpetually rearticulates the Indigenous as only of concern in relation to the object of cultural heritage. Moreover, once that articulation is made, it becomes a technocratic problem of incorporating cultural heritage values into the planning approach, or as one planner described, 'how best to plug the cultural heritage values assessment into our framework' (pers. comm. 12 July 2011).

A closer analysis of the particular object boundary materialized in Victoria through the *Aboriginal Heritage Act* is useful for picking apart a more precise understanding of how this boundary operates. Only when there is a tangible of heritage that is recognizable to the AHA does recognition of political authority to which significant powers are attached suddenly materialize for Aboriginal people. Following archaeological convention, the Act defines Aboriginal cultural heritage as follows: recognized Aboriginal places; objects that relate to Aboriginal life that are culturally significant to Aboriginal people; or Aboriginal human remains (s.4). While temporally expansive in the sense that objects made after colonization can be included, a temporal break is nonetheless instilled into the legislative definitions. Things and places made prior to contact are 'traditional', while things and places made after colonization are deemed 'historical'. This is partly an implicit acknowledgement that colonization processes created all sorts of new kinship, land and cultural connections through forced removal and dispossession. But it can also be read as the placement of non-Western cultures as primitive and pre-historic, with only Western civilization able to be read as the creation of history (see Torgovnick 1990). Discursively splitting 'traditional' pre-contact cultures from post-contact 'historical' cultures is a move enabled by categorizing colonization and modernity as a final rupture of Indigenous societies, one that could not be authentically survived. It signifies the constant search for the irretrievable: an authentic, essentialized and static pre-contact expression of culture (Povinelli 2002).

The *Aboriginal Heritage Act* operationalizes this discourse about authenticity and traditionality by categorizing certain kinds of modern development activities as fatal for Aboriginal cultural heritage interests. Part 2, Division 4 of the AHA provides that where there has been 'significant ground disturbance', this immediately disqualifies that place from being considered an area of cultural heritage sensitivity. In practice, this means any place that has undergone such significant ground disturbance is exempt from any consideration of Aboriginal cultural heritage interest: it presumes that the Aboriginal value of that place has been erased by modern development. This has the much wider material effect of precluding much of the urbanized and settled parts of Victoria from the jurisdiction of Registered Aboriginal Parties, which produces a spatial intensity to this boundary work. Planning legislation and regulations thus operationalize the discourse that Aboriginal values are 'traditional' and that this traditionality (highly essentialized and static) cannot authentically survive modernity. Places like cities, where 'significant ground disturbance' is seen to have removed an Aboriginal presence, are simply not spaces where even a minimal 'interest' in cultural heritage is recognizable.

Object boundaries were also at work in Tsleil-Waututh Nation's negotiation with the District of North Vancouver over development issues on the waterfront at Burrard Inlet. The Tsleil-Waututh Nation was quite forcefully expressing grave concerns about ongoing access to the waterfront for Tsleil-Waututh people in the face of strong development pressures. Other stakeholders in DNV's planning process for preparing the Official Community Plan were also expressing views about access to the waterfront and development along the waterfront, an area of high value land. DNV were largely unwilling to take on board the concerns expressed by Tsleil-Waututh people about their access to the waterfront in the light of balancing other stakeholder and development interests. This ambivalence also operates in the register of a political boundary, as discussed in the previous section. At the same time as this negotiation was unfolding, DNV was much more willing to acknowledge the authority of the Tsleil-Waututh Nation over Cates Park/Whey-ah-Wichen, because that site expressed an obvious materiality of Tsleil-Waututh culture in the form of a recognizable archaeological site, and because certain powers of political authority were afforded the Tsleil-Waututh Nation regarding the protection of that site. Recognition of Tsleil-Waututh authority, along with some rights and interests, was legitimate in relation to the recordable, tangible object of cultural heritage, but neither visible nor legitimate to the planning system when those objects of cultural heritage appeared not to be present.

There is also a significant bounding of Indigenous recognition to the object of 'traditional use and practice', connected to this cultural legitimacy discourse. Recognition becomes possible under this discursive move, in places, times or events where traditional use and practice are present. For example, the economic and cultural importance to Gitanyow of salmon harvesting, which is fixed in planning recognition as a 'traditional use and practice', is possible to recognize. Other uses and practices that are not legitimately fixed as 'traditional' fall outside recognition possibilities. The use and practice, for example, of residential construction is not seen as 'traditional' and therefore not considered a legitimate issue within planning contact zones.

Bounded Recognition as Renewed Dispossession

Our analysis here takes an understanding of bounding work in planning *as renewed dispossession* in a different direction. Here, the dominant power of settler-state planning takes an emergent struggle or practice, which we mapped out in Chapter 9, and reconstructs and reinforces pre-established boundaries around that struggle to enforce or resettle colonial relations of power. In so doing, this particular boundary work of planning works to limit the conditions under which recognition of Indigenous peoples' rights can really be practised in different planning contexts. While Indigenous recognition becomes a 'planning issue', it only does so in the terms already set and rendered legitimate to that system.

By parsing out three distinct boundary mechanisms, we have analyzed the inter-articulation of spatial, political and object boundaries in practice and text. The practices involved in doing so depend upon the stability and reification of certain discourses around property rights, certainty, Indigenous identity and legitimacy. As such, planning contact zones with Indigenous people become visible and articulated around what is possible under the conditions of the security and certainty of private property, of the balancing of the public interest, and only do so when the political authority of Indigenous people being recognized performs a traditional-enough version of culture.

Importantly, however, is the ways those nodal discourses work together and manifest in varying ways across different places and planning contexts. Places apparently fully settled by settler modernity, such as cities, are rendered as lost objects for Indigenous recognition. The construction of Indigenous cultures as unable to authentically survive modernity, and consequently unrecognizable in fully settled landscapes, renders recognition not just off the agenda but obsolete. The complete silence in the urban planning legislative regime in both Victoria and BC should now be clear from the analysis we have presented in this book. That silence is of course itself a discourse and emerges from two quite distinct discursive moves. In Victoria, the regime of extinguishment of native title and the proof tests constructed as part of that regime render cities too settled to be any longer the location of legitimate Aboriginal interests. By contrast, that same silence in BC emerges out of discourses about the right relationship between the province and municipalities and the scope of the Crown.

That silence gives rise to further discursive moves, which are also distinctive in these two different jurisdictions. In Victoria, extinguishment of Aboriginal rights enables a desire to recover a lost past through cultural artefacts. Aboriginality suddenly appears in urban planning bound to the object of cultural heritage, under certain heavily circumscribed spatial and political conditions. In BC, practice norms that inform the strong neighbour-to-neighbour planning approach by municipalities is recontextualized to recognize abutting rights and authority of First Nations spatially contained to their reserve lands. This is a simple recontextualization of a discourse and practice of inter-municipal coordination, one that merely incorporates First Nations into existing settler-state planning practices.

Consequently, the contact zone for planning in both Victoria and BC is *bound to* pre-existing systems and norms of planning, providing heavily prescribed and constrained possibilities for recognition (see Porter and Barry 2015 for further discussion). Indigenous territories are reconstituted in planning systems as additional spatial units through which planning work can continue. Cultural heritage sites, wide areas of exclusion and extinguishment mastered through regulation, the reification of First Nation reserve boundaries as if they marked the edge of territorial jurisdiction – all represent the various and contingent spatial bounding mechanisms through which Indigenous claims are tamed and planning authority reconstituted.

Bureaucratic naming conventions and institutional designs are applied to Indigenous peoples, mirroring established practices and norms. The potential risk that First Nations or Aboriginal people represent to the certainty of planning approaches and settler development rights is managed by regularizing and standardizing Indigenous involvement and engagement within political boundaries, and sharply drawing the limits of recognition through spatial and object boundaries. Tully's conceptualization of monological recognition is insightful for understanding this discursive move in planning, for monological recognition spatially and politically contains the threat of Indigenous challenge to planning authority by demarcating where, who, when and how recognition becomes legitimate.

Conclusion

This chapter has charted the subtle and structural ways that the systems of planning and recognition resettle the authority of settler states and tame Indigenous claims. Occurring through a variety of discursive and material practices, this is achieved through the operationalization of three distinct, yet overlapping, boundary mechanisms: spatial, political and object. The work of producing, regulating and maintaining these boundaries is a core project for planning. Boundaries, edges and margins have been thought to offer transformative potential to planning theory, a perspective on occupying the margins that has offered real insights into the political identity struggles of different groups and their interventions in planning (Sandercock 1999, 2003; Umemoto 2001). Yet in contexts like these, where colonial relations of power and the politics of recognition are seductively normalizing, we see a darker dimension of the work that boundaries do in planning. While settler-state planning is now claiming a role for itself in the politics of recognition, the limits are clear: Indigenous people must simultaneously perform an authentic traditionality alongside a suitably Western form of governance, and limit their claims to sites unaffected by modernity. Such are the costs of recognition in contemporary planning contact zones.

Chapter 11

Developing Intercultural Capacity: Lessons for Planning Practice

Introduction

Everyday practices in the contact zone continuously unsettle and resettle the challenging nature of Indigenous claims on planning. So far, our exploration of these negotiations and contestations has focused on how Indigenous peoples 'speak back' to the systems of state-based planning, using knowledge systems and political processes that will already be familiar to its practitioners. While we have sought to privilege those actions and claims, this is not to suggest that state-based planners did not engage in their own 'arts of the contact zone'. In many of our cases, planners, land managers, staff and managers in government were able to use their professional knowledge and experience to create spaces and possibilities for coexistence. This chapter seeks to bring these stories to the fore.

This chapter is positioned as one of two concluding chapters and is explicitly focused on planning practice. Our intention is to speak directly to the professional institutions and communities of practice of which we (as former state-based planners who became actively engaged in planning education) are a part. We use the experiences of planners and other related professionals from our four case studies to open up new lines of questioning about their role in the shared struggle for coexistence and to explore what those practices might look like. Notably, we deliberately avoid the language of 'best practices'. This term is far too reductive and would fail to do justice to the complexity and contextual specificity of our four stories. Instead, inspired by the work of Howitt and his colleagues (Howitt, Doohan, Suchet-Pearson, Cross, et al. 2013; Howitt, Doohan, Suchet-Pearson, Lunkapis, et al. 2013), we have opted to use the language of capacities and use this chapter to raise questions about the *specific* intercultural capacities (or competencies) that need to be cultivated by state-based planners working in the contact zone.

This chapter highlights some the tangible ways state-based planners have built, and might continue to build, their own intercultural capacities. We begin by unpacking notions of planning capacity and competence, terms that permeate through the planning profession and play a powerful role in shaping the identity of individual planners as well as the culture of the profession as a whole. Current requirements for professional planning competencies in Australia and Canada fall well short of preparing planners to productively engage in the struggle for coexistence. Following the line of thinking sketched out by Howitt and his colleagues (Howitt, Doohan, Suchet-Pearson, Cross, et al. 2013; Howitt, Doohan, Suchet-Pearson, Lunkapis, et al. 2013), we then turn our attention to the development of 'new ethical competencies' (Howitt, Doohan, Suchet-Pearson, Cross, et al. 2013, 130) for intercultural planning practice in (post)colonial contexts. Our thinking is informed by and brought to life through the everyday experience of the non-Indigenous planning and land management practitioners involved in our four case studies.

Intercultural Capacity Deficits in Professional Planning Practice

Indigenous peoples are not the only actors in the contact zone who lack capacity. In fact, 'it is often capacity deficits in government agencies, commercial interests, and non-Indigenous institutions that most dramatically affect collaborative governance of intercultural environmental systems' (Howitt, Doohan, Suchet-Pearson, Lunkapis, et al. 2013, 313). Our four case studies underscore the regressive politics of monological recognition by showing that the perception of Indigenous peoples' lack of planning capacity is often just that: a perception formed by looking only through the privileging lens of Western planning. Indigenous peoples have all kinds of planning capacities, many of which are deeply rooted in their own customary laws and cultural traditions. While settler states clearly have a responsibility to address structural inequity, the fixation with 'Indigenous capacity development' (a phrase we encountered numerous times in our interviews and documentary analysis) may be ill placed and may serve to hide other dimensions. If these agencies and individuals have an equal, if not greater, responsibility to build their own capacities for engaging with Indigenous customary laws and governance systems, then the critical question is how.

It is a matter of extreme concern, then, that the professional institutes in Canada and Australia remain resolutely silent on this particularly important aspect of intercultural capacity development. As in many parts of the world, urban and regional planning is a recognized profession in both Canada and Australia, with professional institutes and standards of accreditation. In Australia, all professional planners must receive an undergraduate or postgraduate degree in urban and regional planning from a program that has been accredited by the Planning Institute of Australia (PIA). Accredited programs must address a series of 'general capabilities and competencies' and 'core curriculum competencies'. The process in Canada is very similar, though the Professional [Planning] Standards Board (PSB) allows individuals without an accredited planning degree to become professional planners after several years of related job experience. Regardless of their entry route into the profession (accredited degree or on-the-job training), all Canadian planners must possess a series of 'enabling' and 'functional' competencies. As illustrated in Table 11.1, not only do the Australian and Canadian accreditation systems share this language of competencies, there is also a great deal of similarity in terms of the specific competencies that need to be possessed by all accredited planners and that must be taught by all accredited planning schools.

These documents are also united in their omission of any direct reference to Indigenous peoples, Indigenous rights or Indigenous governance systems. Knowledge of relevant statutes and case law is seen as a 'core' (Australia) or 'functional' (Canada) competency, but neither document suggests that planners need to have any knowledge of court decisions related to Indigenous rights and title. As this book has shown, these decisions (rightly or wrongly) play a tremendous role in determining the depth and breadth of planning contact zones and really ought to be part of a planner's core knowledge. Similarly, both professional bodies underscore the importance of possessing knowledge of political frameworks that underlie and inform the planning system, but neither makes any reference to how those frameworks also include self-determining Indigenous peoples.

In fact, the only reference to Aboriginal peoples in the Australian document is in its preface, where the PIA expresses an intention to revise the standards to bring them in line with a 2010 discussion paper on how to improve planners' understanding of Aboriginal and Torres Islander Peoples. While the document expresses a commitment to this revision, at the time of writing this commitment had still not been fulfilled. The main document that articulates the Canadian professional standards, on the other hand, makes absolutely no mention of Indigenous peoples. 'Aboriginal peoples' does appear in one of the documents that candidates must complete as part of the accreditation process (Professional Standards Board for the Planning Profession in Canada 2015b), but it is framed in the language of 'inclusiveness' and of being attentive to issues of diversity and particular demographic conditions. This is, of course, the very language that we argued against in Chapter 2, because it provides an insufficient and problematic base for thinking about the nature of coexistence.

Why do we raise these issues here? And how do they come to bear on the contact zones for planning in (post)colonial contexts? Our perspective on these questions is twofold. First, even this cursory examination of the Australian and Canadian accreditation standards reveals significant gaps in the ways in which practitioners are encouraged to consider the unique challenges of planning in (post) colonial contexts. Both sets of standards are grounded in a staid and depoliticized understanding of professional planning practice. Planning professionals in both countries must display a degree competence in public engagement, as well as negotiation and mediation – requirements hinting at the socio-political dimensions of planning practice that have been a frequent subject in the planning literature since at least the early 1980s (see Forester 1989). However, both privilege the technocratic dimensions of planning: the application of existing statutory frameworks, the use of appropriate regulatory and fiscal tools, and the compilation of relevant data – which, in the Canadian system at least, are often framed according to positivist notions of cause and effect (Professional Standards Board for the Planning Profession in Canada 2015b). None of the required competencies

Table 11.1 Planning competencies used in the accreditation of planning professionals in Canada and Australia

CORE CURRICULUM COMPETENCIES	AUSTRALIA	CANADA	*Functional Competencies*
Governance, law, plan implementation & administration	Statutory processes		
	Legal interpretation & drafting	Planning laws	*Government & law*
	Relevant acts & case law		
	Legal/related governmental principles & frameworks	Political & institutional frameworks of planning	
	Appeal systems		
	Planning regulations & policies	Regulatory tools	*Plan & policy implementation*
		Fiscal/financial tools	
		Monitoring & evaluation	
Plan making / land-use allocation, management & design	Reviewing, evaluating & monitoring plans		
	Critiquing planning tools, proposals & outcomes		
	Planning processes & implementation	Visioning, goal setting & problem framing	*Processes of planning & policy making*
	Applying strategic & statutory frameworks		
	Preparing plans & urban designs		
	Processes of governance & participation	Public consultation & deliberation	
	Working with diverse & multidisciplinary groups		
	Gathering data	Information gathering & analysis	*Issues in planning & policy making*
	Theories of urban & regional systems	Environmental, social & economic sustainability	
		Public finance & economics	
		Equity, diversity & inclusiveness	
		Land-use, design & infrastructure	
		Forms, scales & settings	*Human settlements*
		Processes & factors of change	

ENABLING COMPETENCIES

	AUSTRALIA	CANADA	
CORE CURRICULUM COMPETENCIES	Planning theory Key legal principles & practices Using technical tools History of planning in comparative context	Planning theories, principles & practices History of planning in Canada & other countries	*History & principles of planning*
	Planners' roles over time & in various contexts	New developments in planning Planning ethics	
	Engaging diverse groups Mediation & negotiation	Including diverse people & values Mediation, facilitation, negotiation & conflict resolution	*Social interaction & leadership*
	Risk management		
GENERAL COMPETENCIES	Team work	Team-work & team-building Relationship to bosses, officials & the public Handling ethical dilemmas	*Professionalism*
	Work readiness Problem solving	Managing uncertainty & change	
	Self-reflection	Learning from practice	
	Research & analysis Spatial thinking & application Problem identification Strategic thinking	Gathering & analyzing data Thinking at geographic scales Identifying patterns & trends Designing scenarios & plans	*Critical & creative thinking*
	Communication	Written, oral & graphic communication Use of information technology	*Communication*

Source: (Table produced by the authors, derived from Planning Institute of Australia 2011; Professional Standards Board for the Planning Profession in Canada 2015a)

is inherently 'wrong'. In fact, the fulfilment of these competencies is likely to produce planners who are able to attend to the core tasks and responsibilities of professional planning practice – *as it is currently conceived*. However, as we have argued throughout this book, the current conception of planning in relation to Indigenous claims for coexistence is part of the problem.

Yet planning is also potentially part of the answer, as we stated at the very outset of this book. The question, then, is what kind of planning competencies would be required to promote a new conception of planning, one that allows for the coexistence of Indigenous and non-Indigenous modes of governance and social-spatial organization. Some of the foundations for the reconceptualization of planning competence may exist in the current accreditation standards. For example, planning ethics are afforded some prominence and, in both countries, the accrediting bodies draw attention to the importance of personal and professional reflection. The Australian system even speaks of the importance of 'critiquing planning tools, proposals and outcomes' (Planning Institute of Australia 2011). In each case, however, it is entirely unclear what principles and concepts ought to underlie these moments of ethical choice, reflection and critique. Vague and imprecise notions of the 'public interest' and 'common good (see Chapter 4) are the most likely candidates, as these terms are enshrined in the professional codes of conduct that exist in both countries (Planning Institute of Australia 2014; Canadian Institute of Planners 2015) – though the Planning Institute of Australia's Professional Code of Conduct now includes the expectation that decisions be made within the context of a 'considered account of Aboriginal and Torres Strait Islander connections to country' (Planning Institute of Australia 2014, 3).

These observations bring us to our second point. The broad and often imprecise nature of the accreditation standards also holds open possibility for the application of different kind of planning ethic and different ways of evaluating and critically reflecting upon professional practice, ones that are more aligned with, and work to support, the struggle for coexistence. The challenge is how to conceptualize and articulate these different ways of practising, and then inspire non-Indigenous planners to engage in the difficult work of developing these new 'ethical competencies' for intercultural planning practice (Howitt, Doohan, Suchet-Pearson, Cross, et al. 2013, 130). It is to these questions that we now turn.

Towards Intercultural Competence in the Contact Zone

What might these 'ethical competencies' toward a decolonizing practice that engages productively with the politics of coexistence actually look like? This section works to build on this conceptual foundation by adding short empirical vignettes from our case studies to better illustrate some possible emerging principles. Structured in three parts, each highlights a different dimension of intercultural competence organized as a synthesis of Howitt and his colleagues' work and our own analysis of strategic actions taken by planning and other related professionals as they worked to support change in planning contact zones. We begin with the idea of developing competence in the art of 'situated engagement'.

The Art of 'Situated Engagement': Ontological Pluralism and Hybridity

First advanced in the work of Suchet (1999), *situated engagement* refers to the practices through which 'Eurocentric concepts and practices which are assumed to be universal, can be unsettled, challenged and opened up to unimaginable possibilities' (xviii). Situated engagement includes expanding the scope of land and other resource management practices to consciously create space for the expression of specific, contextualized knowledges and governance traditions. The art of situated engagement often begins with small yet meaningful actions that call attention to protocols that purposefully destabilize professional authority.

Enabling such understanding comes, as all our stories show, only from sustained, personal engagement. Regular, sustained engagement, which is without expectation and geared to the agenda of Indigenous people themselves, has the potential to be transformative. It creates a space to better learn, appreciate and be respectful towards the knowledge and values that Indigenous peoples express. That space also provides time and capacity to have those difficult conversations about how to translate values between two coexisting domains, and how to find where they share commonalities and where they are different. All of this demands time and commitment, a willingness to make mistakes and learn from them, and our four case studies are replete with examples of instances when an unusual level of commitment from one or two key individuals in a government agency somewhere enabled different possibilities to emerge.

One such example is a seemingly small initiative that helped catalyze Wurundjeri Council capacity to develop their Narrap Country Plan. In 2009, the State's worst-ever bushfires tore through large swathes of country on Melbourne's northern and eastern fringe, across Wurundjeri and neighbouring Taungerong country. Parks Victoria staff saw Wurundjeri people were showing deep concern about the plight of the victims of those bush fires, and for the ecological and cultural damage that had been done. In response, Parks Victoria staff organized a bus tour to take Elders to the affected areas and meet with local people and land-care groups. Two indirect outcomes emerged from this simple action. First, the closeness of the colonial history of this area suddenly became vivid. As one Parks Victoria manager described it, '[This was the] first time probably that white people had seen that *mountain ash/E regnans* country burnt. The Wallaby Creek catchment had never been burnt since settlement, so essentially the last people to see that area burnt would be Wurundjeri people, their ancestors, as the majority of those mountain ash were over 300 years old' (pers. comm. 27 June 2011). Second, a larger conversation unfolded between Wurundjeri Elders, Parks Victoria and the Catchment Management Authority about broader strategic planning on Wurundjeri country, and this helped catalyze institutional support behind Wurundjeri Council applying for funds to develop the Narrap Country Plan.

These seem small issues and interventions. Indeed, this kind of time and commitment to seemingly small initiatives of little consequence are often not valued in contemporary organizational contexts, especially when the measures of time wasted and time spent are focused on finite, known and contained interactions that privilege non-Indigenous sensibilities and expectations. Yet it is the small interventions within even resoundingly monological instances of recognition that begin to offer the potential to trigger wider possibilities. Much of the action being taken by the Wadi Wadi, Wurundjeri, Tsleil-Waututh and Gitanyow peoples is focused on finding ways to creatively and strategically use very small and limited changes in order to catalyze something bigger. Creative use of small strategic possibilities is also possible among planning practitioners. This is particularly clear for an organization like Parks Victoria. For example, many staff who had long-standing relationships with Aboriginal people acknowledged that the traditional owner boards of management enabled under the new *Traditional Owner Settlement Act (2010)* (TOSA) were insufficient, and indeed, in the words of one, an 'artificial governance arrangement' (pers. comm. 30 June 2011). Yet they represented a way in, a new discourse and framework that expanded the edges of possible alternative practices. Instead of being too concerned with what the legislative framework stipulated, the focus was on relationships and what they made possible.

Officers and senior managers in some government organizations spoke openly and often about the importance of finding creative ways to practise by changing the way that the organization and its staff think about their relationship with traditional owners. For example, even while the regulations required only interaction on cultural heritage – that powerful object boundary – the possibility opened up during that interaction for other kinds of conversation. The initiative, and the risk, had to be taken – but the possibility was there. Part of this practice is shifting the language as well as the expectations and privileges within the operationalization of non-Indigenous governance and process. This takes a lot time and commitment, in a context where moving the language from 'stakeholder group' to 'land owner' or 'regulator' is a massive cultural shift for planning and land management agencies. Much can be done, in other words, in the face of the spatial, political and object boundaries mediating the politics of recognition. This is fragile and 'patchy,' as one officer stated. But the possibility for alternative practices is always present.

The critical challenge, of course, is how to ensure that these practices do not digress into a tokenistic and monological recognition of Indigenous customs and law that fails unsettle the colonial boundaries of the contact zone – and of professional planning practice more broadly. At least part of the answer lies in brokering opportunities to address the structural inequities of settler colonialism. One government officer from Victoria reflected on the huge differential in expectations and capacities between government staff and Indigenous people at planning negotiation tables, issues we foregrounded in Chapter 9:

If our CEO said to us this week … to the staff, 'I want you to go to Mildura [a city in northwest Victoria, 540 kilometres from Melbourne] next week. You need to take your own car and you'll have to book accommodation and pay for it. And your food. And we're not paying you to be there but you've got to go and do the job' – we wouldn't be going, would we? [Yet] we have the same expectations toward Victorian traditional owners back the other way. (pers. comm. 27 June 2011)

Although we remain suspicious of superficial attempts to 'build the planning capacity' of Indigenous people through an uncritical redistribution of state funding and resources, we also encountered state-based planners who were practising the art of situated engagement through the creative allocation of state resources to address precisely these inequities. Although key aspects of the planning process (its timelines and major decisions) were quite resistant to the unsettling effects of Indigenous agency, the contact zone between the Tsleil-Waututh Nation and District of North Vancouver did include a funding arrangement that allowed Tsleil-Waututh to properly engage in the Official Community Plan (OCP) process. As discussed in Chapter 7, the Tsleil-Waututh Nation's *Stewardship Policy* posed significant conceptual and practical challenges for municipalities, many of whom struggled to accept First Nation authority outside the boundaries of the reserve. However, the District of North Vancouver's long-term planning relationship with the Tsleil-Waututh allowed for a *partial* unsettlement of the universalizing and decontextualizing norms of citizen participation and intergovernmental referrals. DNV staff tapped into a funding source that had been originally intended to support innovative approaches to community engagement and were able to creatively extend the boundaries of that fund to accommodate an Indigenous government. The language of accommodation and inclusion is, of course, deeply problematic (see Chapter 2), but, in this instance, it did help open up a zone of interaction that otherwise would not have been possible and that continues to hold the promise of a more mutual approach to Indigenous recognition.

The district manager from the Ministry of Forests, who helped to initiate the Gitanyow's first government-to-government planning relationship with the BC Government, engaged in a somewhat similar practice of creatively interpreting existing planning practices, tools and discourses. This planning process – the Landscape Unit Plan detailed in Chapter 8 – did not conform to universalizing policies of the day, but rather grew out of the specificities of the local context, including the Gitanyow's very specific demands for recognition. Although the process was technically non-compliant, ministry staff were able to carefully frame it according to the prevailing discourse of resource certainty and the duty to consult. The district manager's willingness to take risks and to creatively use existing planning discourses to make way for a different approach to resource management signalled the beginning of a more collaborative relationship. It was through this collaborative relationship that the Gitanyow were able to bring their own customary and highly context-specific law and ancestral knowledge into the planning process and to have it coexist alongside the ontologies that frame BC's approach to strategic natural resource planning.

Planners and land managers, then, have to work well outside their 'normal' duties and practices, facing the likelihood of significant mistakes and setbacks. Or, as one land manager in Victoria put it, 'resourcing things that we might not have thought [are] our role to resource' (pers. comm. 30 June 2011). For some organizations, like Parks Victoria, this shift is already underway – where perhaps 10 years ago blame was laid at the feet of traditional owner communities because they did not have the capacity to engage, even though government 'wanted to'. Realization has dawned for some practitioners that this form of capacity building is the responsibility of settler governments and that 'engagement fatigue' (pers. comm. 30 June 2011) is a real and material problem. Finding a workable solution to support the Wadi Wadi people to come to the table was an example of this kind of practice – working at the creative edges of 'standard practice'. In doing so, senior executives in the Department of Sustainability and Environment, pushed heavily by the Wadi Wadi and their allies in FoE, were able to subvert those structural inequities at least momentarily. It is only through the ongoing implementation of this kind of action, that practitioners can develop an intimate understanding of the specific resources needed for Indigenous people to enter the planning process, not as stakeholders but as a collaborating government authority.

The art of situated engagement therefore requires planners and other related practitioners who possess detailed and intimate knowledge of relevant acts, case law and statutory processes and who are able to reflect upon and critique planning decisions and approaches. These capacities mirror some of the language found in the Australian and Canadian professional standards boards, though these competencies are being used in more expansive ways to *contribute* to the broadening and deepening of the contact zone for planning in (post)colonial contexts. For as the experiences of the professionals involved in our four case studies show, simply ensuring that planners and prospective planners are familiar with the statutory contexts and governance frameworks that guide Indigenous-state planning relations is unlikely to promote real and meaningful change. Planners need to be willing to acknowledge that, while these contexts and framework are thoroughly implicated in the ongoing dispossession of Indigenous lands and Indigenous authorities, they are not static and are open to creative and strategic interpretation. The art of situated engagement therefore demands that planners become more competent in remaining situated in the specificities of Indigenous demands, and the resultant claims to ontological plurality, while also using their professional and institutional knowledge to support Indigenous efforts to wedge open new spaces for planning hybridity.

Thinking with Reference to Indigenous Spatialities and Systems of Governance

Our case studies also revealed a very particular form of situated engagement and ontological pluralism, one that sought to challenge the political and geographic spatialities of state-based planning practice. As we have seen in Part II, these contestations were often at the heart of the 'clashing and grappling' (Pratt 1991) at work in each of these contact zones. Moving beyond these often quite rigid boundaries required the system-transforming agency of not only Indigenous people but also planners whose ethics were 'situated' enough that they were able to alter their own understanding of the spatial boundaries and scales of engagement that mattered most to the planning process. It also required the engagement of non-Indigenous planners who displayed a degree of competence in spatial thinking (a requirement of both the Australian and Canadian accreditation systems). It required them to be willing to learn about – and then find creative ways to allow – the spatial sites and scales that were most relevant to their Indigenous partner(s), so that these could coexist alongside those dictated by the state-based planning system. It is for these reasons that we have decided to highlight this as a particular intercultural competence.

This form of intercultural competency was immediately recognizable in the actions of some of the state-based planners who were involved in the contact zone involving the Gitanyow Huwilp. In fact, the local planning manager spoke at length about his 20-plus years of working in the region and deepening appreciation of the cultural importance of the Huwilp – for not only the Gitanyow but also many of the other Indigenous nations in the region as well. As he describes it, the deep cultural importance of those spatial boundaries and the associated systems of governance was never formally verbalized in any planning meeting. But when he visited the local First Nations, he would see the Wilp Chiefs all sitting around the table, with a large map depicting all of the Lax'yip posted on the wall behind them – a regular occurrence that became a subtle but powerful reminder that the planning boundaries imposed by the provincial forest management system were not the only ones that had meaning.

A shift in the scales in planning is also underway in Victoria, pushed in part by the insistence of Aboriginal people that planning according to park boundaries fails to respect and accommodate the extent of their interests in territory and their political authority. Parks Victoria has begun to discuss preparing plans at the landscape scale (rather than according to park boundaries), which is openly acknowledged to be a much closer match to the interests of traditional owners (pers. comm. 14 July 2011). Because the spatial and political questions are so intrinsically interlinked, that shift also demands counteracting the certainties of political authority and will at some point in the planning process require a suspension of, or direct conflict with, the expectations of settler-state planning systems. In relation to the Wadi Wadi case, government staff acknowledged that the measure of success would have to be that Wadi Wadi people felt that they had exercised their custodial interests and responsibilities; they also acknowledged that these might in fact contravene or be in contra-distinction to the standardized planning outcomes presumed through the legislative framework. In this sense, it becomes clear how important it is for planners and practitioners to 'interpret the rules to suit what [Indigenous people] are telling us' (pers. comm. 30 June 2011).

Embracing the 'Commotion of Co-Motion'

Our third and final intercultural competency is slightly broader. It is less focused on how non-Indigenous planners might promote the coexistence of particular forms of knowledge and social-spatial modes of organization and more on how these planners understand the socio-political and relational aspects of their work. As we have already seen, the accreditation standards that are currently used in Australia and Canada privilege a vision of the profession that is grounded in ideas of deliberation, facilitation, mediation and negotiation. The Australian system also adds 'risk management' to the list, while the Canadian Professional Standards Board references the importance of '*managing* uncertainty and change' (emphasis added). Yet what if risk, uncertainty and change are not things to be managed but rather things that planners need to learn to embrace as essential elements of the shared struggle for coexistence? Howitt and his colleagues refer to this intercultural competence as 'embracing the commotion of co-motion' – an idea that calls attention to the 'hard work of bringing incommensurate systems [of land management] together, to work through what it means to move together towards more just and sustainable outcomes' (Howitt, Doohan, Suchet-Pearson, Cross, et al. 2013, 153).

As we have already argued in Chapter 2, this work cannot be accomplished through post-political planning approaches that presume inclusion and consensus. As the experiences of all of the non-Indigenous parties to our four contact zones attest, the 'commotion of co-motion' is messy and conflict-ridden. In fact, many of the practitioners during this research spoke about the tense nature of many of their meetings with Indigenous peoples, often expressing relief when relationships had progressed to the point that they were no longer being yelled at from the other side of the table. Yet others implicitly or explicitly recognized that conflict was inevitable, if not incredibly productive. They understood that the Indigenous representatives they worked with were not simply 'tough negotiators', as one of the Gitanyow chiefs was referred to (per. comm. 12 May 2011): they were struggling for coexistence, using any opening or avenue that was available to them. And it is through conflicts that intercultural capacity is built within the everyday practices and norms of settler-state planning agencies. When the Growth Areas Authority in Melbourne came into conflict with the Wurundjeri about their rejection of sensitive cultural information provided by Elders for a computer-based model, it at least triggered a profound learning process about what culture meant for Wurundjeri people, how it was expressed and practised, and where it materialised in the landscape.

These lessons about conflict and its role in planning contact zones have significant practical implications for planning competencies, both in everyday practice and for planning education. So much effort in the field of planning practice over the past 20 years has gone into the development of an ethic and orientation toward the mediation of conflict – how to resolve and 'get past' conflict. In (post) colonial contexts, planners are *active agents* in conflict, bringing to the planning table, as they do, the very structural and discursive injustices against which Indigenous people are struggling. There is no way to transcend the inevitability of this conflict – it is a constitutive element of planning contact zones. Understanding this inevitability is quite different, however, from concluding that all is lost, or that all planning action in contact zones is doomed to conflict-ridden failure. Conflict is a vital element in (post)colonial planning contexts, where uncomfortable truths lead to reflexive learning and the possibility of shifting privileged norms, as a more progressive application of the 'arts of the contact zone' appears to demand.

Conclusion

This chapter has shed light on how the struggle for coexistence demands a more nuanced conception of planning practice and of the role of planning practitioners. Context and situated engagement are key dimensions, making attempts to wrap the complexities of these experiences into a neat little package of 'best practices' not only incredibly challenging but also foolhardy. Indigenous claims upon planning are grounded in specific customary laws and knowledge systems, which grow out of particular socio-ecological relationships with actual places. There is not, nor should there be, a definitive set of intercultural capacities that planners need to address. Rather, the art of situated engagement demands that planners find, and/ or create opportunities to step out of the universalizing world of statutory processes and regulatory requirements, so that they can truly listen to, and not merely hear (see Forester 1989 for an excellent discussion of this distinction), the claims that Indigenous peoples are making. Small actions in the tiny corners of monological modes of recognition can unfold in extraordinary ways. The impossible becomes possible when the plurality of ontologies is not merely acknowledged but respected and embraced, and the workings of government reoriented, even if only moderately, to respect and address Indigenous spatialities and governance systems.

As this chapter has also shown, these intercultural capacities and competencies are poorly reflected in the standards that guide professional planning practice in Australia and Canada. These standards present a staid and depoliticized image of planning, one that assumes the spatial scales at which planners are required to think are uncontested and that fails to consider the plurality of ontological and epistemological perspectives. Perhaps most significantly, the accreditation standards are grounded in a belief that planners are the arbiter and mediator of disputes – an assumption that has been, and continues to be, a significant area of debate in planning theory. Although these arguments about the role of planners as both 'critical friends' (Forester 1999) and as agents of deeply oppressive power relations (Yiftachel 1998; Porter 2010; Huxley and Yiftachel 2000), are well rehearsed in the existing literature, they have particular resonance for planning in (post)colonial contexts. This book has shed new light on the system-transforming and systems-maintaining practices of the contact zones. All are at work in a constant dialectic of discursive and practical moves that settle, unsettle and resettle. While their actions are always contingent and just outcomes are never guaranteed, planners can and do play an important role in the struggle for coexistence – a role that needs to be more fully accounted for in both the institutionalized conceptions of the profession and in our theoretical tools for thinking how we practise planning. Thinking through this messy and challenging work of situated engagement as an essential element of any attempt to conceptualize decolonizing planning praxis is our focus in the next and final chapter.

Chapter 12
Towards Coexistence: Rethinking Planning for Indigenous Justice

Introduction

Our aim in this work has been to look closely at what is happening, every day, in contemporary planning contact zones, with an explicit political and ethical interest in creating a decolonizing planning praxis. Our analysis has shown how planning is a site of both resistance and resurgent possibility – at the same time as it is the site of renewed tactics of dispossession. Across urban and environmental planning contexts and across different kinds of planning systems, the essential tension between Indigenous sovereignties and relationships with place, and settler-planning orders of property, certainty and an undifferentiated public interest becomes very clear. The four case studies and the comparative analysis we present in this book all speak to this underlying tension and its essential irreducibility via the dominant modes of recognition currently employed by settler states to manage the unsettling nature of Indigenous claims.

Throughout the book, we have called for a critical appreciation of the liberal politics of recognition when that politics meets planning systems. Where Indigenous people are recognized but in doing so made subject to governmentalities and logics that serve existing orders, then those forms of recognition should be called as they are: regressive, dispossessory, the antithesis of justice and the mutually respectful coexistence that is urgently being demanded. Creating a decolonizing planning praxis demands a different trajectory.

Part of that project of decolonization directly concerns Indigenous cultural resurgence, and is why we have listened closely to the vitally important assertions from Indigenous leaders, activists, scholars and communities in Canada, Australia and beyond. We listen carefully to teachers and leaders like Alfred (1999), Alfred and Corntassel (2005), and Simpson (2014) who ground decolonization in the loving, relational traditions and values of their own cultures, to learn and to have our own presumptions, norms and narratives challenged and turned inside out. Being turned inside out, constantly in discomfort or anxious disquiet, out of our depth – these are the properties of learning required in the process of decolonizing ourselves, as Paulette Regan (2011) also teaches us.

As white scholars, it is not our place to speak about Indigenous resurgence and empowerment. While we hope that this book's stories about struggle and frustration will be useful and informative for Indigenous peoples facing prolonged engagements with Western planning systems in pursuit of their self-determining rights, that is not our purpose, nor should it be. Yet, as it is for other non-Indigenous people who seek to stand beside Indigenous people in solidarity with their struggle, it is our responsibility and our role to learn from their teachings, to listen with quiet joy within our disquieted hearts and learn what responsibilities these teachings demand that we bring to our own field, our own domain.

And so it is with that purpose in mind that we approach concluding this work, bringing what we have learned from those voices clearly and urgently to the domain of our own practice and interest. As Alfred teaches, Indigenous resurgence is a relational dynamic: 'When I speak of restitution, I am speaking of restoring ourselves as peoples, our spiritual power, dignity and the economic bases for our autonomy' (2011, 182–3). We all have to take up our responsibility in this quest. It is our responsibility, then, to ask, What are the necessary conditions for a just relationship between settler societies and Indigenous peoples as they manifest in planning to support this restitution? Our purpose is to find ways to reshape planning contact zones that carefully attend to the persistent power of white privilege; provide space for the transformative agency of Indigenous peoples and resist the reformulation of systems in the interests of renewed settler domination.

Such terms are immensely challenging for planning theory and practice. Yet they are both urgent and important, as this book has shown, in demonstrating the importance that strategic land-use planning represents to the politics of Indigenous recognition and land justice in contemporary settler states. There is a momentum in scholarship and in practice around how to conceive of 'better' outcomes and processes for Indigenous people in relation to land-use planning. Yet much of that thinking has, so far, been unable to shift existing relations of power – it simply 'layers on' Indigenous perspectives into a dominant system and then rather furiously polices the boundaries to ensure that those perspectives cannot disrupt fundamental tenets of planning such as certainty, public interest or property rights. Mutual recognition towards a situation of decolonizing coexistence requires much more than a simple tweaking of process or greater inclusion, through collaborative processes, of Indigenous viewpoints. It demands considerable theoretical and practical deconstruction of how planning sees its own relationship with place and space, and the structures of property rights and governance that make that relationship operational.

Sitting as it does alongside the more practical lessons we outlined in Chapter 11, this second concluding chapter provides a more conceptual conclusion. Here, we take the theoretical insights from critical Indigenous studies and social theory that we outlined in Chapters 1 and 2, alongside the lessons we have learned from the case studies and analysis presented in this book, and ask what these insights demand of us so that we can reimagine a decolonizing planning geared toward what we outlined in Chapter 1 as a normative politics of coexistence. We imagine a mutual, respectful coexistence conceived through negotiation between Indigenous and Western perspectives in which each has equal weight, and neither is positioned as dominant. That negotiation would involve the co-constitution of the political, spatial and material boundaries of the contact zone, and how they are mediated and operationalized. We are mindful that the 'principles of toleration, recognition, and self-determination can guide, but never displace, the formation and exercise of political power' (Williams 2014, 17) and that therefore any framework must remain committed to a 'critical analysis of the relationship between normative principles and structures of power' (ibid.). The next section begins that work by reframing our discussions across the book as demands for a politics of coexistence.

The Demands of a Politics of Coexistence

In Chapters 1 and 2, we aired difficult, uncomfortable challenges that Indigenous voices are mounting to the liberal politics of recognition. Across the rest of the book we showed how land-use planning systems and practitioners are often (though not necessarily always) key actors in the operationalization of that mode of recognition, by practising boundary maintenance, spatial fixity, depoliticization, idealized consensus building and an inclusionary politics stripped of its attention to deep and persistent colonial relations of power and dispossession. The stories we have presented show how tremendously costly these monological forms of recognition are for Indigenous peoples. We also showed the possibilities of more transformative action, with the agency of Indigenous and non-Indigenous actors unsettling those forms of recognition and demanding more. How, then, should we understand and respond to this complex situation? In this section we articulate the key demands for coexistence that crystallize from our reading of critical Indigenous scholarship and the voices of the Indigenous participants in this research.

It is a clear and indisputable fact that settler-colonial states are not, and cannot be seen to be, neutral facilitators of an inclusionary politics of difference in (post) colonial contexts (if, indeed, anywhere else). Instead, just as critical Indigenous scholarship and postcolonial theory teaches us to see, states have a position in, and must be seen as active agents of, the persistent (post)colonial processes of violence, dispossession, marginalization and domination. It should be obvious then, that to settle the essential tension that exists in settler-colonial states between underlying Indigenous sovereignties, and imposed Western orders *through the mechanisms and lenses of those imposed Western orders* is immediately problematic. Conjuring a monological politics of recognition (as Tully identifies it) that cunningly reconstitutes the authority and dominance of colonial orders (as Alfred, Coulthard, I. Watson and Moreton-Robinson show) by seductively enrolling Indigenes to perform their difference in ways that are recognizable, safe and amenable to celebration (as Povinelli explains) comes at profound cost (as Spivak teaches us). Learning from the identification of this key problematic, and really understanding the unacceptable nature of that cost for Indigenous peoples is what the politics of coexistence demands of planning scholarship and practice.

A first lesson to be drawn, then, is about the location of counter-hegemonic agency. For it is clear that such agency must arise from the lifeworlds, laws and teachings of Indigenous people themselves. As Fanon reminds us, the wellspring of liberation is in the *transformative praxis* (1967) of colonized peoples. As colonizers sitting within constructed systems of colonial domination and authority, we must look toward Indigenous law, culture and ontologies for our essential teachings about how to proceed. Let us be clear about a critical difference: this is learning from, not co-opting or appropriating. Learning from so that we, too, can be part of the untying of colonial forms of domination. A relational ethic of learning from the peoples for whom the cost of monological recognition is greatest is profoundly important.

This role as learners, then, signals a break with anti-colonial thinkers like Fanon on the question of the role of the colonizing state and colonizer subject-positions. While we agree that settler-states are conditioned with inherent tendencies toward resettling colonial authority and relations of domination, neither can they be accurately conceived of as monolithic, uncomplicated or ultimately hegemonic. Nor is it to say there is no agency or counter-hegemonic possibility among non-Indigenous planning agents. As the shifting scales and dynamics of analysis presented in this book has endeavoured to show, there are *always* contingent and alternative possibilities, moments when things might be different, even while they often remain unrealized. As a tradition of critical planning also teaches us, counter-hegemonic practices can occur within and against the state without necessarily seeking to smash the state (see, for example, Sandercock 1998a). The four stories in this book very precisely charted the vital lines of connection with state-based resources, systems of control and authority as intrinsically important to the possibilities of resurgent Indigenous law and culture.

Considering the trajectory and relationship of texts toward practice, where both are agents of planning activity, as neither predetermined nor determining also reminds us of this important point. While texts, as we have shown in this book, act as powerful mediators of planning contact zones, they also exist as a strategic resource, differently deployed in the struggle over coexistence and recognition. Texts simultaneously hold open the possibility for and constrain the conception of different kinds of relationship between Indigenous and state-based planning agencies. Sometimes, the very text that has constrained the recognition of an Indigenous authority over land becomes a strategic resource, providing powerful ways for Indigenous people to articulate their demands for recognition and to contest or reframe both the processes and outcomes of planning. Texts are, therefore, involved in the exercise of *power over* the contact zone and in assembling the *power to* struggle for coexistence. A key contribution of this work, to which we spoke directly in Chapters 9 and 11, is toward the more hopeful practice of seizing openings and alternatives within existing systems, and making space for counter-hegemonic practices and options that might sow the seeds of more systemic transformation.

A second lesson to be drawn is that a more relational, mutual politics of coexistence is not impossible and offers enormous transformative potential. Taking the normative politics of coexistence seriously means finding ways to respectfully work within and between overlapping, coexisting jurisdictions of authority, and fostering the existence of plural ontologies and epistemologies. It demands listening to how Indigenous ontologies and sovereignties are best served and, then, holding the actions of state-based planning to account. Some of the seeds of these orientations are present already, even if only fleeting and fragile, in the arts of the contact zone. Many of the stories presented here show how productive the tension between coexisting jurisdictions of authority can be when there is respectful attention and care paid to that coexistence. Alternative actions can be pursued, new relationships are forged, different temporalities and spatialities helpfully unsettle old methods and assumptions. As we set out in Chapter 11, none of these are possible without building the capacity of non-Indigenous planning professionals, the profession generally and the systems within which they work.

Yet while we have seen that there is room for transformation, this book has also highlighted how difficult it is to change and challenge historically constituted relations of power when these establish spatial, political and material boundaries constrain the contact zone. Planning contact zones are, in the main, profoundly mediated by state-based systems of planning and state-based systems of recognition that have not in any way changed or shifted the parameters within which 'planning' and 'recognition' is conceived and performed. What, then, must change, and how? What might a mutually constituted contact zone look like? It perhaps should go without saying that there are no universal or standard prescriptions that can, or indeed should, be made about the contours, orientation and methods that might work towards this more radical, relational and political contact zone. The very notion of a 'relational' contact zone must reject outright any formula or prescription as completely anathema to its philosophical and ethical orientations. What can be developed are some analytical, ethical and philosophical orientations for developing conceptual positions, practices and interventions that are counter-hegemonic, agonistic and decolonizing. Using agonistic pluralism as a core framework, the next four sections sketch out four different threads in this complex web of decolonizing praxis: the centrality and vitality of conflict and forgiveness; a reimagination of communicative ethics; the essential but discomforting process of 'flipping the table' of recognition; and, finally, an orientation toward the outcome of Indigenous justice and self-determination.

Performing the Delicate Dance of Conflict and Forgiveness

The phrase 'planning is political' is an important reminder of just how far we have come in the field from the days when planning was largely considered a technical exercise done by experts. Yet there is a danger that it has become so overused, and in such common-sense and normalized ways, that it is evacuated of any meaning or actual *politics*. Responding to that danger, we are inspired by a rich seam of thinking in planning and geography, taking Chantal Mouffe's (2000) idea of agonistic pluralism to help reformulate just how planning is political in the contact zone, and what kinds of politics should be cherished and cultivated. Agonism, perhaps best defined as a domestication of antagonism (Hillier 2003, 42), respects conflict and identifies the incommensurable plurality of values existing in reality as the heart of politics and a lively democratic ethos. For those reasons, agonism presents enormous possibilities for reimagining planning in the light of these demands for a politics of coexistence.

Central to Mouffe's conceptualization of agonism is the inevitability of conflict at the heart of political decision making. Mouffe rejects, quite explicitly, the building of democratic theory on the 'belief [in] the inner goodness and original innocence of human beings' (2005, 2–3). This, she says, has for too long been asserted as the cornerstone of a viable democratic society when it is in fact nonsense. Instead, she wants to 'elaborate the democratic project on an anthropology which acknowledges the ambivalent character of human sociability and the fact that reciprocity and hostility cannot be dissociated' (Mouffe 2005, 3).

Antagonism, struggle, hostility – these are part of our human sociality and cannot be denied – they are 'the political' (Mouffe 2005, 9). Instead of pushing them out of sight, ignoring and disavowing the political, an alternative could be to design a 'public sphere of contestation where different hegemonic political projects can be confronted' (Mouffe 2005, 3). Judith Butler also sees this productive conflict as the heart of a lively democratic ethos when she eschews the 'synthesis' of conflicts and seeks 'a *mode of sustaining conflict in politically productive ways*, a practice of contestation that demands that these movements articulate their goals under the pressure of each other without therefore actually becoming each other [emphasis in original]' (Butler 1998, 37).

Agonism, then, potentially provides a more helpful way to conceive of struggles that are rooted in different identity positions, where conflicting interpretations of history, reality and the future are being performed. The political – the conflict and antagonism that is never far from the surface in the human social condition – is something to be harnessed: passions to be mobilized rather than risks to be tamed and problems to be regulated away.

The four stories told in this book highlight just how central and important conflict is to the practices and realities of the contact zone. Each case exhibits a range of types of conflict, from overt and direct confrontation to simmering discontent and dissatisfaction. Conflict is as inherent to the more positive and productive outcomes in these cases as it is to those in which the battles have been harder and longer and whose outcomes are less than satisfactory from the perspective of Indigenous justice. Moreover, any of the agreements or brief moments of consensus that have been arrived at in any of these four cases is not so much fleeting (though that may be true also), as always open to future disagreement and contest. We interpret the centrality of conflict in these stories of planning contact zones to be emblematic of the political contest at the heart of this field of practice and the reason why an agonistic approach to planning in the contact zone heralds such possibilities.

What we find, however, is that there is much more to conflict than simply the raw rub of incipient discontent, or the outright disagreement over terms and possibilities, or reactions of anger at yet another example of incontrovertible injustice. For all of our stories also provide ample evidence of the role of forgiveness and tolerance in the face of – indeed right in the thick of – those very same moments of conflict. And here we are referring specifically to the willingness of Indigenous parties to planning processes to accommodate, respect and tolerate what amount to often grave incursions on and the abrogation of the rights, interests and laws of those nations. Our findings in this regard resonate deeply with research in many other and very different contexts, where conflict is not only present but a core part of the story of breaking new ground, challenging assumptions and stereotypes, and changing long-standing norms and practices. While conflict, forgiveness and tolerance have not been identified quite so overtly as core practices in the contact zone, they are clearly an important dimension.

Reimagining Communicative Ethics as a Core Practice of Planning for Coexistence

How, then, to proceed in this context of incommensurability, conflict and discomfort? What practices are possible? Many years ago, John Forester implored planning practice and scholarship to 'not leave pain at the door' but to allow passion, unease, pain and sorrow to move and inform decision making. Many others have contributed to this widening of planning practice, rethinking the contours of planning action to encompass story, film, narrative and the hopeful politics of love (Sandercock and Attili 2010; Sandercock 1998a; *Finding Our Way* 2010; Eckstein 2003; Beauregard 2003; Porter et al. 2012; Porter 2010, see Chapter 7).

In an insightful paper theorizing at the interface of Habermasian and Mouffeian thinking, Sophie Bond (2011) takes this invocation and deepens a conceptual framing for planning action. Drawing from Seyla Benhabib and Iris Marion-Young's recasting of deliberative democracy, Bond argues that potentially conflicting differences in values and identity must be the starting point of any deliberative process. In that sense, she is keen (as Hillier was earlier) 'not to throw the Habermasian baby out with the bathwater' (2003, 38). Both scholars argue that a choice between Habermasian and Mouffeian approaches would be a false one; there are trajectories in each that can help shape our field in progressive and socially just ways.

To this end, Bond argues for adoption of a Mouffian ontology, one that is rooted in the political, where radical contingency and the ineradicability of conflict are central but rely on a 'recast communicative approach' (2011, 163) to provide the normative framework for actually making decisions. Framed in this way, the political is also an essentially communicative domain. The most sensible way we have to proceed within a context of incommensurability and conflict is to talk and listen – to learn and through learning 'come to terms' through a deliberative process.

In each of the cases we have discussed in this book, people talked, listened and learned together. Indigenous peoples in each of these cases have placed enormous emphasis – drawing on their cultures and traditions – on this process of talking, listening and learning. Much of this talking was one sided, with one side's voice was louder and more powerful than the other. And much of the talk was neither heard nor listened to, or when it was heard it was misrecognized as something else. Nonetheless, there was also willingness and courage to argue, fall out, and meet again to try to reframe, reposition and come to an agreement.

This communicative process was at its weakest and most vulnerable, in terms of the demands of coexistence, when the privilege of the planning system went unremarked and unquestioned by non-Indigenous planning agents. In situations where Indigenous people were invited to the table, but only as a specific culture inserted into a standard process, misrecognition, thin listening and regressive outcomes resulted. When there was a more careful attentiveness to the lifeworlds, sovereignty, law and planning intelligence Indigenous people expressed, different opportunities began to unfold.

These stories have much to teach us, then, about a communicative ethics fit for the agonistic coexistence of Indigenous peoples and planning systems. Indigenous peoples are planning agents in their own right. What this means is that the process, content, direction and ratification of land-use planning must be the subject of co-constituted negotiation and agreement. This must include the following: what the planning table and its negotiations will look like, over what time frame and according to what terms; the agenda of the plan, its shape, content, direction and purpose; the processes for agreement and ratification; the decisions about who is a stakeholder and who is not, and on what terms each stakeholder comes to the table; and the types of knowledge and information that will be used, when, by whom and for what ends. This reimagined communicative moment is at the same time the site of figuring out the terms and contours of relational coexistence.

Flipping the Table:[1] Relational Politics and the Co-constitution of Political, Spatial and Object Boundaries

While our own conclusions are influenced and inspired by critical planning scholars such as Sandercock and Forester in their quite differently articulated calls for more deliberative, accountable, reflexive, political and justice-oriented actions for planning, this is where we break substantively. Much of that debate has been couched in an inclusionary politics of difference and voice, envisaging that 'a culturally pluralist democracy needs to practise a politics of inclusion by providing mechanisms for the effective recognition and representation of the distinct voices and perspectives of oppressed and disadvantaged groups' (Sandercock 1998a, 198). As we have seen in this book, such a politics of inclusion and recognition does not sufficiently unsettle and deprivilege the norms and authorities of settler-colonial positions. As we flagged in Chapter 2, participation and inclusion are the

---

1   Paraphrased, with inspiration from Leanne Simpson 2014, 17.

most cunningly seductive moments in planning, tending to produce monological forms of recognition.

Again, we look to a Mouffian ontology for a way out of this problematic. Mouffe contends that an agonistic politics shifts the stakes in any conflict, changing fundamentally what the struggle is actually *about*. As we have shown, the contemporary politics of monological recognition is of Indigenous Others struggling 'for' recognition and celebration of their difference from settler-states. Agonistic politics shifts that dynamic by reframing the terms of recognition. Indigenous claims are not requests for inclusion; they are expressions of self-determining sovereignty. The mode of deliberation itself, then, must be made subject to those same demands. The struggle then becomes about 'the very configuration of power relations around which a given society is structured' (Mouffe 2005, 21). This has a potentially transformative effect on the 'sides' that take up their positions in any struggle, and the terms over which that struggle plays out. Instead of an antagonistic relation, agonism is a 'relation where the conflicting parties, although acknowledging that there is no rational solution to their conflict, nevertheless recognize the legitimacy of their opponents. They are "adversaries", not enemies' (Mouffe 2005, 21).

The tables must be flipped. The spatial boundaries assumed by settler planning to be static and normal would be suspended, made subject to negotiation. Indigenous spatialities would be carefully taught and expressed. The coexisting and overlapping nature of these spatial ontologies would be visualized, drawn and sung in a process of mutual learning to decide the terms of negotiating across those boundaries. The political authority of settler planning would also be suspended and subject to negotiation, no longer the final arbiter on land-use disputes; the political authority of Indigenous peoples would be afforded parity. There would be no presumed process for decision making, but instead a negotiation about what the right decision rules might be in any given context. Decisions would involve the presence of country, of ancestor spirits, of the non-humans relationally involved in caring for place as much as they would statistics, projections and regulations. All of the dimensions of that caring and responsibility would be present and negotiated. Culture would be appreciated as the world view through which all of the different ontologies are lived and known. Planning would offer its cultural view as willingly as Indigenous people would offer their world view. This brief sketch of a relational politics of coexistence would suspend existing boundaries and make them subject to negotiation and co-constitution.

As the stories and analysis in this book attest, the possibility of agonistic dissent is always present. Those negotiations will not always result in easy agreements. It will not always be possible to reconcile competing jurisdictions and claims. The struggle is a constant one, particularly as we have noted because the broader structures of power and dominance and the ways they are made manifest and reconstituted through settler-colonial state practices cannot be transcended. The tendencies of domination and co-optation are inherent to the settler-Indigenous tension. There is no permanent fix, then, only contested relationships that must be durable enough to survive countless rounds of negotiation.

Being Alive to the Costs of Recognition: Planning with and for Indigenous Justice

For those struggling against hegemonic and dominant interests, those who are asserting voices long marginalized, or peoples oppressed, there is never a moment when any wins or gains signal the end of the need for struggle. All 'wins' are vulnerable, and any victory produces its own new dogmas and potential hegemonic practices (Spivak 1993). This brings us to the final but critical point in this rethinking of planning outside of the cunning fantasy of monological recognition. We find ourselves back at the question of plural ontologies and values. Values conflict because of the differences between them, differences that arise from the identities and social realities of the people expressing those values. In other words, they are not matters of rationality, but matters of identity and historical contingency – demanding a respectful learning from plural ontologies. Not all values are equal, or equally recognized, nor do we propose that all values are politically and morally acceptable. The elephant in the room is how to assess the content of values and determine who should do that assessing. If everybody has the right to be in the domain of the political, in agonistic conflict with other lifeways and values, then what do we do when faced with values that assert regressive, oppressive or environmentally and socially unjust positions?

Mouffe (2005) again offers a way forward, suggesting that we can and should distinguish progressive politics by analyzing *for whom hegemonic orders are articulated, in whose service they work and to what ends.* Are those hegemonic orders working in the interests of the powerful, or the interests of those marginalized in social relations of power? Taking this into planning thinking, Bond (2011) asserts that the point is to be alert to logics and orders that normalize assumptions about what should be done, by whom and to what ends. These are precisely the contours of monological recognition the relational politics of coexistence we are trying to chart here must carefully subvert.

Hegemony must therefore be the central focus of critical planning inquiry – any hegemonic practice (including counter-hegemonic practice, following Gramsci [1971]) contains exclusions and marginalizations. Such practices must always be questioned, not because they are 'wrong' and there exists something better or purer, but because certain rationalities become dogmatic and hegemonic. They become unquestioned practices, norms that universalize and constrain. These hegemonic practices are never far from the horizon of any deliberative, collaborative or agonistic practice – not in planning, nor anywhere else. This is why conflict and struggle is the dynamic that keeps us alert to the possibilities of hegemonic repression.

A more relational, just and radical mode of recognition should, then, take very seriously the notion of hegemony. There is no possibility of transcending power

(Laclau and Mouffe 2001), because power works as hegemony (such as through the manufacture of consent) and does so in productive as well as repressive ways, as Foucault teaches us (1988a, 1980). The task is to expose the mechanisms and workings of power and hegemony and not fall for the conceit of consensus, simplistic participation and the reification of white power.

Seeing the relational ways by which planning and Indigenous peoples interactively negotiate and renegotiate the terms of recognition enables attention to both the operations of colonial relations of power – the hegemonic tendencies of planning practice, especially when it is in its 'stakeholder inclusion' mode – as well as the possibilities for progressive transformation. Where there is hegemonic practice, there is always the possibility for things to be different. What the stories and concepts presented in this book teach us is to be awake to the possibilities of counter-hegemonic practices not just emerging but becoming transformative. The political dimension will always remain, heralding the vitality of conflict to any social field and its inherent hopeful possibility.

Relational, decolonizing, agonistic modes of recognition are possible and vital. An agonistic democratic approach offers the possibility of recognizing the demand for self-determination and sovereignty that Indigenous claims make. For one thing is quite clear: the source of liberation, of decolonization, does not come from the patriarchal benevolence of colonizers bestowing and granting rights and protections. 'The political' in planning contact zones might best be seen as a right – the right to express an identity position potentially at odds with dominant, mainstream perspectives on the proper relationship of humans with land, and who gets to say. An agonistic approach urges a spirit of reciprocity – *everyone* recognizing their historically constituted positions, their Otherness, their right to be incommensurably different and for that difference to matter to the deliberations. These core lessons, ethics that *all* of us in the planning field – scholars, students, communities, practitioners, analysts, decision makers and policy designers – will have to learn and relearn countless times, will be the beating heart of our efforts toward the decolonization of planning.

References

Aboriginal Affairs and Northern Development Canada. 2012. *'First Nations Commercial and Industrial Development Act'*. *Aboriginal Lands and Economic Development*. https://www.aadnc-aandc.gc.ca/eng/1100100033561/11001000 33562.

Agyeman, Julian, and Jennifer Erickson. 2012. 'Culture, Recognition, and the Negotiation of Difference: Some Thoughts on Cultural Competency in Planning Education'. *Journal of Planning Education and Research* 32 (3): 358–66.

Alfred, Taiaiake. 2011. 'Restitution Is the Real Pathway to Justice for Indigenous Peoples'. In *Response, Responsibility and Renewal: Canada's Truth and Reconciliation Journey*, edited by Greg Younging, Jonathon Dewar and Mike De Gagné, 179–90. Ottawa: Aboriginal Healing Foundation. http://www.ahf.ca/downloads/trc2.pdf.

Alfred, Taiaiake. 1999. *Peace, Power, Righteousness: An Indigenous Manifesto*. Don Mills, ON: Oxford University Press.

———. 2001. 'Deconstructing the British Columbia Treaty Process'. *Balayi: Culture, Law and Colonialism* 3: 37–65.

Alfred, Taiaiake, and Jeff Corntassel. 2005. 'Being Indigenous: Resurgences against Contemporary Colonialism'. *Government and Opposition* 40 (4): 597–614.

Allmendinger, Phil, and Graham Haughton. 2012. 'Post-Political Spatial Planning in England: A Crisis of Consensus?' *Transactions of the Institute of British Geographers* 37 (1): 89–103.

Altman, J. & Markham, F., 2015. Burgeoning Indigenous land ownership: Diverse values and strategic potentialities. In *From Mabo to Akibo: A vehicle for change and empowerment?*, edited by Sean Brennan, Megan Davis, Brendan Edgeworth and Leon Terrill. Sydney: The Federation Press.

Atkinson, Wayne. 2002. 'Mediating the Mindset of Opposition: The Yorta Yorta Case'. *Indigenous Law Bulletin* 5 (15): 8–11.

Barry, Janice. 2011. 'Building Collaborative Institutions for Government-to-Government Planning: The Nanwakolas Council's Involvement in Central Coast Land and Resource Management Planning' (PhD diss., University of British Columbia).

Barry, Janice, and Libby Porter. 2012. 'Indigenous Recognition in State-Based Planning Systems: Understanding Textual Mediation in the Contact Zone'. *Planning Theory* 11 (2): 170–87.

Barwick, Diane. 1988. 'Aborigines of Victoria'. In *Being Black: Aboriginal Cultures in "Settled" Australia*, edited by Ian Keen, 27–32. Canberra: Aboriginal Studies Press.

Bauman, Toni, Smith, Sally, Lenffer, Anoushka, Kelly, Tony, Carter, Rodney & Harding, Mick, 2014. 'Traditional Owner agreement-making in Victoria: The Right People for Country Program'. *Australian Indigenous Law Review* 18(1):78–98.

BC Integrated Land Management Bureau. 2006. *A New Direction for Strategic Land Use Planning in BC*. https://www.for.gov.bc.ca/tasb/slrp/policies-guides/new%20direction%20synopsis.pdf.

———. 2007. *New Direction for Strategic Land Use Planning in BC: Initiating Planning Projects and Developing a Business Case: Policies and Procedures.* https://www.for.gov.bc.ca/tasb/slrp/policies-guides/Approved_Project_Initiation_and_Business_Case_Policy_Dec_11_07.pdf.

BC Treaty Commission. 2003. *'Where Are We': BC Treaty Commission Annual Report 2003.* http://www.bctreaty.net/files/pdf_documents/2003 Annual Report.pdf.

———. 2009. 'Stage 1 Criteria'. *Six Stages: Policy and Procedures.* http://www. bctreaty.net/files/sixstages-2.php.

———. 2010. 'Sparrow case moved BC Government to negotiate Treaties'. BC Treaty Commission press release, 31 May 2010. http://www.bctreaty. net/files/pdf_documents/newsrelease_sparrow-case-moved-bc-gov-to-nego tiate.pdf.

Beauregard, Robert. 2003. 'Democracy, Storytelling and the Sustainable City'. In *Story and Sustainability: Planning, Practice and Possibility for American Cities*, edited by Barbara Eckstein and James A. Throgmorton, 65–77. Cambridge, MA: MIT Press.

Beebeejaun, Yasminah. 2004. 'What's in a Nation? Constructing Ethnicity in the British Planning System'. *Planning, Theory and Practice* 5 (4): 437–51.

Berke, P.R., N. Ericksen, J. Crawford and J. Dixon. 2002. 'Planning and Indigenous People: Human Rights and Environmental Protection in New Zealand'. *Journal of Planning Education and Research* 22: 115–34.

Bhabha, Homi K. 1994. *The Location of Culture*. London: Routledge.

Bohman, James. 1999. 'Practical Reason and Cultural Constraint: Agency in Bourdieu's Theory of Practice'. In *Bourdieu: A Critical Reader*, edited by Richard Shusterman, 129–52. Oxford: Blackwell.

Bond, Sophie. 2011. 'Negotiating a "Democratic Ethos": Moving beyond the Agonistic-Communicative Divide'. *Planning Theory* 10 (2): 161–86.

Borrini-Feyeraband, Grazia, Ashish Kothari and Gonzalo Oviedo. 2004. *Indigenous and Local Communities and Protected Areas: Towards equity and enhanced conservation*, Gland: International Union for Conservation of Nature (IUCN), available at https://cmsdata.iucn.org/downloads/pag_011.pdf.

Bourdieu, Pierre. 1977. *Outline of a Theory of Practice*. Cambridge: Cambridge University Press.

Boyce, James. 2011. *1835: The Founding of Melbourne and the Conquest of Australia*. Collingwood: Black Inc. Books.

Brennan, Sean. 2011. 'Statutory Interpretation and Indigenous Property Rights'. UNSW Faculty of Law Research Paper No. 2011-19.

British Columbia. 2005. *The New Relationship*. http://www2.gov.bc.ca/assets/gov/zzzz-to-be-moved/9efbd86da302a0712e6559bdb2c7f9dd/9efbd86da302a0712e6559bdb2c7f9dd/agreements/new_relationship_accord.pdf.

Brownhill, Sue, and Juliet Carpenter. 2007. 'Increasing Participation in Planning: Emergent Experiences of the Reformed Planning System in England'. *Planning, Practice and Research* 22 (4): 619–34.

Burayidi, M. 2003. 'The Multicultural City as Planners' Enigma'. *Planning Theory & Practice* 4 (3): 259–73.

Butler, Judith. 1998. 'Merely Cultural'. *New Left Review* I/227 (52/53): 33–44.

———. 1999. 'Performativity's Social Magic'. In *Bourdieu: A Critical Reader*, edited by Richard Shusterman. Oxford: Blackwell.

———. 2010. 'Performative Agency'. *Journal of Cultural Economy* 3 (2): 147–61.

Butler, Judith, and Athena Athanasiou. 2013. *Dispossession: The Performative in the Political*. Cambridge: Polity Press.

Campbell, Marie, and Frances Mary Gregor. 2002. *Mapping Social Relations: A Primer in Doing Institutional Ethnography*. Toronto, ON: University of Toronto Press.

Canadian Institute of Planners. 2015. 'CIP Code of Professional Conduct' *Becoming a Planner*. https://www.cip-icu.ca/Becoming-a-Planner/Codes-of-Professional-Conduct/CIP-Code-of-Professional-Conduct#.

Cardinal, Nathan. 2006. 'The Exclusive City: Identifying, Measuring and Drawing Attention to Aboriginal and Indigenous Experiences in an Urban Context'. *Cities* 23 (3): 217–28.

Cavanagh, Edward, and Lorenzo Veracini. 2013. 'Editors Statement'. *Settler Colonial Studies* 3 (1): 1.

Chouliaraki, Lilie, and Norman Fairclough. 1999. *Discourse in Late Modernity: Rethinking Critical Discourse Analysis*. Edinburgh: Edinburgh University Press.

Christophers, Brett. 2014. 'From Marx to Market and Back Again: Performing the Economy'. *Geoforum* 57: 12–20.

Clark, Ian. 1998. '"That's My Country Belonging to Me": Aboriginal Land Tenure and Dispossession in Nineteenth Century Western Victoria'. Beaconsfield: Heritage Matters.

Clark, Ian D. 1995. Map of Massacre Sites in Western Victoria. Canberra: Australian Institute of Aboriginal and Torres Strait Islander Studies (AIATSIS).

Coates, Ken. 2008. 'The Indian Act and the Future of Aboriginal Governance in Canada', National Centre for First Nation Governance, Research Paper, May. http://fngovernance.org/ncfng_research/coates.pdf.

Corntassel, Jeff. 2012. 'Re-Envisioning Resurgence: Indigenous Pathways to Decolonization and Sustainable Self-Determination'. *Decolonization: Indigeneity, Education, & Society* 1 (1): 86–101.

Coulthard, Glen S. 2007. 'Subjects of Empire: Indigenous Peoples and the "Politics of Recognition" in Canada'. *Contemporary Political Theory* 6 (4): 437–60.

———. 2014. *Red Skin, White Masks*. Minneapolis: University of Minnesota Press.

Dale, Norman. 1999. 'Cross-Cultural Community-Based Planning: Negotiating the Future of Haida Gwaii (British Columbia)'. In *The Consensus Building Handbook: A Comprehensive Guide to Reaching Agreement*, edited by Lawrence E. Susskind, Sarah McKearnen and Jennifer Thomas-Lamar, 923–50. Thousand Oaks, CA: SAGE.

District of North Vancouver. 2009. 'Launch Event: Our Places.' Summary Report, June 25, 2009. North Vancouver, BC.

———. 2011. 'Our Official Community Plan for a Sustainable Future'. North Vancouver, BC. https://www.dnv.org/property-and-development/our-official-community-plan-ocp.

Dodson, Mick. 1994. 'Towards the Existence of Indigenous Rights: Policy, Power and Self-Determination'. *Race and Class* 35 (4): 65–76.

———. 1996. 'Indigenous Peoples, Social Justice and Rights to the Environment'. In *Ecopolitics IX: Conference Papers and Resolutions*, edited by R. Sultan, P. Josif and C. Mackinolty. Darwin: Northern Territory University.

Dorries, Heather. 2012. 'Rejecting the "False Choice": Foregrounding Indigenous Sovereignty in Planning Theory and Practice' (PhD diss., University of Toronto).

Eckstein, Barbara. 2003. 'Making Space: Stories in the Practice of Planning'. In *Story and Sustainability: Planning, Practice, and Possibility for American Cities*, edited by Barbara Eckstein and James A Throgmorton, 13–36. Cambridge, MA: MIT Press.

Edmonds, Pauline. 2010. *Urbanizing Frontiers: Indigenous Peoples and Settlers in 19th Century Pacific Rim Cities*. Vancouver: University of British Columbia Press.

Fairclough, Isabela, and Norman Fairclough. 2012. *Political Discourse Analysis: A Method for Advanced Students*. Abingdon,UK: Routledge.

Fairclough, Norman. 1992. *Discourse and Social Change*. Bristol, UK: Polity Press.

———. 2003. *Analyzing Discourse: Textual Analysis for Social Science*. London: Routledge.

———. 2005. 'Critical Discourse Analysis'. *Marges Linguistiques* 9: 76–94.

Fairclough, Norman, Bob Jessop and Andrew Sayer. 2004. 'Critical Realism and Semiosis'. In *Realism, Discourse and Deconstruction*, edited by J. Joseph and J. Roberts, 23-42. London: Routledge.

Fanon, Frantz. 1967. *Black Skin, White Masks*. Translated by Charles Lam Markmann. St. Albans, UK: Paladin.

Fenster, Tovi. 2003. *The Global City and the Holy City: Narratives on Knowledge, Planning and Diversity*. Harlow, UK: Pearson Education.

Fincher, Ruth, and Kurt Iveson. 2008. *Planning for Diversity: Redistribution, Recognition and Encounter*. Basingstoke, UK: Palgrave Macmillan.

Finding Our Way. 2010. Documentary film. Directed by Leonie Sandercock and Giovanni Attili. Vancouver: Moving Images Distribution.

Fischer, Frank. 2003. *Reframing Public Policy: Discursive Politics and Deliberative Practices*. Oxford: Oxford University Press.

Forester, John. 1989. *Planning in the Face of Power*. Berkeley: University of California Press.

———. 1999. *The Deliberative Practitioner: Encouraging Participatory Planning Processes*. Cambridge, MA: MIT Press.

ForTech Consulting and Magellan Digital Mapping. 2007. *Gitanyow Road Liabilities Report*. Gitanyow Hereditary Chiefs Office, Unpublished document.

Foucault, Michel. 1980. *Power/Knowledge: Selected Interviews and Other Writings 1972–1977*. Edited by Colin Gordon. Brighton, UK: The Harvester Press.

———. 1984. 'Nietzsche, Genealogy, History.' In *The Foucault Reader*, edited by Paul Rabinow, 76–100. London: Penguin.

———. 1988a. 'On Power.' In *Michel Foucault: Politics, Philosophy, Culture: Interviews and Other Writings 1977–1984*, edited by L.D. Kritzman, 96–109. New York: Routledge.

———. 1988b. *The History of Sexuality: The Will to Knowledge*. London: Penguin.

Fraser, Nancy. 1995. 'From Redistribution to Recognition? Dilemmas of Justice in a "Post-Socialist" Age'. *New Left Review* I (212): 68–93.

———. 1997a. *Justice Interruptus: Critical Reflections on the "Postsocialist" Tradition*. New York: Routledge.

———. 1997b. 'A Rejoinder to Iris Young'. *New Left Review* I/223: 126–29.

———. 2000. 'Rethinking Recognition'. *New Left Review* 3: 107–20.

Fredericks, Bronwyn. 2013. '"We don't leave our identities at the city limits": Aboriginal and Torres Strait Islander people living in urban localities.' *Australian Aboriginal Studies* 1: 4-16.

Gitanyow Hereditary Chiefs. 2006. 'Building a New Relationship: Recognition, Reconciliation, Respect & the Gitanyow Huwilp'. In *BC's Northern Interior Forests: Planning for Sustainability in a Dynamic Landscape*. Prince George, BC: Forrex.

Gitanyow Hereditary Chiefs Office, BC Hydro, and Rescan. 2010. *Proposed Northwest Transmission Line Project: Hanna-Tintina Route Alternatives Evaluation Report*. Vancouver, BC: Prepared for BC Hydro by Gitanyow Hereditary Chiefs Office, BC Hydro and Rescan Environmental Services Ltd. July 2010.

Gitanyow Hereditary Chiefs and Government of British Columbia. 2012. *Gitanyow Huwilp Recognition and Reconciliation Agreement*. http://www.gitanyowchiefs.com/images/uploads/land-use-plans/Gitanyow-R-R-Agreement-2012.pdf.

Gitanyow Nation. 2009. *The Gitanyow Ayookxw: The Constitution of the Gitanyow Nation*. http://www.gitanyowchiefs.com/images/uploads/constitution/Gitanyow_Constitution_2009.pdf.

Gleeson, Brendan, and Nicholas Low. 2000. 'Revaluing Planning: Rolling Back Neo-Liberalism in Australia'. *Progress in Planning* 53 (2): 83–164.

Godlewska, Christina, and Jeremy Webber. 2007. 'The Calder Decision, Aboriginal Title, Treaties, and the Nisga'a'. In *Let Right Be Done: Aboriginal Title, the Calder Case, and the Future of Indigenous Rights*, edited by Hamar Foster, Heather Raven and Jeremy Webber, 1–33. Vancouver: University of British Columbia Press.

Gramsci, Antonio. 1971. *Selections from the Prison Notebooks*. Edited by and translated by Q. Hoare and G. Nowell-Smith. London: Lawrence and Wishart.

Haig-Brown, Celia, and Jo-Ann Archibald. 1996. 'Transforming First Nations Research with Respect and Power'. *International Journal of Qualitative Studies in Education* 9 (3): 245–67.

Hajer, Maarten. 1993. 'Discourse Coalitions and the Institutionalisation of Practice: The Case of Acid Rain in Great Britain'. In *The Argumentative Turn in Policy Analysis and Planning*. London: UCL Press.

———. 2003. 'Policy without Polity? Policy Analysis and the Institutional Void'. *Policy Sciences* 36: 175–95.

Harvey, David. 1996. *Justice, Nature and the Geography of Difference*. Oxford: Blackwell.

Harwood, Stacy Anne. 2005. 'Struggling to Embrace Difference in Land-Use Decision Making in Multicultural Communities'. *Planning Practice and Research* 20 (4): 355–71.

Healey, Patsy. 1997. *Collaborative Planning: Shaping Places in Fragmented Societies*. Hampshire: Macmillan Press.

———. 1998. 'Collaborative Planning in a Stakeholder Society'. *Town Planning Review* 69 (1): 1–21.

Hibbard, Michael, Marcus B. Lane and Kathleen Rasmussen. 2008. 'The Split Personality of Planning: Indigenous Peoples and Planning for Land and Resource Management'. *Journal of Planning Literature* 23 (2): 136–51.

Hillier, Jean. 2003. 'Agon'izing over Consensus: Why Habermasian Ideals Cannot Be "Real."' *Planning Theory* 2 (1): 37–59.

Hodge, Gerald, and David Gordon. 2013. *Planning Canadian Communities*, 6th ed. Scarborough, ON: Nelson Education.

Hooper, Barbara. 1992. '"Split at the Roots": A Critique of the Philosophical and Political Sources of Modern Planning Doctrine'. *Frontiers: A Journal of Women's Studies* XIII (1): 45–80.

Howitt, R., J. Connell, and P. Hirsch. 1996. 'Resources, Nations and Indigenous Peoples'. In *Resources, Nations and Indigenous Peoples: Case Studies from Australasia, Melanesia, and South East Asia*, edited by R. Howitt, J. Connell and P. Hirsch, 1–30. Melbourne: Oxford University Press.

Howitt, Richard, Kim Doohan, Sandie Suchet-Pearson, Sherrie Cross, Rebecca Lawrence, Gaim James Lunkapis, Samantha Muller, Sarah Prout and Siri Veland. 2013. 'Intercultural Capacity Deficits: Contested Geographies of Coexistence in Natural Resource Management'. *Asia Pacific Viewpoint* 54 (2): 126–40.

Howitt, Richard, Kim Doohan, Sandie Suchet-Pearson, Gaim Lunkapis, Samantha Muller, Rebecca Lawrence, Sarah Prout, Siri Veland and Sherrie Cross. 2013. 'Capacity Deficits at Cultural Interfaces of Land and Sea Governance'. In *Reclaiming Indigenous Planning*, edited by Ryan Walker, David Natcher and Ted Jojola, 313–38. Montreal: McGill-Queen's University Press.

Howitt, Richard, and Gaim James Lunkapis. 2010. 'Coexistence: Planning and the Challenge of Indigenous Rights'. In *The Ashgate Research Companion to Planning Theory: Conceptual Challenges for Spatial Planning*, edited by Jean Hillier and Patsy Healey. Farnham: Ashgate Publishing Ltd.

Howitt, Richard, and Sandra Suchet-Pearson. 2003. 'Ontological Pluralism in Contested Cultural Landscapes'. In *Handbook of Cultural Geography*, edited by Kay Anderson, Mona Domosh, Steve Pile and Nigel Thrift. London: SAGE.

Howitt, Richie. 2006. 'Scales of Coexistence: Tackling the Tension between Legal and Cultural Landscapes in Post-Mabo Australia'. *Macquarie Law Journal* 6: 49–64.

Huxley, Margo. 2000. 'The Limits to Communicative Planning'. *Journal of Planning Education and Research* 19: 369–77.

Huxley, Margo, and Oren Yiftachel. 2000. 'New Paradigm or Old Myopia? Unsettling the Communicative Turn in Planning Theory'. *Journal of Planning Education and Research* 19: 333–42.

Integrated Land Management Bureau and Gitanyow Hereditary Chiefs Office. 2005. *Nass South Sustainable Resource Management Plan (SRMP): Terms of Reference*. Unpublished document.

Imai, Shin, and Ashley Stacey. 2014. 'Municipalities and the Duty to Consult Aboriginal Peoples: A Case Comment on Neskonlith Indian Band v. Salmon Arm (City)'. *UBC Law Review* 47 (1): 293–312.

Indian and Northern Affairs Canada. 2003. 'Resolving Aboriginal Claims: A Practical Guide to Canadian Experience'. http://www.aadnc-aandc.gc.ca/eng/1 100100014174/1100100014179, last accessed 29 August 2015.

———. 2010. 'Fact Sheet: Treaty-Related Measures', November.

Innes, Judith, and David E. Booher. 2010. *Planning with Complexity: An Introduction to Collaborative Rationality for Public Policy*. Abingdon, UK: Routledge.

Innes, Judith E., and David E. Booher. 2004. 'Reframing Public Participation: Strategies for the 21st Century'. *Planning Theory & Practice* 5 (4): 419–36.

Jackson, Sue. 1997. 'A Disturbing Story: The Fiction of Rationality in Land Use Planning in Aboriginal Australia'. *Australian Planner* 34 (4): 221–26.

Jacobs, Jane M. 1996. *Edge of Empire: Postcolonialism and the City*. London: Routledge.

Jaireth, Hanna, and Dermot Smyth. 2003. 'Introduction and Overview'. In *Innovative Governance: Indigenous Peoples, Local Communities, and Protected Areas*, edited by Hanna Jarieth and Dermot Smyth, xi–xxxi. New Delhi: Ane Books.

Jentoft, Svein, Henry Minde and Ragnar Nilsen. 2003. *Indigenous Peoples: Resource Management and Global Rights*. Delft, Netherlands: Eburon.

Jojola, Ted. 2003. 'Notes on Identity, Time, Place and Space'. In *American Indian Thought: Philosophical Essays*, edited by Anne Waters, 89–96. Malden, Mass.: Wiley-Blackwell.

———. 2008. 'Indigenous Planning – An Emerging Context'. *Canadian Journal of Urban Research* 17 (1): 37.

Jojola, Theodore. 1998. 'Indigenous Planning: Clans, Intertribal Confederations, and the History of the All Indian Pueblo Council'. In *Making the Invisible Visible: A Multicultural Planning History*, edited by Leonie Sandercock. Berkeley: University of California Press.

Jones, Elizabeth R. 2007. 'Three Management Challenges for Protection of Aboriginal Cultural Heritage in a Tasmanian Multiple-Use Conservation Area'. *Australian Geographer* 38 (1): 93–112.

King, A.D. 1990. *Urbanism, Colonialism and the World Economy: Cultural and Spatial Foundations of the World Urban System*. London: Routledge.

Kovach, Margaret. 2009. *Indigenous Methodologies: Characteristics, Conversations, and Contexts*. Toronto, ON: University of Toronto Press.

Laclau, Ernesto, and Chantal Mouffe. 2001. *Hegemony and Socialist Strategy: Towards a Radical Democratic Politics*, 2nd ed. London: Verso.

Lane, Marcus B, and Michael Hibbard. 2005. 'Doing It for Themselves – Transformative Planning by Indigenous Peoples'. *Journal of Planning Education and Research* 25 (2): 172–84.

Lane, Marcus B., and Liana J, Williams. 2008. 'Color Blind: Indigenous Peoples and Regional Environmental Management'. *Journal of Planning Education and Research* 28: 38–49.

Lane, Marcus, and Stuart Cowell. 2001. 'Land and Resource Planning and Indigenous Interest: Reproducing or Transforming the Social Relations of Resource Use'. In *The Power of Planning: Spaces of Control and Transformation*, edited by Oren Yiftachel and Margo Huxley, 155–70. The Hague: Kluwer Academic Publishers.

Langton, Marcia. 2001. 'Dominion and dishonour : a treaty between our nations'. *Postcolonial Studies*, 4(1): 13–26.

———. 2002. 'The Edge of the Sacred, the Edge of Death: Sensual Inscriptions'. In *Inscribed Landscapes: Marking and Making Place*, edited by Bruno David and M. Wilson, 253–69. Honolulu: University of Hawai'i Press.

Lloyd-Smith, Jane. 2009. 'New Approaches: Gitanyow Experience'. Presentation to Skeena Salmon Habitat Conference. Smithers, BC. http://bvcentre.ca/files/Conferences/SkeenaSalmon/7-JaneLloyd-Smith.pdf.

Lovell, Terry. 2003. 'Resisting with Authority: Historical Specificity, Agency and the Performative Self'. *Theory, Culture and Society* 20 (1): 1–17.

Lower Mainland Treaty Advisory Committee. 2011. *LMTAC Discussion Paper: Local Government Issues and Interests on the First Nations Commercial and Industrial Development Act and the First Nations Certainty of Land Title Act*. http://www.surrey.ca/bylawsandcouncillibrary/CR_2011_R071.pdf.

Lukes, Steven. 1973. *Individualism*. Colchester, UK: ECPR Press.

MacCallum Fraser, Clara, and Leela Viswanathan. 2013. 'The Crown Duty to Consult and Ontario Municipal–First Nations Relations: Lessons Learned from the Red Hill Valley Parkway Project'. *Canadian Journal of Urban Research* 22 (1) (Supplement): 1–19.

Maclean, Kirsten, Catherine Robinson and David Natcher. 2014. 'Consensus Building or Constructive Conflict? Aboriginal Discursive Strategies to Enhance Participation in Natural Resource Management in Australia and Canada'. *Society and Natural Resources: An International Journal* 28 (2): 197-211.

Matunga, Hirini. 2013. 'Theorizing Indigenous Planning'. In *Reclaiming Indigenous Planning*, edited by Ryan Walker, Ted Jojola and David Natcher, 35–59. Montreal: McGill-Queen's University Press.

McGuirk, Pauline. 2001. 'Situating Communicative Planning Theory: Context, Power, and Knowledge'. *Environment and Planning* A 33: 195–217.

Metro Vancouver Aboriginal Relations Legal and Legislative Services. 2015. *Metro Vancouver Profile of First Nations*. Burnaby, BC. http://www. metrovancouver.org/services/first-nation-relations/AboriginalPublications/ ProfileOfFirstNations-2015.pdf.

Minister of Indian Affairs and Northern Development. 1987. 'Comprehensive Land Claims Policy.' Ottawa.

Ministry of Aboriginal Relations and Reconciliation. 2012. 'Agreement Creates New Opportunities for Gitanyow'. https://news.gov.bc.ca/stories/agreement-creates-new-opportunities-for-gitanyow.

Moreton-Robinson, Aileen. 2004. 'The Possessive Logic of Patriarchal White Sovereignty: The High Court and the Yorta Yorta Decision'. *Borderlands E-Journal* 3 (2).

Mouffe, Chantal. 2000. 'Deliberative Democracy or Agonistic Pluralism'. No. 72, Political Science Series. Vienna: Institute for Advanced Studies.

———. 2005. *On the Political*. Abingdon, UK: Routledge.

Mountjoy, Terry. 1999. 'Municipal Government Perspectives on Aboriginal Self-Government'. In *Aboriginal Self-Government in Canada: Current Trends and Issues*, edited by John Hylton, 2nd ed., 310–28. Saskatoon: Purich Publishing Ltd.

Murrundi Ruwe Pangari Ringbalin (River Country Spirit Ceremony): Aboriginal Perspectives on River Country. 2010. Documentary film. Directed by Eleanor Gilbert and Ben Pederick. Australia: Talkinjeri Dance Group, goodmorningbeautifulfilms and Enlightning Productions.

Murtagh, Brendan, Brian Graham and Peter Shirlow. 2008. 'Authenticity and Stakeholder Planning in the Segregated City'. *Progress in Planning* 69 (2): 41–92.

Nadasdy, Paul. 2003. *Hunters and Bureaucrats: Power, Knowledge, and Aboriginal-State Relations in the Southwest Yukon*. Vancouver: University of British Columbia Press.

Newman, Dwight G. 2009. *The Duty to Consult: New Relationships With Aboriginal Peoples*. Saskatoon: Purich Publishing Ltd.

Perlman, D., and J. Milder. 2005. *Practical Ecology for Planners, Developers, and Citizens*. Washington, DC: Island Press.

Peters, Evelyn. 1992. 'Self-Government for Aboriginal People in Urban Areas'. *The Canadian Journal of Native Studies* 12 (1): 51–74.

———. 2005. 'Indigeneity and Marginalisation: Planning for and with Urban Aboriginal Communities in Canada'. Special issue of *Progress in Planning* 63 (4).

———. 2006. '"[W]e Do Not Lose our Treaty Rights Outside the … Reserve": Challenging the Scales of Social Service Provision for First Nations Women in Canadian Cities'. *GeoJournal* 65 (4): 315–27.

Philpot Forestry Services. 2006. *Gitanyow Landscape Unit Plan*. https://www.for.gov.bc.ca/ftp/dss/external/!publish/Web/Gitanyow_LUP/Gitanyow%20LUP%20Draft%205%20030506%20(Final).doc

Pieris, Anoma. 2012. 'Occupying the Centre: Indigenous Presence in the Australian Capital City'. *Postcolonial Studies* 15 (March 2015): 221–48.

Planning Institute of Australia. 2011. *Accreditation Policy for the Recognition of Australian Planning Qualifications for the Urban and Regional Planning Chapter*. Kingston, ACT. http://www.planning.org.au/documents/item/3406.

———. 2014. *Professional Code of Conduct*. Kingston, ACT. http://www.planning.org.au/documents/item/6014.

Pløger, John. 2004. 'Strife: Urban Planning and Agonism'. *Planning Theory* 3 (1): 71–92.

Pollon, Christopher. 2012. 'In the Nass, New Power Line Jolts First Nations Relations'. *The Tyee*, November 6. http://thetyee.ca/News/2012/11/06/Northwest-Transmission-Line-Through-Nass/.

Porter, Libby. 2006a. 'Rights or Containment? The Politics of Aboriginal Cultural Heritage in Victoria'. *Australian Geographer* 37 (3): 355–74.

———. 2006b. 'Unlearning One's Privilege: Reflections on Cross-Cultural Research with Indigenous Peoples in South-East Australia'. *Planning Theory & Practice* 5 (1): 104–9.

———. 2007. 'Producing Forests A Colonial Genealogy of Environmental Planning in Victoria, Australia'. *Journal of Planning Education and Research* 26 (4): 466–77.

———. 2010. *Unlearning the Colonial Cultures of Planning*. Aldershot: Ashgate Publishing Ltd.

———. 2013. 'Coexistence in Cities: The Challenge of Indigenous Urban Planning'. In *Reclaiming Indigenous Planning*, edited by Ryan Walker, Ted Jojola and David Natcher, 283–310. Montreal: McGill-Queen's University Press.

———. 2014. 'Possessory Politics and the Conceit of Procedure: Exposing the Cost of Rights under Conditions of Dispossession'. *Planning Theory* 13 (4): 387–406.

Porter, Libby, and Janice Barry. 2015. 'Bounded Recognition: Urban Planning and the Textual Mediation of Indigenous Rights in Canada and Australia'. *Critical Policy Studies* 9 (1): 22–40.

Porter, Libby, Leonie Sandercock, Karen Umemoto, Lisa K. Bates, Marisa A. Zapata, Michelle C. Kondo, Andrew Zitcer et al. 2012. 'What's Love Got To Do With It? Illuminations on Loving Attachment in Planning'. *Planning Theory & Practice* 13 (4): 593–627.

Povinelli, Elizabeth A. 1998. 'The State of Shame: Australian Multiculturalism and the Crisis of Indigenous Citizenship'. *Critical Inquiry* 24 (2): 575–611.

———. 2002. *The Cunning of Recognition: Indigenous Alterities and the Making of Australian Multiculturalism.* Durham, NC: Duke University Press.

Pratt, Mary Louise. 1991. 'The Arts of Contact Zone'. *Profession* 91: 33–40.

Presland, Gary. 2010. *First People: The Eastern Kulin of Melbourne, Port Phillip & Central Victoria.* Melbourne: Museum Victoria Publishing.

Professional Standards Board for the Planning Profession in Canada. 2015a. 'Overview of University Planning Degree Program Accreditation.' http://www.psb-planningcanada.ca/UNIVERSTYACCREDITATION/index.php.

———. 2015b. *Prior Learning Assessment and Recognition: Self-Assessment Against Competencies.* http://www.psb-planningcanada.ca/APPLY/PDF/PLAR_Self-Assessment_Grid.docx.

Quick, K.S., and M.S. Feldman. 2011. 'Boundaries and Inclusive Public Management'. Syracuse, NY: Public Management Research Association. http://www.maxwell.syr.edu/uploadedFiles/conferences/pmrc/Files/Quick_Feldman boundaries inclusive public management PMRC 2011.pdf.

Rahder, Barbara, and Richard Milgrom. 2004. 'The Uncertain City: Making Space(s) for Difference'. *Canadian Journal of Urban Research* 13 (1) (Supplement): 27–45.

'Raven Woods – A Distinct Community'. 2014. http://www.ravenwoods.com/developer/.

Regan, Paulette. *Unsettling the Settler Within: Indian Residential Schools, Truth Telling, and Reconciliation in Canada.* 2011. Vancouver: University of British Columbia Press.

Sandercock, Leonie. 1998a. *Towards Cosmopolis: Planning for Multicultural Cities.* Chichester, UK: John Wiley & Sons.

———. 1998b. *Making the Invisible Visible: A Multicultural Planning History.* Berkeley: University of California Press.

———. 1999. 'Translations: From Insurgent Planning Practices to Radical Planning Discourses'. *Plurimondi* I (2): 37–46.

———. 2000. 'When Strangers Become Neighbours: Managing Cities of Difference'. *Planning Theory & Practice.*

———. 2003. *Cosmopolis II: Mongrel Cities in the 21st Century.* London: Continuum.

Sandercock, Leonie, and Giovanni Attili. 2010. 'Digital Ethnography as Planning Praxis: An Experiment with Film as Social Research, Community Engagement and Policy Dialogue'. *Planning Theory & Practice* 11 (1): 23–45.

Sandercock, Leonie, and Ann Forsyth. 1992. 'A Gender Agenda: New Directions for Planning Theory'. *Journal of the American Planning Association* 58: 49–59.

Scott, James C. 1987. *Weapons of the Weak: Everyday Forms of Peasant Resistance.* Newhaven, CT: Yale University Press.

———. 1990. *Domination and the Arts of Resistance: Hidden Transcripts.* Newhaven, CT: Yale University Press.

Shaw, Wendy. 2007. *Cities of Whiteness.* Malden, MA: Blackwell.

Simpson, Leanne Betasamosake. 2014. 'Land as Pedagogy: Nishnaabeg Intelligence and Rebellious Transformation'. *Decolonization: Indigeneity, Education & Society* 3 (3): 1–25.

Smith, Dorothy E. 2001. 'Texts and the Ontology of Organizations and Institutions'. *Culture and Organization* 7: 159–88.

———. 2005. *Institutional Ethnography: A Sociology for People.* Lanham, MD: AltaMira Press.

Smith, Laurajane. 2004. *Archaeological Theory and the Politics of Cultural Heritage.* London: Routledge.

Smith, Linda Tuhiwai. 1999. *Decolonizing Methodologies: Research and Indigenous Peoples.* London: Zed Books.

Smith, Benjamin, and Morphy, Frances. 2007. 'The Social Effects of Native Title: Recognition, translation, coexistence.' Research Monograph No. 27, Centre for Aboriginal Economic Policy Research (CAEPR): Canberra.

Somerville, Margaret, and Tony Perkins. 2003. 'Border Work in the Contact Zone: Thinking Indigenous/non-Indigenous Collaboration Spatially'. *Journal of Intercultural Studies* 24 (3): 253–66.

Spivak, Gayatri Chakravorty. 1990. *The Post-Colonial Critic.* New York: Routledge.

———. 1993. *Outside in the Teaching Machine.* London: Routledge.

———. 2003. *Death of a Discipline.* New York: Columbia University Press.

Stanger-Ross, Jordan. 2008. 'Municipal Colonialism in Vancouver: City Planning and the Conflict over Indian Reserves, 1928–1950s'. *Canadian Historical Review* 89 (4): 541–80.

Statistics Canada. 2012. 'North Vancouver, British Columbia (Code 5915046) and Greater Vancouver, British Columbia (Code 5915) (table)'. *Census Profile. 2011 Census.* Statistics Canada Catalogue no. 98-316-XWE. Ottawa. Released October 24, 2012. http://www12.statcan.gc.ca/census-recensement/2011/dp-pd/prof/index.cfm?Lang=E.

Sterritt, Neil J., Susan Marsden, Robert Galois, Peter R. Grant and Richard Overstall. 1998. *Tribal Boundaries in the Nass Watershed.* Vancouver: University of British Columbia Press.

Stevens, Stan. 1997. *Conservation Through Cultural Survival: Indigenous Peoples and Protected Areas.* Washington, DC: Island Press.

Suchet, Sandra. 1999. 'Situated Engagement: A Critique of Wildlife Management and Post-Colonial Discourse'. Unpublished PhD Thesis, Macquarie University.

Swyngedouw, Erik. 2009. 'The Antinomies of the Postpolitical City: In Search of a Democratic Politics of Environmental Production'. *International Journal of Urban and Regional Research* 33 (3).

Tarrow, Sidney. 1994. *Power in Movement: Social Movements, Collective Action and Politics*. Cambridge: Cambridge University Press.

Tennant, Paul. 1990. *Aboriginal Peoples and Politics: The Indian Land Question in British Columbia*, 1849–1989. Vancouver: University of British Columbia Press.

Thomas, Huw. 2000. *Race and Planning: The UK Experience*. London: UCL Press.

Thompson, Susan, and Paul Maginn. 2012. *Planning Australia: An Overview of Urban and Regional Planning*, 2nd ed. Port Melbourne: Cambridge University Press.

Tobias, Terry N. 2000. *Chief Kerry's Moose : A Guidebook to Land Use and Occupancy Mapping, Research Design and Data Collection*. Vancouver: Union of British Columbia Indian Chiefs, Ecotrust Canada.

———. 2009. *Living Proof : The Essential Data-Collection Guide for Indigenous Use-and-Occupancy Map Surveys*. Vancouver: Union of British Columbia Indian Chiefs, Ecotrust Canada.

Torgovnick, M. 1990. *Gone Primitive: Savage Intellects, Modern Lives*. Chicago: University of Chicago Press.

Tsleil-Waututh Nation. 2009. 'Stewardship Policy'. North Vancouver, BC: Tseil-Waututh Nation. http://www.twnation.ca/en/About TWN/~/media/Files/Stewardship January 2009.ashx.

———. 2015. 'Mapping and GIS.' *About TWN: Stewardship*. http://www.twnation.ca/About%20TWN/Stewardship/Mapping%20and%20GIS.aspx.

Tsleil-Waututh Nation and District of North Vancouver. 2006. 'Cates Park/Whey-Ah-Wichen Park Master Plan and Cultural Resources Interpretation Management Plan.' District of North Vancouver, BC.

———. 2007. 'Cooperation Protocol between the Tsleil-Waututh Nation and District of North Vancouver'. https://www.civicinfo.bc.ca/Library/First_Nations_Service_Agreements/Cooperation_Protocol_Agreement--DNV_and_TsleilWaututh_Nation--2007.pdf.

Tsleil-Waututh Nation, Her Majesty the Queen in Right of Canada, and Her Majesty the Queen in Right of British Columbia. 1996. *Openness Protocol*. Vancouver: Ministry of Aboriginal Affairs.

Tsleil-Waututh Nation, Treaty Lands and Resources Department. 2012. Treaty, Lands and Resources Department 2012-2013 Work Plan and Budget. Unpublished document.

Tully, James. 1995. *Strange Multiplicity: Constitutionalism in an Age of Diversity*. Cambridge: Cambridge University Press.

———. 2000. 'The Struggles of Indigenous People for and of Freedom'. In *Political Theory and the Rights of Indigenous People*, edited by D. Ivison, P. Patton and W. Sanders. Cambridge: Cambridge University Press.

———. 2004. 'Recognition and Dialogue: The Emergence of a New Field'. *Critical Review of International Social and Political Philosophy* 7 (3): 84–106.

Ugarte, Magdalena. 2014. 'Ethics, Discourse, or Rights? A Discussion about a Decolonizing Project in Planning'. *Journal of Planning Literature* 29 (4): 403–14.

Umemoto, Karen. 2001. 'Walking in Another's Shoes: Epistemological Challenges in Participatory Planning'. *Journal of Planning Education and Research* 21 (1): 17–31.

Union of British Columbia Municipalities. 1994. 'Local Government and Aboriginal Treaty Negotiations: Defining the Municipal Interest'. http://www.ubcm.ca/assets/Resolutions~and~Policy/Policy~Papers/1994/LG%20and%20Aboriginal%20Treaty%20Negotiations-Defining%20the%20Municipal%20Interest-1994.pdf.

———. 1997. 'UBCM's Response to Provincial Government Mandates: BC's Approach to Treaty Settlements. http://www.ubcm.ca/assets/Resolutions~and~Policy/Policy~Papers/1997/UBCM's%20Response%20to%20Provincial%20Government%20Mandates-BC's%20Approach%20to%20Treaty%20Settlements%201997.pdf.

Victorian Environmental Assessment Council. 2008. 'River Red Gum Forests Investigation: Final Report'. East Melbourne: VEAC.

Wagenaar, Hendrik. 2012. *Meaning in Action: Interpretation and Dialogue in Policy Analysis*. Armonk, NY: M.E. Sharpe.

Walker, Ryan. 2003. 'Engaging the Urban Aboriginal Population in Low-Cost Housing Initiatives: Lessons from Winnipeg'. *Canadian Journal of Urban Research* 12 (10): 99–118.

———. 2006. 'Searching for Aboriginal/Indigenous Self-Determination: Urban Citizenship in the Winnipeg Low-Cost Housing Sector, Canada'. *Environment and Planning A* 38: 2345–63.

Walker, Ryan, and Manuhuia Barcham. 2010. 'Indigenous-Inclusive Citizenship: The City and Social Housing in Canada, New Zealand, and Australia'. *Environment and Planning A* 42 (2): 314–331.

Watson, Irene. 2002. 'Buried Alive'. *Law and Critique* 13: 253–69.

———. 2005. 'Illusionists and Hunters: Being Aboriginal in This Occupied Space'. *Australian Feminist Law Journal* 22: 15–28.

———. 2007. 'Settled and Unsettled Spaces: Are We Free to Roam?' In *Sovereign Subjects: Indigenous Sovereignty Matters*, edited by Aileen Moreton-Robinson, 15–32. Crows Nest NSW: Allen and Unwin.

———. 2015. *Aboriginal Peoples, Colonialism and International Law: Raw Law*. Abingdon, UK: Routledge.

Watson, Vanessa. 2003. 'Conflicting rationalities: implications for planning theory and ethics.' *Planning Theory and Practice*, 4(4): 395–407.

———. 2005. 'Teaching Planning in a Context of Diversity'. *Planning Theory & Practice* 5 (2): 252–54.

———. 2006. 'Deep Difference: Diversity, Planning and Ethics'. *Planning Theory* 5 (1): 31–50.

Weber, Max. 1979. *Economy and Society: An Outline of Interpretive Sociology*. Berkeley: University of California Press.

Williams, Melissa. 2014. 'Introduction: On the Use and Abuse of Recognition in Politics'. In *Recognition vs Self-Determination: Dilemmas of Emancipatory Politics*, edited by Jeremy Webber and Glen Coulthard. Vancouver: University of British Columbia Press.

Wilson, Shawn. 2009. *Research Is Ceremony: Indigenous Research Methods*. Black Point, NS: Fernwood Publishing.

Wolfe, Patrick. 2006. 'Settler Colonialism and the Elimination of the Native'. *Journal of Genocide Research* 8 (4): 387–409.

Wood, Patricia. 2003. 'Aboriginal/Indigenous Citizenship: An Introduction'. *Citizenship Studies* 7 (4): 371–78.

Woolford, Andrew. 2005. *Between Justice and Certainty: Treaty-Making in British Columbia*. Vancouver: University of British Columbia Press.

———. 2011. 'Transition and Transposition: Genocide, Land and the British Columbia Treaty Process.' *New Proposals: Journal of Marxism and Interdisciplinary Inquiry* 4 (2): 67–76.

Wurundjeri Tribe Land and Cultural Heritage Compensation Council Incorporated, 2012. 'Narrap Country Plan', Abbotsford: Wurundjeri Tribe Land and Cultural Heritage Compensation Council.

Wurundjeri Tribe Land and Cultural Heritage Compensation Council Incorporated 2015. Website, available online at <www.wurundjeri.com.au>, last accessed 18 August 2015.

Yanow, Dvora. 1996. *How Does a Policy Mean? Interpreting Policy and Organizational Actions*. Washington, DC: Georgetown University Press.

———. 2000. *Conducting Interpretive Policy Analysis*. Thousand Oaks: SAGE.

———. 2007. 'Interpretation in Policy Analysis: On Methods and Practice'. *Critical Policy Analysis* 1 (1): 110–22.

Yiftachel, Oren. 1998. 'Planning and Social Control: Exploring the "Dark Side"'. *Journal of Planning Literature* 12 (4): 395–406.

———. 2009. 'Critical Theory and "Gray Space": Mobilization of the Colonized'. *City* 13 (2–3).

Yiftachel, Oren, and Tovi Fenster. 1997. 'Frontier Development and Indigenous Peoples'. Progress in Planning. UK: Pergamon.

Young, Iris Marion. 1990. *Justice and the Politics of Difference*. Princeton: NJ: Princeton University Press.

―――. 1997. *Intersecting Voices: Dilemmas of Gender, Political Philosophy, and Policy*. Princeton, NJ: Princeton University Press.
―――. 2000. *Inclusion and Democracy*. Oxford: Oxford University Press.
Zaferatos, NC. 2004. 'Tribal Nations, Local Governments, and Regional Pluralism in Washington State.' *Journal of the American Planning Association* 70: 81–94.
Zizek, Slavoj. 2001. *Did Someone Say Totalitarianism?* London: Verso.
―――. 2009. *First as Tragedy, Then as Farce*. London: Verso.

Cases cited

Delgamuukw v. British Columbia [1997] 3 SCR 1010. 1997.
Gitxsan and other First Nations v. British Columbia (Minister of Forests) [2002] BCSC 1701. 2002.
Haida Nation v. British Columbia (Minister of Forests) [2004] 3 S.C.R. 511, 2004 SCC 73
Mabo v. State of Queensland (No. 2) [1992] 175 CLR 1. 1992.
R. v. Sparrow – [1990] 1 SCR 1075. 1990.
Taku River Tlingit First Nation v. British Columbia (Project Assessment Director). [2004] 3 SCR 550. 2004.
Wii'litswx v. British Columbia (Minister of Forests) (2008) BCSC 1139

Statutes cited

Aboriginal Heritage Act (Vic) (2006)
Aboriginal and Torres Strait Islander Heritage Protection Act (Cwth) (1983)
Community Charter [SBC 2003] Chapter 26
Conservation Forests and Lands Act (Vic) (1987)
Crown Land (Reserves) Act (Vic) (1979)
Forest and Range Practices Act [SBC 2002] Chapter 69
Indian Act [RSC 1985] Chapter I-5
Land Act [RSBC 1996] Chapter 245
Local Government Act [RSBC 1996] Chapter 323
Local Government Act (Vic) (1989)
National Parks Act (Vic) (1975)
Native Title Act (Cwth) (1993)
Planning and Environment Act (Vic) (1987)
Traditional Owner Settlement Act (Vic) (2010)

Index